Europe and Asia as a Legal Area for Fundamental Rights

Masahisa Deguchi · Kimio Yakushiji
Editors

Europe and Asia as a Legal Area for Fundamental Rights

Springer

Editors
Professor Dr. Masahisa Deguchi
Faculty of Law
Ritsumeikan University
Kyoto, Japan

Professor Emeritus Kimio Yakushiji
School of Law
Ritsumeikan University
Kyoto, Japan

ISBN 978-981-19-7541-7 ISBN 978-981-19-7542-4 (eBook)
https://doi.org/10.1007/978-981-19-7542-4

This Springer imprint is published by the registered company Springer Nature Singapore Pte Ltd.
The registered company address is: 152 Beach Road, #21-01/04 Gateway East, Singapore 189721, Singapore

Preface

This book is mainly the academic collaborative result of the International Symposium on the topic: "Europe and Asia as a legal area for peace, fundamental rights, democracy and the rule of law", which was organized at Ritsumeikan University in Kyoto/Japan from February 21–23, 2019.

Based on the history and development of the European unification process, this conference asked the question of to what extent Asia can look to Europe as a model and what lessons can be learned. We invited as Keynote Speaker the vice-president of the European Court of Human Rights, Prof. Dr. h.c. Angelika Nussberger, University of Cologne, and former Federal Minister of Defence, Prof. Dr. Rupert Scholz, University of Munich, to share their views on Europe as a legal sphere and the current challenges. We also invited prominent representatives from East and Southeast Asia to the symposium who have discussed these issues and shared the perspective and challenges of their respective countries. This symposium is a thematic follow-up to the 4th Meeting of the East-Asian Germany-Alumni for Jurists on the subject "Protection of Fundamental Rights in legal practice and dogmatics—Aspects of European and Asian constitutional, civil and criminal law" at Ritsumeikan University in Kyoto 2017[1].

From an economic point of view, East Asia is a highly developed region; despite the huge differences between the political systems, the region has grown together—not only economically but in recent times also in the demand for (and examples of) cooperative legal frameworks. However, the legal systems of the respective countries have to be further developed and improved with mutual respect to create the necessary conditions for peaceful coexistence. It is precisely in this respect that we can learn from the European experience. It is important to create legal institutions in the East-Asian region following the examples of the European Union or the Council of Europe to legally implement the principles of the rule of law, democracy, and guarantee of human rights. This would also contribute to the improvement of the quality of life in the entire region.

---

[1] *See in details,* http://www.ritsumei.ac.jp/acd/cg/law/lex/rlr35/002deguchimasahisa.pdf

The Council of Europe and the European Union succeeded in building legal and political institutions after WWII, and in establishing effective judicial systems. The protection of human rights has emerged as the highest good for the co-existence in Europe. Without it, Europe could not have developed a community in such a peaceful and harmonious way.

This is why we consciously decided to focus on human rights for the three-day international symposium in 2017 on the subject "Protection of Fundamental Rights in legal practice and dogmatics—Aspects of European and Asian constitutional, civil and criminal law" with distinguished lecturers and legal experts from the EU and Asia.

The symposium opened with a keynote speech about "The European Fundamental Rights' Protection System" by Jean-Paul Costa, former judge and president of the European Court of Human Rights. His speech specifically covers "The General Protection System—and the Specific Problem of the European Union Accession to the European Convention in Human Rights (The Lisbon Treaty and its Follow Up)". As a human rights issue in the European Union and the Council of Europe, it has implications for the Asian legal space. This was followed by lectures and discussions about the situation and challenges in Japan, China, Korea, and Taiwan. We also invited guests from Southeast Asia for the discussions to broaden the perspective.

For the symposium in 2019, we decided to move the discussion further and focus on the possibility of establishing an Asian legal sphere, considering the example of Europe. In this connection, it was important not to stop at one-sided descriptions of facts and situations, but to discuss what options we have in Asia to initiate a similar development like in Europe, what precisely would be the experiences in Europe that may be applicable to Asia, and which conditions might allow for this to happen, and, if there are elements in Asia that might be interesting to be considered in Europe.

The movement for European unity has always seen itself as value-based. At present, however, these common values seem to be under threat and are no longer shared by all who see themselves as belonging to Europe.

Europe came together in various ways: it began with an initial economic and political focus within the framework of the European Union (EU) while the focus within the framework of the Council of Europe lay from the outset exclusively on the nations' common values. Both forms of unions can only be understood by taking into account the historical background, the close community among the European states bound by a common destiny, and the almost complete mutual destruction during the Second World War.

On the one hand, a narrow legal framework has emerged for 27 states (after Brexit), which creates a "supranational" community with the EU, which is quite different from a typical international organization or from a state which is regularly called upon to explain, develop, and preserve its own specific characteristics. On the other hand, there exists a union of a further circle of 47 European states, the Council of Europe[2], which functions as a classical international organization.

The form of integration has changed fundamentally over the decades, especially after 1989. The states belonging to the socialist block at the time of the "Cold War" with a decidedly different political heritage were admitted to both organizations, but to a different extent: in the Council of Europe all states except Belarus and Russia, in the EU only the Central and South-Eastern European states. Moreover, the EU now no longer defines itself as a mere economic community but also as a community of values, so that the contents of the two unions are increasingly overlapping and thus partly strengthening, but also partly competing with each other.

The current challenges have to be seen against this historical background. In economic and legal terms, the withdrawal of one of the "core states", the United Kingdom, is particularly difficult to manage. However, the questioning of a consensus on values considered fundamental can be seen as especially problematic for a community of values. This applies not only to the controversial issue of migration but also to the understanding of the rule of law and democracy, which is being called into question by recent structural changes, particularly in Poland and Hungary. And the Russian invasion of Ukraine, which began in February 2022, poses an extremely difficult challenge for the Council of Europe and the European Union.

These current challenges and the history of the movement for European unity are important lessons to study and debate. Asia is not Europe, and current-day Asia differs from the circumstances that led to the unification of Europe: Besides the issues of huge economic gaps between neighboring countries and a wide variety of political forms of government, Asia also does not share the unifying narrative of post-WWII Europe, nor can it be described as a community of shared values.

These vast differences in history, economies, culture, traditions, and values make it a particularly difficult environment to set up binding legal and political institutions comparable to the European Union or the Council of Europe. And yet, there have been encouraging developments besides the mere economic relationships in recent years.

Human rights may sound like an area where it's difficult to find a consensus among the Asian nations. However, if one looks at the differences between the 1950s (or probably even the 1990s) and present Asia, an increasing number of developments in constitutional and international practices—especially the development of judicial review and interaction between different courts at the domestic, regional, and international levels—can be interpreted as an entry point to an Asian Human Rights court.

[2] The Council of Europe held an extraordinary meeting of a committee of ministers from member states on March 16 2022 to condemn Russia's invasion of Ukraine and to expel Russia, a decision that took effect immediately.

Recently, the establishment of the ASEAN Intergovernmental Commission on Human Rights (AICHR) suggests that there is the possibility of creating a transnational system to address human rights in Asia.

At the 3rd Congress of the World Conference on Constitutional Justice in Seoul in September 2014, the President of the Constitutional Court of the Republic of Korea, Park Han-Chul, proposed the establishment of a Court of Human Rights in Asia.

Economically and politically, there are several multilateral organizations in Asia that were founded for different purposes (ASEAN: Association of South-East Asian Nations, SAARC: South Asian Association for Regional Cooperation, ECO: Economic Cooperation Organization) and have led to closer integration among Asian nations.

All these developments indicate that there may indeed be a way to create a common legal Asian sphere. That is why we chose the ambitious topic of “a European and Asian legal area for peace, fundamental rights, democracy and the rule of law”.

We invited scholars and legal experts from Europe and East- and Southeast Asia (Taiwan, Korea, China, Vietnam, Thailand, and Japan) to ensure that the lectures and ensuing discussions will provide the platform for lively exchanges and the opportunity to identify the relevant aspects for all countries concerned. We hope this book could lead readers to have an increasing interest in and appreciation of “Europe and Asia as a legal area for peace, fundamental rights, democracy and the rule of law”.

I therefore am pleased to also include in this volume the keynote speech in the international symposium in 2017 on the topic: “Former President of the European Court of Human Rights, Honorary President of the Foundation René Cassin-International Institute of Human rights” by President Jean-Paul Costa. Prof. Dr. Michael Reiterer (Distinguished Professor, EU-Ambassador ret., Centre for Security, Diplomacy & Strategy) who has spoken on the topic: “The EU as Defender of the Liberal International Oder and the Rule of Law” prior to the Symposium, also gave a very important lecture at Ritsumeikan University in February 2022 on the topic: “The primacy of EU law over national law: Rule of law contested—Reflections on the Case of the Polish Constitutional Court”. The principle of primacy of EU law is an issue that is fundamental to the EU institutions and is also extremely important to the legal space in Asia, so it is also included in this book.

I would like to thank the Konrad-Adenauer-Foundation, Kyoto Museum for World Peace, and the Faculty of Law and Research Office of Ritsumeikan University for their generous financial support on behalf of my co-editors. I would like to thank my conference assistant Mr. Tha-Phuong Vo from Freiburg/Germany and my colleagues, staff, and students at Ritsumeikan University in Kyoto/Japan who have supported our international symposium.

Lastly, I dedicate this book to my dear father-in-law, the late Professor emeritus. Dr. Yoshio Cho, Osaka Prefecture University in Japan, who had supported my international exchange activity behind the scenes since my marriage with my wife Yukiko Deguchi.

July 2022

On behalf of my co-editors,
Professor Dr. Masahisa Deguchi
Faculty of Law, Honorary Vice
President of International Association
of Procedural Law (IAPL)
Ritsumeikan University
Kyoto, Japan

The original version of this book was revised: The name "Dr. Oshio Cho" has been changed to "Dr. Yoshio Cho" in Preface. The correction to the book is available at https://doi.org/10.1007/978-981-19-7542-4_14

Contents

The European Union and the Council of Europe as Legal Area of Freedom, Fundamental Rights and Rule of Law

Angelika Nußberger

1 Legal Concepts in Their Cultural and Historical Embedding

Law is not something abstract. Rather, it is deeply rooted in culture. It is constantly being formed and modified and adapted to new societal requirements and developments. Good ideas can be transferred from one legal system to another one, convincing concepts can be implanted and work in different environments, but that is rather the exception than the rule. The transfer of legal ideas and concepts from Europe to Asia in the twentieth century—e.g. German and American constitutionalism to Japan—is one of the most interesting examples of such a transfer. We can learn from the past what might be possible for the future.

1.1 Value-Oriented Approach in Europe

Europe is proud of its values. Both the EU and the Council of Europe identify themselves as value-oriented close forms of cooperation between States on an equal basis. In this context the concepts of rule of law, democracy, and human rights are deemed to be of fundamental importance. We find them in the preambles and in the first articles of all the major legal texts, be it the Statute of the Council of Europe or the EU Treaty.

When I speak about EU and Council of Europe I speak of course of the Europe of the second half of the twentieth century.

A. Nußberger (✉)
Faculty of Law, University of Cologne, Cologne, Germany
e-mail: angelika.nussberger@uni-koeln.de

M. Deguchi and K. Yakushiji (eds.), *Europe and Asia as a Legal Area for Fundamental Rights*, https://doi.org/10.1007/978-981-19-7542-4_1

Nothing similar can be found in the new world order after the First World War. There was no close connection between the European States, there was no common frame-work, there was no pride of being "European".

Let's have a short look at the very different starting points after for rebuilding and re-inventing Europe after the first and the second World War, first the period after 1918 and then the period after 1945. Both are right now reference points for commemoration: the end of the first World War in 1918 was remembered and celebrated in 2018, the Versailles Peace Conference of 1919 is an important event to reflect upon in 2019. The beginning of the work on the Statute of the Council of Europe was started in 1949, 70 years ago—another reason to celebrate and look back in 2019. Commemoration is important for identity-building. If the elaboration of international treaties is part of a common commemorative culture, this is a good sign.

1.2 Lessons Learnt After Two World Wars

The aim both after the First and the Second World War was to secure long-lasting peace. But the analysis of what had gone wrong and led to crisis and war first in 1914 and then in 1939 and what consequences should be drawn from the mistakes made was very different.

The analysis of the catastrophe of the first World War was focused on three aspects: the oppression of people forced to be citizens of multiethnic Empires, the disastrous and ruthless economic competition between the national States, and the lack of a mechanism for effective conflict resolution for interstate conflicts. The legal recipes worked out by Woodrow Wilson, Georges Clemenceau and David Lloyd George in Paris in 1919 were meant to respond to these deficiencies. Three new concepts were developed: self-determination, international standards for labour law and social policies, (the ILO), and the creation of a universal framework for the cooperation of States, i.e. the creation of the League of Nations.

This peace project failed. Only two decades later the Second World War started.

After 1945 the analysis of what had led to such a disastrous war was different even if the concepts developed after the First World War were not abandoned. Rather there was a shift in the perception of what was important. In his famous Zurich speech Winston Church in 1949 spoke about the "vast, quivering mass of tormented, hungry, careworn and bewildered human beings."[1] Thus, by then, the suffering of the individuals was seen as primordial. It was understood that the root of the tragedy was the absolute power of the State over the individual, the State developing into a machine destroying the individuals instead of allowing them to live and "strive for happiness", the State doing whatever it wanted without being bound by any rules. The answer was therefore the discovery of individual human rights and rule of law. At the same time, cooperation between States was seen to be crucial, but not only on

---

[1] Speech on a Council of Europe, Zurich 19 September 1946, http://aei.pitt.edu/14362/.

the universal level, but also on the European level. It was also Churchill who spoke in the same Zurich speech about the "European family in a regional structure".

This was the basis, and on this basis two parallel legal frameworks were created in Europe, on the one hand the Council of Europe with its focus on the protection of human rights and rule of law, and on the other hand the European communities with their focus on economic cooperation.

In history it does not make much sense to ask the "if-question" or the "if-not-question"—what would have happened if there had not been a Second World War? Nevertheless, I think it is fair to say that without the catastrophes of the first half of the twentieth century the rebuilding of Europe based on common values such as human rights and rule of law and the creation of European institutions in Brussels, Luxembourg and Strasbourg would not have been likely.

1.3 Different Heritage in Asia

What does that mean for Asia, for its quest for a closer cooperation in the field of human rights and rule of law?

We all understand that the situation in Asia nowadays is very different. Obviously, there is no "point zero" for rebuilding a new world order. Neither are human rights a new discovery. All Asian States are—more or less intensely—bound by universal human rights treaties. Even if in the 1940s Asian States did not contribute to the elaboration of the Universal Declaration of Human Rights on an equal footing with "Western States" as many Asian States were still under the yoke of colonialism or were excluded as "enemy states" or for other reasons, Asian philosophies, e.g. Confucianism, had been integrated into the universal human rights project. In Eleanor Roosevelt's team there was Peng-chun Chang as Chinese delegate; Chinese and Indian philosophers such as Mahatma Gandhi and Chung-Shu Lo were being heard. Later on Asian States were fully integrated in drafting further UN human rights treaties.

Nevertheless, unlike in other parts of the world such as Africa, South America and in the Arab countries, up to now in Asia there is no institutional framework for the systematic protection of human rights and rule of law comparable to the one elaborated in Europe after 1945. It will be for Asian countries to decide if they need and want something similar.

What we—Europeans—can do is to explain where we stand in a legal area that is called a "legal area of freedom, human rights and rule of law". The question is how optimistic we should be.

I would argue that there are two narratives about Europe—a success story and a story of lost illusions. I will tell you both stories and reflect with you where we stand and what can be learnt from our experience.

2 Human Rights and Rule of Law—A Success Story for Europe?

2.1 Bridging the Differences Between East and West

Half a century ago, when Europe started from the scratch, only half of the European States were in a position to accept rule of law and human rights as basic principle for organizing State and society. There was a huge divide between the countries of Western Europe and Eastern Europe. It was the time of the Cold War. All the countries of the so-called "socialist block" were disconnected from a vital part of the European heritage. Rule of law remained an outcast in the socialist value system. Although long lists of human rights were codified in the constitutions, they followed the model of Stalin's Soviet Constitution, remained only on paper and were null and void because of the State-centered communist ideology which did not allow individuals to decide for themselves. Rule of law was considered to be a remnant of the bourgeois capitalist worldview and was replaced by what was first called "revolutionary legality" and later on "socialist legality". There was a positivist and formal approach to written law which could at any time be given up for the sake of what was demanded for the accomplishment of revolutionary aims. Instead of legal certainty legal uncertainty and arbitrariness reigned. Civil and political rights were sacrificed to the aims to be achieved by socialist societies. It was only in the late 1980s that the idea of a State based on rule of law and real civil and political rights and freedoms were "discovered" by the Eastern European States and taken up in the newly elaborated constitutions after what was called "velvet revolutions".

The sudden career of the principle of rule of law and the elaboration of comprehensive human rights codifications as part of the new constitutions after the break-down of communism can be seen as one pillar of the success story of the new world-view in Europe. By now, rule of law and human rights are substantive elements in all written constitutions in Europe and they are a vital part of the discourse in all European States.

2.2 Institutionalization and Judicialisation

Without exaggeration we may say that Europe is especially good at instituting legal mechanisms to secure the implementation of its fundamental values. Thus, the two European courts, the European Court of Justice of Luxemburg and the European Court of Human Rights in Strasbourg are unique. While the first one is "supranational" and its judgments have binding force in all member States of the EU—now 28 and after Brexit 27—, the second one is "international", i.e. based on the mechanisms of international law. Nevertheless, the Strasbourg Court with its over sixty years of elaborate jurisprudence in all human rights questions, with its workload of about 60.000 cases per year, with its sophisticated implementation mechanism, is exemplary for all other international courts world-wide. Other international human rights courts such as the African Court of Human and Peoples' Rights and the Inter-American Court of Human Rights are inspired by its case-law and by its efficiency.

Without any doubt the fact that judges watch over the implementation of human rights and rule of law in the member States is one of the most important factors of the success story.

2.3 "Acquis" in Human Rights and Rule of Law

The third pillar of the success story is the development of the relevant legal concepts step by step, an approach made possible by investing courts with the power to decide on individual cases and thus to resolve problems of interpretation as they arise.

Thus the concept of rule of law is not just a vague idea, but has become workable. Lord Bingham enumerated in his famous book "Rule of Law" the eight "ingredients": Accessibility and predictability of the law, exclusion of discretion in the application of rights and liabilities, equality, good faith, adequate protection of human rights, conflict resolution on the basis of law, fair trial, and compliance with the obligations under international law. These "ingredients" coincide to a large extent with what the European Court of Human Rights has elaborated in its jurisprudence over the last decades. Rule of law is considered to be part of the "spirit" of the Convention and to underlie all the Convention provisions.The starting point can be a negative one: Rule of law is the opposite of arbitrariness.

Rule of law and human rights are intrinsically linked. In the following I will introduce what is considered to be fundamental. It can be called the European "acquis" in human rights and rule of law.

2.3.1 Basic Substantive Rights

Fair Trial

First and foremost the relevant provision of the ECHR is Article 6, the right to fair trial and independence of the judiciary. This article enumerates the most essential features of the concept of rule of law based on experience throughout the centuries such as the right to the presumption of innocence, the right to be heard, the right to defend oneself or through legal assistance, and the right to equality of arms. At the same time the basic notion of "fair trial", i.e. an overall assessment, remains relevant.

Prohibition of Torture and Inhuman Treatment

Rule of law elements are not exclusively to be found in Art. 6. Article 3 enshrines the fundamental principle that the State must not torture or treat people in an inhuman or degrading way. An almost philosophical challenge was posed by the case Gäfgen v. Germany.[2] A police officer threatened a child's kidnapper with torture in order to save the child's life. Because of the threat the kidnapper led the police to the hiding place, but the child was already dead. Although Germany had sanctioned the police officer on the basis of criminal and disciplinary law, the Court still found a violation as the sanction had not been hard enough. The Court accepted that such a case was not comparable to other cases concerning arbitrary and serious acts of brutality by State agents. Nevertheless it emphasized that sanctions which are "manifestly disproportionate to a breach of one of the core rights of the Convention", do not have the "necessary deterrent effect in order to prevent further violations of the prohibition of ill-treatment in future difficult situations."[3]

Right to Freedom

The gist of Article 5, the right to liberty and security, is the protection against arbitrariness, another essential feature of "rule of law". The same is true for Article 7, the guarantee that there should be no punishment without law, an idea that can be traced back to the old maxime of "nulla poena sine lege", for the first time spelt out explicitly by Cesare Beccaria. The jurisprudence of the Court has refined this principle in many ways. Closely linked to it is the right not to be punished twice, laid down in Article 4 of Protocol No. 7. In this context the Court was in this context confronted with the problem in how far somebody can be held accountable for a war crime after having been granted amnesty. The Court held that the protective clause of Article 4 Protocol No. 7 was not applicable to such a situation. On the contrary, the States were under an obligation to prosecute acts such as torture and intentional killings.

Prohibition of Discrimination

Last but not least Art. 14 guarantees the principle of equality of individuals before the law and thus also contains an essential element of "rule of law".

---

[2] ECtHR, 01.06.2010, no. 22978/05 – Gäfgen v. Germany.

[3] ECtHR, 01.06.2010, no. 22978/05 – Gäfgen v. Germany, para 124.

Freedom of Expression and Freedom of Religion

There are two more rights that are deemed to be especially important, freedom of expression and freedom of religion. While they are also emphasized in international treaties the ECHR's jurisprudence is especially farreaching in its interpretation. It has developed what we may call "formula" or perhaps "confessions" which are repeated again and again in the jurisprudences. The central one on freedom of religion is the following:

"As enshrined in Article 9, freedom of thought, conscience and religion is one of the foundations of a "democratic society" within the meaning of the Convention. This freedom is, in its religious dimension, one of the most vital elements that go to make up the identity of believers and their conception of life, but it is also a precious asset for atheists, agnostics, sceptics and the unconcerned. The pluralism indissociable from a democratic society, which has been dearly won over the centuries, depends on it. That freedom entails, inter alia, freedom to hold or not to hold religious beliefs and to practise or not to practise a religion."[4] The central one on freedom of expression reads:

"The Court has consistently held that freedom of expression constitutes one of the essential foundations of a democratic society and one of the basic conditions for its progress and for each individual's self-fulfilment. Subject to paragraph 2 of Article 10, it is applicable not only to "information" or "ideas" that are favourably received or regarded as inoffensive or as a matter of indifference, but also to those that offend, shock or disturb. Such are the demands of pluralism, tolerance and broadmindedness without which there is no "democratic society."[5]

These two formula sound quite similar. They summarize what we can call "European heritage", or, even better, "lessons learnt"—individual freedom is seen as the basis for society, restrictions of the individual's freedom are accepted only when "necessary". It is not an "egoistic" view, but a view that balances the rights of the individual and society. But the individual is clearly in the focal point. Why do I say that these is the result of lessons learnt?—Because in totalitarian regimes it was the other way round—the State (not society) was the focal point and the individuals had to try to fit into a pre-defined narrow frame.

2.3.2 Institutional Guarantees and Fundamental Principles in Resolving Conflicts

Independence of the Judiciary

The implementation of rule of law and human rights will not be possible without an independent of the judiciary; that is the cornerstone of the whole system.

[4] ECtHR, 25.05.1993, no. 14307/88 – Kokkinakis v. Greece, para. 31.

[5] ECtHR, 30.04.2019, nos. 60921/17 and 7202/18 – Elvira Dmitriyeva v. Russia, para. 74; ECtHR, 30.04.2019, nos. 48310/16 and 59663/17 – Kablis v. Russia, para. 79.

Could we imagine a State without courts? We could, but we would immediately understand how threatening such a vision would be.—I know that in some Asian countries, e.g. in Japan, going to Court is seen as disgrace. Other mechanisms of conflict resolution are deemed to be much more helpful and adequate, perhaps based on the Confucian ideal of a just and brotherly society. But nevertheless, courts do exist, and be it only as last resort.

The Strasbourg Court has called the judiciary "guarantor of justice, a fundamental value in a law-governed State."

But the very existence of courts is not sufficient. They are of no help if they are not independent and impartial.

The Court has elaborated a differentiated jurisprudence on the notions of "independence" and "impartiality". In order to determine if a court is "independent" the Court focuses on many aspects such as the manner of appointment of its members and their term of office, the existence of safeguards against external pressure and the question whether the body presents an appearance of independence. Although the Convention does not require States to comply with any theoretical constitutional concepts regarding the permissible limits of the powers' interaction, the Court emphasizes in its jurisprudence the principle of "separation of powers".

An important case the Court has decided in this context is the case of Oleksandr Volkov against Ukraine[6] concerning the dismissal of the President of the Military Chamber of the Supreme Court of Ukraine. He had been charged with what was called "gross procedural violations" and was therefore dismissed by Parliament because of "breach of oath", a vague "crime" that could be easily used as an accusation against an unwanted judge. Another important case concerned Hungary where the new Constitution was worded in such a way as not to allow the President of the Supreme Court to continue his mandate or to be re-elected. The Court held that this was a consequence of critical statements he had made about political reforms. Although judges are—having regard to their status—not completely free to comment on politics, in this case the Court found a violation of freedom of speech.

One of the problems of the Court's jurisprudence in this context is that the same legal regulations can have very different effects depending on the legal culture of a country. The legal culture is, however, difficult to "measure" and difficult to evaluate. Cases on judicial independence are therefore difficult to adjudicate, first, because many important facts might not be known, and second, because there might be not only black and white, but also a lot of grey tones. It is rare that, as in the case of Sovtransavto v. Ukraine,[7] a letter of the President of the Republic advising the judge on how to decide can be found in the file.

[6] ECtHR, 09.01.2013, no. 21722/11 – Oleksandr Volkov v. Ukraine.

[7] ECtHR, 25.07.2002, no. 48553/99 – Sovtransavto Holding v. Ukraine.

Legal Certainty

Independent judges decide on the basis of the law. The essential guarantee for the implementation of rights in this context is legal certainty. On the basis of the Convention restrictions are only allowed "on the basis of law". For the Court the existence of a legal provision in the respective national legal order as such is, however, not sufficient. It also controls what it called the "quality" of the law. Thus the Court often repeats the following standard formula:

> "The requirement of lawfulness … is not satisfied merely by compliance with the relevant domestic law; domestic law must itself be in conformity with … the principle of the rule of law, …. The notion underlying the expression "in accordance with a procedure prescribed by law" is one of fair and proper procedure …"

It is important that norms are formulated with sufficient precision in order to enable the individual to regulate his or her conduct accordingly. The individual "must be able—if need be with appropriate advice—to foresee, to a degree that is reasonable in the circumstances, the consequences which a given action may entail. This is for example very important in case of regulations giving the executive power large discretion. "The law must indicate the scope of any such discretion conferred on the competent authorities and the manner of its exercise with sufficient clarity, having regard to the legitimate aim of the measure in question, to give the individual adequate protection against arbitrary interference".[8]

Proportionality

A further essential principle elaborated in the Strasbourg court's jurisprudence is proportionality, a principle well known in the German tradition. It was first developed in the administrative courts in Prussia dealing with interventions by the police. In the Court's case-law the question of the proportionality of a measure is often decisive. Interests are weighed, e.g. privacy rights on the one hand, freedom of speech on the other hand. The symbol of the balance, a traditional symbol for justice in Europe, is as important now as it was in Antiquity when it was the attribute of the Goddess "Iustitia".

Proportionality is also relevant in the difficult fight against terrorism. Even if the individual's rights are protected under Article 3 of the Convention which is considered to be an absolute right, in defining the threshold of what is to be considered "inhuman" the Court applies the proportionality principle, even if in a hidden manner. Thus, to give just one example, in the case Ramirez Sanchez v. France,[9] the Court did not find a violation of Article 3 although the applicant was held in solitary confinement for eight years. In this context that Court took into account that the applicant was

---

[8] ECtHR, 04.12.2015, no. 47143/06 – Roman Zakharov v. Russia, para. 230; ECtHR, 12.01.2016, no. 37138/14 – Szabó and Vissy v. Hungary, para. 65.

[9] ECtHR, 04.07.2006, no. 59450/00 – Ramirez Sanchez v. France.

considered to be the most dangerous terrorist in the 1970s and that he was convicted for terrorist-related offences. The Court explained:

> "The Court shares the CPT's concerns about the possible long-term effects of the applicant's isolation. It nevertheless considers that, having regard to the physical conditions of the applicant's detention, the fact that his isolation is "relative", the authorities' willingness to hold him under the ordinary regime, his character and the danger he poses, the conditions in which the applicant was being held during the period under consideration have not reached the minimum level of severity necessary to constitute inhuman treatment within the meaning of Article 3 of the Convention."[10]

Enhanced Responsibility for the State's Actions and Omissions

Last but not least, it has to be emphasized that the Court has added a specific new dimension to the meaning of rule of law. State authorities are not only responsible for human rights violations they commit themselves, but also for those they enable to be committed. A State based on rule of law cannot close its eyes to the consequences of its actions and omissions even if they happen outside its territory. This might be called responsibility "beyond one's one nose". The famous first example of the relevant jurisprudence is the case Soering v. United Kingdom[11] concerning death penalty. A Convention State is not allowed to extradite someone to another State where he or she would be exposed to torture or inhuman treatment or even to the death penalty.

This approach has been stretched to potential violations of Article 6 of the Convention, the right to fair trial:

> "It is established in the Court's case-law that an issue might exceptionally be raised under Article 6 by an expulsion or extradition decision in circumstances where the fugitive had suffered or risked suffering a flagrant denial of justice in the requesting country."[12]

Thus, rule of law is, to a certain extent, exported to countries outside Europe. Nevertheless, not all potential Convention violations are relevant in this context. Rather, the Court has defined a sort of "second (lower) level" of rule of law comprising only the most basic principles. In this context flagrant violations of fair trial are outlawed such as convictions in absentia with no possibility subsequently to obtain a fresh determination of the merits of the charge, trials which are summary in nature and conducted with a total disregard for the rights of the defense, detention without any access to an independent and impartial tribunal to have the legality the detention reviewed, and the deliberate and systematic refusal of access to a lawyer, especially for an individual detained in a foreign country.

The narrative of the success story of rule of law in Europe is based on solid grounds. It suggests that real progress has been achieved: The "East" has accepted what had been developed in the "West", institutions have been built up that are models for

---

[10] ECtHR, 04.07.2006, no. 59450/00 – Ramirez Sanchez v. France, para. 150.

[11] ECtHR, 07.07.1989, no. 14038/88 – Soering v. The United Kingdom.

[12] ECtHR, 17.01.2012, no. 8139/09 – Othman (Abu Qatada) v. United Kingdom, para. 258.

other world regions, the contents of rule of law and human rights has been clarified in abundant case-law.

Nevertheless, it has to be asked if this success story is really true. A deeper analysis might lead to a less optimistic result. It is also possible to play the role of the advocatus diaboli and to argue that rule of law and progress in the implementation of human rights in Europe form part of, is a story of lost illusions.

3 Spreading Rule of Law in Europe—A Story of Lost Illusions?

3.1 Discrepancies Between Legal Obligations and Reality

The cases brought to the European Court of Human Rights every year do not suggest that there would be any progress in implementing human rights based on rule of law. There are many cases which might be called "anti-rule-of-law-cases" as they manifest complete arbitrariness and violence on the part of the State authorities, above all the police and the prison guards. The following short anecdote may be revealing. In a Ukrainian file a report on a short interview of a policeman was reproduced. He was asked if he had mistreated the detainee and answered: "No, I have not mistreated him. He had already confessed." This proves an attitude towards others in a vulnerable situation which should have been outlawed already many centuries ago. Nevertheless, the finding of a Convention violation because of the use of violence in order to obtain confessions can be regarded as routine in Strasbourg. There are no signs that this will improve in the future.

Other "hard cases" concern flagrant violations of the right to liberty where arbitrariness reigns. Thus the Court had for example to deal with pretrial detention ordered to prevent people from participating in demonstrations or to silence political opponents. The case of Mammadov v. Azerbaijan might serve as an example:

> "The Court considered that Mr Mammadov, who had a history of criticising the Government, had been arrested and detained without any evidence to reasonably suspect him of having committed the offence with which he was charged, namely that of having organised actions leading to public disorder. The Court concluded that the actual purpose of his detention had been to silence or punish Mr Mammadov for criticising the Government and publishing information it was trying to hide."[13]

The Court judgment dates back to 2014. Only five years later, after having served more than two thirds of the prison sentence, in summer 2019, Mr. Mammadov was released, after a procedure under Article 46 para. 4 of the Convention had, for the first time in the Court's history, been started, a violation was found.

[13] ECtHR, 22.05.2014, no. 15172/13 – Ilgar Mammadov v. Azerbaijan, paras. 92, 143.

Similar cases are to be reported from other countries where basic guarantees of rule of law are denied during trials and pretrial detention is ordered without any or without sufficient reasoning.

There are also cases illustrating that courts in Europe apply the law in a completely arbitrary manner. A good illustration is provided by the case of Khamidov v. Russia in which the house of a Chechen family was occupied by Russian police without any legal basis. The damage to the house was acknowledged by the authorities as well as in one court judgment. Nevertheless the court judgment was ignored and the relevant reports were not accepted by the competent Russian court. The European Court used very strong language:

> "The Court is perplexed by this conclusion and cannot see how it could be reconciled with the abundant evidence to the contrary, and, first of all, with the findings made in the judgment of 14 February 2001, or the replies from public officials. In the Court's view, the unreasonableness of this conclusion is so striking and palpable on the face of it that the decisions of the domestic courts in the 2002 proceedings can be regarded as grossly arbitrary, and by reaching that conclusion in the circumstances of the case the domestic courts in fact set an extreme and unattainable standard of proof for the applicant so that his claim could not, in any event, have had even the slightest prospect of success."[14]

Confronted with such repetitive cases it may be allowed to ask if the inscription of the principle of rule of law in constitutions and the ratification of an international treaty based on rule of law is more than a lip-service.

Looking back at the decades of human rights jurisprudence it might even be asked if the standards already achieved are lowered again. Is progress an illusion?

One sign of retrogression might be that the Court's authority is undermined by the deliberate non-execution of its judgments. One example is the introduction of a special procedure in Russia to contest the enforcement of binding judgments deemed not to be compatible with the Constitution. This mechanism was already used twice—a clear sign of disrespect towards the Court, long time before Russia was expelled from the Council of Europe due to its aggressive war against Ukraine.

3.2 Controversies About the Core Meaning of the Principle of Rule of Law

Furthermore, even if the Court has clarified many different aspects of the principle of rule of law in the last decades, essential questions remain unanswered. One important controversy concerns for example jury trial, on the one hand deemed to be especially fair and transparent, on the other hand heavily criticized as the judgments are, as a rule, not reasoned. The critique of the jury trials touches upon the constitutional identity of some member States of the Convention system They consider the introduction of jury trials as a major achievement in implementing rule of law. It is worth quoting

[14] ECtHR, 15.11.2007, no. 72118/01 – Khamidov v. Russia, para 174.

the arguments of the Irish Government who acted as a Third Party intervener in the case Taxquet v. Belgium:

> "In the Irish Government's submission, the system of jury trial in Ireland was the unanimous choice of accused persons and of human-rights advocates and was viewed as a cornerstone of the country's criminal-law system. There had never been a complaint that the system lacked transparency or impinged on or inhibited the rights of the accused. The system inspired confidence among the Irish people, who were very attached to it for historical and other reasons. ..."[15]

Thus, for some jury trials it inspires confidence, for others they have to be reformed as they leaves the accused without an explanation of why he or she was found guilty—completely different approaches, no consensus about what is right and wrong. The Court's jurisprudence is lukewarm in this context. It accepts jury trials, but at the same time checks the results on a case-by-case basis.

Similar seemingly insurmountable differences are seen in the attitude towards trials in absentia. While Italian procedural law accepts them under specific circumstances, the German Constitutional Court considers then as incompatible with human dignity and rule of law. It argues that in such a case an extradition would even violate German constitutional identity.

3.3 Reforms Challenging the Common Heritage

Even more important than controversies about the contents of rule of law and human rights—what seemed to be accepted by all is more and more often called into question again. Although the ideological divide between East and West seemed to be overcome, once again there are major differences between Western European countries on the one hand and Poland, Romania and Hungary on the other hand. They cannot agree on recent reforms of the judiciary which—for the one side—are meant to strengthen independence and—for the other side—to undermine it. The controversy is about measures such as lowering the age limit for judges with the consequence of ending the judicial careers of a large amount of especially experienced judges and then raising the age limit again, or sacking active investigators of corruption. While EU law in the field of judicial policy is theoretically built on "mutual trust", it seems that quite a few of the most recent judgments of national courts and the EU Court in Luxembourg show an evident lack of trust. Clashes show that there might be less common ground than assumed.

If, however, Europe loses its belief in rule of law, it loses its identity.

---

[15] ECtHR, 16.11.2010, no.926/05 – Taxquet v. Belgium, para. 76.

4 Response to the Challenges

The decisive question therefore is which narrative is true. Where do we stand 100 years after the Versailles Treaty, 70 years after the foundation of the Council of Europe, 30 years after the end of the Cold War, 15 years after the accession of many Eastern European States to the European Union? Building up a new and united Europe with a European Court of Justice, a European Court of Human Rights and rule of law—is it a success story or a story of lost illusions?

There is some truth in both narratives, the optimistic and the pessimistic one.

The mission of all those striving for societies based on rule of law resembles the task of Sisyphus. We have a huge boulder in front of all of us. We have to push it up on top of a mountain. We can never exclude that the boulder might roll down again, but we must never give up. This mythological story can be interpreted in the perspective of Albert Camus. The last words of his philosophical study are:

> "La lutte elle-même vers les sommets suffit à remplir un cœur d'homme. Il faut imaginer Sisyphe heureux."[16]

5 Europe as a Model?

But for Asian countries the question remains if the European model is inspiring for them, if they want to coordinate their efforts in order to create a similar institutionalized system. Perhaps it is helpful not to have utopian visions, but to see reality as it is. Some questions and answers might be helpful.

Has the European model brought peace?

Generally, yes. EU countries have never resorted to violence against one another, despite important controversies, e.g. during the financial crisis in Greece. The same is, however, not true for the countries of the Council of Europe. It is sufficient to mention the armed conflicts between Georgia and Russia, as well as between Ukraine and Russia. Nevertheless, even in such a desperate situation the Convention is helpful. The Court can provide a platform for conflict resolution in inter-State cases. The judgment on compensation in the first case Georgia v. Russia was just adopted; Russia has to pay to Georgia 10 million Euros. But it never paid, and after its expulsion from the Council, refused categorically to abide by the judgment.

Has the European model helped to create a "European identity"?

Yes, if something like a European identity exists, it is mainly built on common values that were elaborated over many years step by step, not least concerning women's rights and minorities' rights. However, this convergence is undermined by new populist movements claiming back (absolute) sovereign rights for the national States. Brexit is an example for such developments.

Has the European model a future?

---

[16] "The struggle itself toward the heights is enough to fill a man's heart. One must imagine Sisyphus happy."

Yes. The European model has overcome already many crises. Even if the present crisis seems to be deeper and more threatening than other crises before, there are no signs of a general abandonment of the project. Rather, there seems to be consensus that some re-orientation might be useful. "More" is not always "better". The principle of "subsidiarity" is leading the way. But, as long as all main players reflect together what to do and how to overcome the difficulties there is a chance to profit from the crisis and to improve what was achieved.

For Asian countries Europe is far away. Observing with distance what is going on might help to find out what mistakes should not be repeated and what is positive and inspiring.

Protection of Human Rights in East and Southeast Asian Countries After World War II: A Short Comment on the Keynote Speech of Vice-President Judge Nußberger

Kimio Yakushiji

Please allow me first to express my heartfelt thanks to Vice-President Nußberger for her wonderful and very stimulating keynote speech. I would like to make a short comment on her speech by touching upon the reality of, and possible way forward in the near future for, human rights protection in countries in East and Southeast Asia including Japan from the perspective of a Japanese academic specializing in international human rights law.

1 The General Circumstances of the Countries in East and Southeast Asia After World War II: Contrast with Europe

In contrast with Europe, after the catastrophe of World War II, East and Southeast Asia (E + SE Asia), not to mention Asia as a whole, have been unable to build up regional or sub-regional institutions or mechanisms based on common values such as human rights, rule of law, and democracy. After WWII, the main influential powers such as the US and the USSR tried to expand their spheres of influence in this region mainly through political and military alliances, and certain colonial States tried to recover their colonies after the collapse of the "Empire of Japan." Peoples in the territories of this region could not draw pictures on the future order because most of them were under the yoke of the reconstructed colonial rule of Western Powers, were occupied by the American or Soviet troops, or, as in the case of China were in the midst of civil war. After the cold war started between the US and the USSR, the Chinese Communist Party won the Chinese Civil War on mainland China and established the People's Republic of China in 1949, although the Republic of China

K. Yakushiji (✉)
Emeritus Professor of Ritsumeikan University, Kyoto, Japan
e-mail: yakusiji@fc.ritsumei.ac.jp

M. Deguchi and K. Yakushiji (eds.), *Europe and Asia as a Legal Area for Fundamental Rights*, https://doi.org/10.1007/978-981-19-7542-4_2

led by the Kuomintang government in Taiwan continued to represent China in the UN until 1971. On the Korean peninsula, which was divided at the 38th parallel into two zones of occupation by either the US or the USSR after the collapse of the Japanese colonial rule, the Republic of Korea and the Democratic People's Republic of Korea were established in each zone in 1948, but the Korean war was waged with the invasion from the North Korea from 1950 until the Korean Armistice Agreement was signed in 1953. It was only in August 1991 that both States were simultaneously admitted to the UN. As for Japan, the Allied Powers' Peace Treaty with Japan was concluded in 1951 and Japan recovered its independence, but Japan had to wait for her comeback to international society until 1956, when Japan was accepted as a member of the UN.

On the other hand, decolonization movements in this region became active after WWII and many newly independent States were established, sometimes through harsh struggles against colonial powers before or after proclamations of independence. Indonesia declared its independence in 1945 but had to fight against the Netherlands until 1949; the US officially recognized the independence of the Philippines in 1946; the Union of Burma as a fully independent republic was established in 1948, and the UK recognized the establishment of the Federation of Malaya as an independent sovereign country within the Commonwealth in 1957. But, as is well known, on the Indochina peninsula, after the declaration of independence of Vietnam in 1945, the First Indochina War continued between Vietnam and France until 1954 when the Geneva Accords were concluded. During this war, Laos won autonomy in 1949 and became independent in 1953 although internal armed conflict continued until 1975, and Cambodia also gained independence in 1953 through an agreement with France. Vietnam was divided into two parts with the Democratic Republic of Vietnam in the north and the Republic of Vietnam in the south, but after the Vietnam War was over and all US troops withdrew according to the Paris Peace Accords, the two parts merged into the Socialist Republic of Vietnam in 1976 and one year later the country was admitted to the UN.

Under these circumstances, the principles the Asian-African countries regarded as most important from their perspective were reflected in the Declaration adopted at the Asian-African conference of Bandung held in 1955. The declaration included among others the following principles: respect for the sovereignty and territorial integrity of all nations; recognition of the equality of all races and of all nations large and small; abstention from intervention or interference in the internal affairs of another country; and a pledge to refrain from acts or threats of aggression or the use of force against the territorial integrity or political independence of any country.[1]

[1] Final Communiqué of the Asian-African conference of Bandung (24 April 1955), "G. Declaration on the promotion of world peace and co-operation", http://www.cvce.eu/obj/final_communique_of_the_asian_african_conference_of_bandung_24_april_1955-en-676237bd-72f7-471f-949a-88b6ae513585.html. In addition to five sponsoring countries (Burma, Ceylon, India, Indonesia and Pakistan), twenty-four Asian and African countries participated in the Conference. From East Asia and Southeast Asia region eight more countries (Cambodia, People's Republic of China, Japan, Laos, Philippines, Thailand, Democratic Republic of Vietnam and Republic of Vietnam) attended the Conference.

The Member States of the UN from E + SE Asia had comprised only four countries, that is, China (Republic of China), the Philippines, Thailand, and Burma before the Bandung Conference was convened. Thus, the contributions of the countries of this region to the adoption of the Universal Declaration of Human Rights (UDHR) and 1954 Draft International Covenants on Human Rights were limited. Furthermore, a strong movement promoting Asian or E + SE Asian unity or integration, equivalent to that in Europe was never organized or grown up in the aftermath of World War II. It seems that the basic prerequisites for establishing institutional mechanisms based on human rights or the rule of law were lacking in this region at that time. In Southeast Asia, it is true that the Association of Southeast Asia was organized in 1961 and then the Association of Southeast Asian Nations (ASEAN)[2] was established by Indonesia, Malaysia, the Philippines, Singapore and Thailand in 1967 in order to accelerate economic growth, social progress, and cultural development in the region, to promote peace and stability through abiding respect for justice and the rule of law in the relationship among countries of the region, and so on. But it was also established in the circumstances of Cold War conflicts, military coups, events such as the so-called Indonesian massacre in 1965–1966, and inter-ethnic conflicts in the region. Thus no mention was made of human rights in the Bangkok Declaration of 1967. It is worth mentioning that the first principle in the Bandung Declaration of 1955 had already referred to respect for fundamental human rights, and the communiqué of the conference had stated: "The Asian-African Conference declared its full support of the fundamental principles of Human Rights as set forth in the Charter of the United Nations and took note of the Universal Declaration of Human Rights as a common standard of achievement for all peoples and all nations," and also gave its full support of the principle of self-determination of peoples and nations as "a pre-requisite of the full enjoyment of all fundamental Human Rights."[3] However, different from the principle of self-determination of all people, human rights still remained only a symbol on the documents of the 1950s and 1960s for many Asian-African countries. The African Commission on Human and Peoples' Rights itself recognized that:

> In spite of the [OAU's] endorsement of the principles of the Universal Declaration on Human Rights of 1948 in the preamble of the OAU Charter, the promotion and protection of human rights within OAU members states was not a major priority. As such, it concentrated its efforts on political and economic independence, non-discrimination and the liberation of Africa, the eradication of colonialism on the continent and apartheid in Southern Africa, at the expense of individual liberty.[4]

In Africa, however, pressure was applied by media groups, the Church, and inter-governmental and non-governmental organizations against the OAU, which was accused of using a double standard in condemning apartheid in South Africa while failing to condemn the massive human rights violations committed by some of its

[2] The ASEAN Declaration (Bangkok Declaration) Bangkok, 8 August 1967, available at https://asean.org/the-asean-declaration-bangkok-declaration-bangkok-8-august-1967/.

[3] *Supra* note 1, "C. Human rights and self-determination".

[4] African Commission on Human and People's Rights, "History," available at https://www.achpr.org/history.

own members. After more pressure and support by the UN, the OAU Assembly of Heads of State and Government decided to call on the OAU Secretary General to form a committee of experts to draft an African Charter on Human and People's Rights (ACHPR) providing for mechanisms to promote and protect the rights embodied in the Charter, which was finally adopted in 1981.[5] The existence of the OAU in Africa seems to have been an essential and significant prerequisite for the adoption of the ACHPR and creation of its implementing mechanisms.

Contrary to this, Asia as a whole, which has no regional intergovernmental organization equal to the OAU, has not yet found the key to creating Asian human rights conventions and institutional mechanisms for the promotion and protection of human rights. However, at the level of Southeast Asian countries, the ASEAN has made new progress towards the creation of new sub-regional mechanisms for protecting human rights. That said, in eastern Asia, we have no regional standing organization or multilateral mechanism to constantly monitor human rights issues. Therefore, I would like to mention some aspects of the human rights situation in this region merely by referring to the ways E + SE Asian countries address human rights issues under the UN mechanisms to promote and protect human rights.

A few words should be added about Japan. The Constitution of Japan, promulgated in 1946, allocated thirty-one articles covering the fundamental rights and duties of nationals (Chapter III: Rights and Duties of the People). Many articles of the Constitution, drafted with the involvement of the US occupying forces, covered most civil and political rights as well as economic, social, and cultural rights prescribed in the UDHR. In 1951, the Treaty of Peace with Japan was signed by 48 Allied Powers and Japan, and in the preamble of the Treaty, Japan declared its intention "to strive to realize the objectives of the Universal Declaration of Human Rights" and "to seek to create within Japan conditions of stability and well-being as defined in Articles 55 and 56 of the Charter of the United Nations and already initiated by post-surrender Japanese legislation" as a condition of its recovery of independence.[6] Based on the Peace Treaty of 1951, Japan concluded peace or other treaties to build new relationships with other countries such as the Treaty of Peace Between Japan and the Republic of China in 1952, the Joint Declaration by the USSR and Japan in 1956 (Japan was admitted to the UN that year), Treaty on Basic Relations Between Japan and the Republic of Korea in 1965, Treaty of Peace and Friendship Between Japan and the People's Republic of China in 1978 (a Joint Communiqué of the Government of Japan and the Government of the People's Republic of China had been issued in 1972). In parallel with this, the US-Japan Security Treaty was signed in 1951, to be superseded by the Treaty of Mutual Cooperation and Security in 1960, and in 1972 the Okinawa islands were returned to Japan by the US. Japan became one of the high GNP countries in the world via the so-called high economic growth period from

[5] *Ibid*. See G. Naldi, "The African Union and the Regional Human Rights System," M. Evans & R. Murray, The African Charter on Human and Peoples' Rights: The System in Practice, 1986–2006, 2nd ed. (2008, Cambridge), pp. 20–48.

[6] Treaty of Peace with Japan, paragraph 2 of preamble, UN Treaty Series, No. 1832 (1952), p. 46. Fifty-one Allied Powers took part on the San Francisco Conference, but the USSR, Poland and Czechoslovakia did not sign the Treaty.

1954 thru 1970. Japan ratified the International Covenant on Economic, Social and Cultural Rights (ICESCR) and International Covenant on Civil and Political Right (ICCPR) in 1979, marking the first time Japan became a State party to the UN core human rights conventions.

2 Two Trends Which May Improve the Human Rights Situation in East and Southeast Asian Countries

With the end of the Cold War, so-called "development dictatorship" regimes in the E + SE Asian region were deprived of their justifiability. After the end of the Cold War in Europe and against the background of East Asia's remarkable economic growth in the 1980s and 1990s, there arose two trends which affected the human rights situation in the E + SE Asian region. First was the progress among ASEAN countries in the field of human rights, and the second was the participation of E + SE Asian countries in the UN's process for promoting and protecting human rights. On the one hand, ASEAN began to change from a regional security organization to a regional community consisting of a Political-Security Community, Economic Community, and Socio-Cultural Community. One month after the World Conference on Human Rights held in 1993, the 26th ASEAN Ministerial Meeting agreed that "ASEAN should coordinate a common approach on human rights and actively participate and contribute to the application, promotion and protection of human rights," and "ASEAN should also consider the establishment of an appropriate regional mechanism on human rights."[7] On the other hand, the Vienna Declaration and Action Programme of 1993 accelerated the ratification of or accession to the core UN human rights conventions in particular the Convention on the Elimination of All Forms of Discrimination Against Women (CEDAW) and the Convention on Rights of the Child (CRC) by E + SE Asian countries. Japan agreed to support ASEAN's efforts to further implement and disseminate the ASEAN Human Rights Declaration (AHRD), to support the work of the ASEAN Inter-Governmental Commission on Human Rights (AICHR) and the ASEAN Commission on the Promotion and Protection of the Rights of Women and Children (ACWC) through training, capacity-building and technical cooperation aimed at enhancing the promotion and protection of human rights and fundamental freedoms, and to continue to strengthen the capacity in the law and justice sector to strengthen the rule of law, judicial systems, and the legal infrastructure.[8] Owing to the

---

[7] Joint Communique of the Twenty-Sixth ASEAN Ministerial Meeting Singapore, 23–24 July 1993, paras. 16–18. Available at https://humanrightsinasean.info/wp-content/uploads/files/documents/ASEAN%20Joint%20Communique%2026th%20ASEAN%20Ministerial%20Meeting%201993.pdf.

[8] Revised Implementation Plan of the Vision Statement on ASEAN-Japan Friendship and Cooperation: Shared Vision, Shared Identity, Shared Future, 6 August 2017, Manila, paras. 1.11–1.13. Available at https://asean.org/storage/2017/08/Revised-IP-of-ASEAN-Japan-Vision-Statement-Final.pdf.

limit of my knowledge, I will only give a basic outline of the ASEAN's mechanisms for promoting and protecting human rights.

2.1 The Progress in ASEAN's Human Rights Promotion Mechanism and Its Challenges

The Final Declaration of the Regional Meeting for Asia of the World Conference on Human Rights held at Bangkok in 1993 (Bangkok Declaration of 1993) mentioned that, "while human rights are universal in nature, they must be considered *in the context of a dynamic and evolving process of international norm-setting*, bearing in mind *the significance of national and regional particularities and various historical, cultural and religious backgrounds* (emphasis added)."[9] However, the Vienna Declaration adopted by the World Conference on Human Rights mentioned that, "[w]hile the significance of national and regional particulars and various historical, cultural and religious backgrounds must be borne in mind, it is *the duty of States, regardless of their political, economic and cultural systems, to promote and protect all human rights and fundamental freedoms* (emphasis added)."[10] The two documents are in sharp contrast in that the former gives weight to the significance of national and regional particularities and various historical, cultural, and religious backgrounds of human rights, while the latter emphasizes the universality and globally equal applicability of human rights.

The Bangkok Declaration of 1993, which has been regarded as a symbolic document that reflected the Asian countries' common stance on international protection of human rights,[11] gave importance to the following principles: respect for national sovereignty and territorial integrity as well as non-interference in the internal affairs of States, and non-use of human rights as an instrument of political pressure (para. 5); the interdependence and indivisibility of economic, social, cultural, civil, and political rights, and the need to give equal emphasis to all categories of human rights (para. 10); the right to development as a universal and inalienable right and integral part of fundamental human rights, which must be realized through international

[9] Para. 8 of the Declaration adopted on 2 April 1993, in the Report of the regional meeting for Asia of the World Conference on Human Rights, Bangkok, 29 March–2 April 1993, A/CONF.157/ASRM/8; A/CONF.157/PC/59, p. 5. Among thirty-five Asian countries that took part in the Regional Meeting there were fourteen E + SE Asian countries except Cambodia (KHM). Timor-Leste (TLS) was not yet an independent country until 2003.

[10] Para. 5 of the Declaration adopted on 25 June 1993, in the World Conference on Human Rights, Vienna, 14–25 June 1993, Vienna Declaration and Programme of Action, Note by a Secretariat, U.N. Doc. A/CONF.157/23, p. 5.

[11] See Li-ann Thio, "Implementing Human Rights in ASEAN Countries: "Promises to Keep and Miles to Go before I Sleep"," *Yale Human Rights and Development Journal*, Vol. 2 (1999), pp. 22–29; Suzannah Linton, "ASEAN States, Their Reservations to Human Rights Treaties and the Proposed ASEAN Commission on Women and Children", *Human Rights Quarterly*, Vol. 30 (2008), pp. 437–441; Jun Zhao, "China and the Uneasy Case for Universal Human Rights," *Human Rights Quarterly*, Vol. 37 (2015), pp. 45–46.

cooperation (para. 17); the primary responsibility of States for the promotion and protection of human rights through appropriate infrastructure and mechanisms and the remedies which must be sought and provided primarily through such mechanisms and procedures (para. 9); and the universality, objectivity and non-selectivity of all human rights and the need to avoid the application of double standards in the implementation of human rights and its politicization (para. 7).[12] Both China and the ASEAN States are said to have played an important role in formulating the Bangkok Declaration of 1993.[13] Some of the alleged principles in the Bangkok Declaration such as those mentioned in paragraphs 10 and 17 above were incorporated into the Vienna Declaration (paras. 5 and 10), but others were not. Thus, the Vienna Declaration and Programme of Actions set forth common basic principles which all States of the world should observe, and the foreign ministers of ASEAN welcomed the international consensus achieved in Vienna, although they expressed their conviction that "freedom, progress and national stability are promoted by a balance between the rights of the individual and those of the community, through which many individual rights are realized[14]" in the 26th ASEAN Ministerial Meeting mentioned above.

About 30 years have passed since the Vienna Conference. During this period ASEAN has expanded its membership to ten by accepting Brunei Darussalam (1984), Vietnam (1995), Lao PDR (1997), Myanmar (1997), and Cambodia (1999) as new members. As for activities in the field of human rights, the ASEAN Charter was signed in 2007 and its article 2(i) prescribed "respect for fundamental freedoms, the promotion and protection of human rights, and the promotion of social justice" as principles ASEAN and its member States shall respect, and article 14(1) provided that "ASEAN shall establish an ASEAN human rights body."[15] In 2009 AICHR, an inter-governmental consultative body consisting of representatives nominated by their respective governments, was inaugurated as an overarching institution with overall responsibility for the promotion and protection of human rights. According to the Terms of Reference (TOR) of AICHR, the following functions are included as its mandate: to develop strategies for the promotion and protection of human rights and fundamental freedoms (4.1); to develop the AHRD and other instruments dealing with human rights (4.2); to promote capacity building for the effective implementation of international human rights treaty obligations undertaken by ASEAN Member States (4.4); and to encourage ASEAN Member States to consider acceding to and ratifying international human rights instruments (4.5). AICHR shall be guided in exercising its mandate by the principles embodied in 2.1 thru 2.5 of the TOR, including respect for the independence, sovereignty, equality, territorial integrity, and national identity of all ASEAN Member States, and non-interference in their

[12] Bangkok Declaration, *supra* note 9, pp. 4–5.

[13] Jun Zhao, *supra* note 11, p. 45; see also Li-ann Thio, supra note 11, pp. 25–29.

[14] *Supra* note 7, para. 17.

[15] ASEAN Charter, Articles 2 & 14. Available at https://asean.org/storage/2012/05/The-ASEAN-Charter-14042020-final.pdf.

internal affairs.[16] Following the creation of AICHR, the ASEAN Commission on the Promotion and Protection of the Rights and Women and Children (ACWC) was established in 2010.[17] In 2012 the ASEAN Human Rights Declaration (AHRD) was adopted at the twenty-first ASEAN Summit, and the ASEAN Convention Against Trafficking in Persons, Especially Women and Children was concluded in 2015.[18]

The AHRD listed not only most of the civil, political, economic, social, and cultural rights set forth in the UDHR, including the right to freedom of expression and peaceful assembly (with the exception of the right to freedom of association) (articles 23 & 24), but also so-called third-generation human rights such as right to development and right to peace (articles 35 thru 38). The AHRD has no legally binding force and it is sometimes criticized since it may allow wide-ranging restrictions of human rights by admitting that "[t]he enjoyment of human rights and fundamental freedoms must be balanced with the performance of corresponding duties" and that "the realization of human rights must be considered in the regional and national context bearing in mind different political, economic, legal, social, cultural, historical and religious backgrounds (articles 5 & 6)." Though the AHRD reflects a compromise made in 2012, it also confirms an important principle that "[e]very person has the right to an effective and enforceable remedy, to be determined by a court or other competent authorities, for acts violating the rights granted to that person by the constitution or by law" (article 5), on which an efficient domestic judicial system for the protection of human rights should be built. As far as the AICHR is concerned, its mandate and functions are limited to promoting human rights and, unlike the Inter-American Commission on Human Rights, it is not authorized to receive and investigate individual petitions alleging human rights violations. Moreover, unlike working groups under the Human Rights Council Complaint Procedure, it has no competence to examine written communications from alleged victims of

---

[16] TOR of the AICHR, "2 Principles" and "4 Mandate and Functions". Available at https://aichr.org/wp-content/uploads/2018/10/TOR-of-AICHR.pdf.

[17] With regard to the purpose, principles and mandate and functions of the ACWC, see TOR of the ACWC. Available at https://www.asean.org/wp-content/uploads/images/2012/Social_cultural/ACW/TOR-ACWC.pdf.

[18] ASEAN Human Rights Declaration, adopted at the 21st ASEAN Summit in Phnom Penh, 18 November 2012. Available at https://asean.org/asean-human-rights-declaration/ and Convention Against Trafficking in Persons, Especially Women and Children concluded in 2015. Available at http://agreement.asean.org/media/download/20160303122945.pdf.

With regard to the history, backgrounds and contents of these documents see John D. Ciorciari, "Institutionalizing Human Rights in Southeast Asia," *Human Rights Quarterly*, Vol. 34 (2012), pp. 695–725; Catherine Shanahan Renshaw, "The ASEAN Human Rights Declaration 2012," *Human Rights Law Review*, Vol. 13 (2013), pp. 557–579; Gerard Clarke, "The Evolving ASEAN Human Rights System: the ASEAN Human Rights Declaration of 2012," *Northwestern Journal of International Human Right*, Vol. 11 (2012), pp. 1–27; Hien Bui, "The ASEAN Human Rights System: A Critical Analysis," *Asian Journal of Comparative Law*, Vol. 11 (2016), pp. 111–140; Robin Ramcharan, "ASEAN's Human Rights Commission: Policy Considerations for Enhancing Its Capacity to Protect Human Rights," *UCL Human Rights Review*, Vol. 3 (2010), pp. 199–235; Deborah Basham-Jones, "ASEAN's Intergovernmental Commission on Human Rights: A Pale Shadow of What It Could Have Been," *Asia–Pacific Journal on Human Rights and the Law*, Vol. 13, Issue 2 (2012), pp. 1–26.

human rights violations or to bring consistent patterns of gross and attested violations of human rights to an upper organ. Though AICHR's 2019 Annual Report only mentions abstractly that "[c]onsistent with its Terms of Reference, AICHR has seen encouraging progress in its efforts to promote human rights; however challenges remain to the protection of human rights,"[19] there are some severe criticism about its incapability to deal with serious human rights violations such as the use of systematic violence, discrimination and segregation against the ethnic minority Rohingya in Myanmar, and large-scale extrajudicial killings in the name of a "war on drugs" in the Philippines. Therefore, civil society organizations such as Forum-Asia call on the AICHR and ASEAN Foreign Ministers to actively respond to serious human rights violations, including through (1) the establishment of a robust complaints mechanism that would receive, examine individual complaints and seek their solutions independently and professionally, and (2) the drafting of an ASEAN convention on human rights which at least reflects minimum international human rights standards.[20] Though, it cannot be denied that the creation and operation of the ASEAN regional human rights mechanisms seems to have contributed to the promotion of human rights in the ASEAN Member States especially in the field of suppression of trafficking in persons (especially women and children) and promotion of the rights of immigrant workers and their family, ASEAN's mechanisms for human rights protection face a crucial juncture. The institution by Gambia of proceedings against Myanmar concerning application of the Genocide Convention before the International Court of Justice in 2019 was a symbolic action from outside ASEAN countries in case the regional human rights mechanisms are unable to properly deal with the serious violation of human rights. But, in the end, it is the people of the ASEAN countries who must decide the most appropriate regional human rights protection mechanism. If the attitudes of the leaders of ASEAN Member States towards the protection of human rights do not change, the human rights situation in these countries will also never change.

---

[19] The AICHR Annual Report 2019, "10 Years of the AICHR: An Overview," p. 7. Available at https://aichr.org/wp-content/uploads/2019/08/AICHR-Annual-Report-2019.pdf.

[20] See, *e.g.*, Forum-Asia, A Decade in Review: Assessing the Performance of the AICHR to Uphold the Protection Mandates, pp. 3–13; Forum-Asia, Joint Statement: ASEAN needs a stronger Human Rights Mechanism. Available at https://www.forum-asia.org/?p=28741.

2.2 Progress of Ratification of and Accession to Core UN Human Rights Conventions by East and Southeast Asian Countries and Stagnancy of Acceptance of Individual Communications Procedure

The Vienna Conference of 1993 called for the universal ratification of human rights treaties and set target years for CRC (1995) and CEDAW (2000).[21] At that time the core UN human rights treaties were six: International Convention on the Elimination of All Forms of Racial Discrimination (ICERD), ICESCR, ICCPR, CEDAW, Convention against Torture and Other Cruel, Inhuman or Degrading Treatment or Punishment (CAT), and CRC. Table 1[22] shows that before the Vienna Conference the E + SE Asian countries which had already ratified or acceded to all or most of the six core conventions were only MNG (five), KOR (six), KHM (six), PHL (six), and VNM (five). KOR became a State party to ICESCR, ICCPR, and CRC under its Sixth Republic established in 1987 and after the Cold War was over in 1989, and KHM's Supreme National Council acceded to ICESCR, ICCPR, CEDAW, CAT, and CRC in 1992 under the administration and support of the United Nations Transitional Authority in Cambodia. After the Vienna Conference, fifteen among sixteen E + SE Asian countries (except TLS) became State parties to the CRC by the end of 1995, and CEDAW's State parties increased to thirteen (all except PRK, BRN, and TLS) by the end of 2000. Since the International Convention on the Protection of the Rights of All Migrant Workers and Members of Their Families (ICRMW, 2003), Convention on the Rights of Persons with Disabilities (CPRD, 2008) and International Convention on Enforced Disappearance (CPED, 2010) entered into force after the Vienna Conference, now nine core conventions and four of their protocols are in force setting forth international standards of substantive human rights and freedoms. It is beyond doubt that both the start of the Universal Periodic Review in 2008 according to the resolution 5/1 on Institution-Building of the Human Rights Council (HRC) and, as for ASEAN countries, the entry into force of the TOR of the AICHR in 2009 propelled the ratification of and accession to the nine core conventions and their four protocols by E + SE Asian countries.[23] As of 30 September 2020, Table 1 shows that all sixteen E + SE Asian countries have become State parties to CEDAW and to CRC and fifteen have become State parties to the Optional Protocol to CRC on

[21] Para 26 of the Vienna Declaration and para. 4 of the Vienna Programme of Action A/CONF.157/23, pp. 5 and 13; Para. 21 of the Vienna Declaration and para. 39 of the Vienna Programme of Action, *ibid.*, pp. 8 and 19.

[22] Hereinafter the names of the E + SE Asian countries are abbreviated as follows: CHN (China), PRK (the Democratic People's Republic of Korea), JPN (Japan), MNG (Mongolia), KOR (the Republic of Korea), BRN (Brunei Darussalam), KHM (Cambodia), IDN (Indonesia), LAO (the Lao People's democratic Republic), MYS (Malaysia), MMR (Myanmar), PHL (the Philippines), SGP (Singapore), THA (Thailand), TLS (Timor-Leste), VNM (Vietnam).

[23] Typical examples are as follows: IDN ratified CRPD (2011), ICRMW (2012), OP-CRC-AC and OP-CRC-SC (2012); Malaysia ratified CRPD (2010), OP-CRC-AC, and OP-CRC-SC (2012); Myanmar ratified CPRD (2011), OP-CRC-SC (2012), and ICESCR (2017); MNG ratified and acceded to CPRD (2009), ICCPR-OP2 (2012), OP-CAT (2015), and CPED (2015).

the involvement of children in armed conflict (OP-CRC-AC), the Optional Protocol to CRC on the sale of children, child prostitution, and child pornography (OP-CRC-SC) and CRPD. The universal character of the rights prescribed in these five treaties is accepted by all or nearly all States in this region. Thus, all or almost all countries in the E + SE Asian region have come to the stage of having common instruments for implementation as well as for bilateral or multilateral co-operation and coordination in the field of protection of the human rights of women, children, and persons with disabilities, elimination of discrimination based on gender, and suppression of human trafficking and exploitation. However, with regard to ICERD, ICESCR, ICCPR, and CAT, several States still resist or hesitate to become State parties, and few States have agreed to be bound by the Second Optional Protocol to ICCPR on abolition of the death penalty (ICCPR-OP2) or the Optional Protocol to CAT (OP-CAT), ICRMW and ICPED. Consequently, they have not yet reached a common standpoint to undertake all obligations to protect basic civil and political rights set forth in ICCPR as well as to eliminate all forms of racial and ethnic discrimination provided for in ICERD.

Another disappointing feature is the refusal by many E + SE Asian countries of accepting the treaty bodies' competence to receive and consider the individual communications prescribed in each of the UN human rights conventions. Now each of the nine core conventions has its own individual communications procedure and its follow-up system. However, State parties to the Optional Protocol to ICCPR in this region are only MNG (1991), KOR (1990), and PHL (1989), and State parties to Optional Protocol to CEDAW are MNG (2002), KOR (2006), KHM (2010), PHL (2003), and THA (2000) as of 30 September 2020. The State parties to the Optional protocol to CRC on a communications procedure and the Optional Protocol to CRPD remain two countries each, that is, MNG (2015) and THA (2012) for the former and the same MNG (2009) and THA (2016) for the latter, and in the case of article 14 of ICERD, the Optional Protocol to ICESCR, and article 22 of CAT, only one State party has accepted the individual communications procedure that is, KOR (1997), MNG (2010), and KOR (2007) respectively. Eleven other E + SE Asian countries, that is, CHN, PRK, JPN, BRN, IDN, LAO, MYS, MMR, SGP, TLS, and VNM, have not yet accepted the individual communications procedure. Considering that the possessors of rights under UN human rights conventions are individuals, it is essential that any person whose rights or freedoms recognized in the conventions are violated shall have an effective remedy by competent judicial authorities first, and, if the remedy is denied, the right to have his or her claims for remedies considered objectively by independent monitoring bodies established by the conventions. As long as influential countries in the region continue to reject individual complaint procedures, it will be difficult to create effective regional human rights mechanisms, not to mention a regional human rights court. In this connection China repeated its position in its 3rd Universal Periodic Review (UPR) (2019): "The primary responsibility for the implementation of international human rights treaties falls on national

Table 1 Ratification of or accession to the core UN human rights conventions by E + SE countries

		CHN	PRK	JPN	MNG	KOR	BRN	KHM	IDN	LAO	MYS	MMR	PHL	SGP	THA	TLS	VNM
	Entry into Force																
ICERD	04 Jan 1969	29 Dec 1981a	×	15 Dec 1995a	06 Aug 1969	05 Dec 1978	×	28 Nov 1983	25 Jun 1999a	22 Feb 1974a	×	×	15 Sep 1967	27 Nov 2017	28 Jan 2003a	16 Apr 2003a	9 Jun 1982a
ICESCR	03 Jan 1976	27 Mar 2001	14 Sep 1981a	21 Jun 1979	18 Nov 1974	10 Apr 1990a	×	26 May 1992a	23 Feb 2006a	13 Feb 2007	×	06 Oct 2017	07 Jun 1974	×	5 Sep 1999a	16 Apr 2003a	24Sep 1982a
ICCPR	23 Mar 1976	1998 S	14 Sep 1981a	21 Jun 1979	18 Nov 1974	10 Apr 1990a	×	29 Oct 1992	23 Feb 2006a	25 Sep 2009	×	×	23 Oct 1986	×	29 Oct 1996a	18 Sep 2003a	24 Sep 1982a
ICCPR-OP2	11 Jul 1991	×	×	×	13 Mar 2012a	×	×	×	×	×	×	×	20 Nov 2007	×	×	18 Sep 2003a	×
CEDAW	03 Sep 1981	04 Nov 1980	27 Feb 2001a	25 Jun 1985	20 Jul 1981	27 Dec 1984	24 May 2006a	15 Oct 1992a	13 Sep 1984	14 Aug 1981	5 Jul 1995a	22 Jul 1997a	05 Aug 1981	5 Oct 1995a	9 Aug 1985a	16 Apr 2003a	17 Feb 1982
CAT	26 Jun 1987	04 Oct 1988	×	29 Jun 1999a	24 Jan 2002a	9 Jan 1995a	2015 S	15 Oct 1992a	28 Oct 1998	26 Sep 2012	×	×	18 Jun 1986a	×	2 Oct 2007a	16 Apr 2003a	05 Feb 2015
OP-CAT	22 Jun 2006	×	×	×	12 Feb 2015	×	×	30 Mar 2007	×	×	×	×	17 Apr 2012a	×	×	2005 S	×

(continued)

Table 1 (continued)

		CHN	PRK	JPN	MNG	KOR	BRN	KHM	IDN	LAO	MYS	MMR	PHL	SGP	THA	TLS	VNM
CRC	02 Sep 1990	02 Mar 1992	21 Sep 1990	22 Apr 1994	05 Jul 1990	20 Nov 1991	27 Dec 1995a	15 Oct 1992a	05 Sep 1990	8 May 1991a	17 Feb 1995a	15 Jul 1991a	21 Aug 1990	5 Oct 1995a	27 Mar 1992a	16 Apr 2003a	28 Feb 1990
OP-CRC-AC	12 Feb 2002	20 Feb 2008	×	02 Aug 2004	06 Oct 2004	24 Sep 2004	17 May 2016a	16 Jul 2004	24 Sep 2012	20 Sep 2006a	12 Apr 2012a	27 Sep 2019	26 Aug 2003	11 Dec 2008	27 Feb 2006a	2 Aug 2004a	20 Dec 2001
OP-CRC-SC	18 Jan 2002	03 Dec 2002	10 Nov 2014	24 Jan 2005	27 Jun 2003	24 Sep 2004	21 Nov 2006a	30 May 2002	24 Sep 2012	20 Sep 2006a	12 Apr 2012a	16 Jan 2012a	28 May 2002	X	11 Jan 2006a	16 Apr 2003a	20 Dec 2001
ICRMW	01 Jul 2003	×	×	×	×	×	×	2004 S	31 May 2012	×	×	×	05 Jul 1995	×	×	30 Jan 2004a	×
CRPD	03 May 2008	01 Aug 2008	06 Dec 2016	20 Jan 2014	13 May 2009a	11 Dec 2008	11 Apr 2016	20 Dec 2012	30 Nov 2011	25 Sep 2009	19 Jul 2010	7 Dec 2011a	15 Apr 2008	18 Jul 2013	29 Jul 2008	×	05 Feb 2015
CPED	23 Dec 2010	×	×	23 Jul 2009	12 Feb 2015	×	×	27 Jun 2013a	2010 S	2008 S	×	×	×	×	2012 S	×	×
Total	**9 + 4Pts**	**6 + 2pts**	**5 + 1Pt**	**8+ 2Pts**	**8 + 4Pts**	**7 + 2Pts**	**3 + 2Pts**	**8 + 3Pts**	**8+ 2Pts**	**7 + 2Pts**	**3 + 2Pts**	**4 + 2Pts**	**8 + 4 Pts**	**4 + 1 Pt**	**7 + 2Pts**	**7 + 3Pts**	**7 + 2Pts**

Produced from Status of Treaties of the UN Treaty Collection, Chap. IV (as of 30 June 2022)
The letter “a” means accession. The letter “S” means signature

governments. Citizens should resort to domestic complaint institutions for remedies and solutions when their rights were violated."[24] Vietnam did not accept the recommendation requesting ratification of the OP-CEDAW without mentioning any reason in its 3rd UPR (2019).[25] Indonesia supported the recommendations requesting consideration of ratifying OP-ICESCR or acceding to OP-ICCPR, but only took note of the recommendation requesting ratification of OP-ICCPR without explaining any reason in its 3rd UPR (2017).[26] Japan, which accepted the state communications procedure under CAT and ICED, stated in its national report in its 3rd UPR (2017) that "The [Government of Japan] considers the procedure to be noteworthy in a sense that it could effectively guarantee the implementation of Human Rights Treaties. At the same time, consideration has been given to questions such as whether there are any problems in relation to Japan's Judicial system and legislative policy, and the kind of system that would need to be established for implementation of the individual communications procedure in the case where Japan accepts it based on further discussion among the relevant ministers. ...The GOJ will continue to engage in the discussion on this matter, while taking various opinions into account."[27] Though the reasons are different from country to country, eleven countries do not seem to be ready to accept an individual communications procedure in the near future. This attitude towards individual communications procedure has made it difficult for the people in this region to become familiar with UN human rights conventions and to make use of them and consequently prevents convention procedures from providing remedies to the stakeholders.

3 Heterogeneity of Contemporary East and Southeast Asian Countries: The Backgrounds of Their Contextual Approaches

3.1 Different Circumstances Surrounding Human Rights and Rule of Law Between Europe and East and Southeast Asia

The wide differences of approach towards UN human rights processes among E + SE Asian countries mentioned above may derive from the diversity of political, economic, religious, ethnic, and historical situations which each country has been and is faced with. Though the difference of attitudes towards human rights protection between Western European countries and former Eastern European countries may still be wide, almost all of them are now member States of the Council of

---

[24] A/HRC/40/6/Add.1, para. 2, reply to 28.3.

[25] A/HRC/41/7, para. 38, 38.38 and A/HRC/41/7/Add.1, para. 15, No. 38.

[26] A/HRC/36/7, para. 141, 141.1–141.3 and A.HRC/36/7/Add.1, para. 10.

[27] A/HRC/WG.6/28/JPN/1, para.83.

Europe which promotes common values of rule of law, democracy, and human rights. However, the E + SE Asian region may consist of the most heterogeneous countries in the world, which may make necessary a step-by-step approach towards creating regional mechanisms for human rights protection. The Bangkok Declaration of 1993 mentioned above may have been the first step—a common external expression by heterogeneous Asian countries of the position they could take or adjust themselves to in order to incorporate human rights, rule of law, and democracy into their national and regional order in the post-Cold War and ever globalizing world.

According to Vice-President Nußberger's keynote speech, the success of the new world-view in Europe after the breakdown of the Soviet bloc consists of three pillars, that is, the principle of rule of law and comprehensive human rights (first pillar); institutionalization and judicialization by which judges watch over the implementation of human rights and rule of law (second pillar), and "acquis" in human rights and rule of law (third pillar).[28] She points out that among the European "acquis" in human rights and rule of law are included: fair trial (provided for in article 6 of the European Convention on Human Rights (ECHR)), prohibition of torture and inhumane treatment (article 3), right to freedom (articles 5 & 7), prohibition of discrimination (article 14), and freedom of expression and freedom of religion (articles 9 & 10) as basic substantive rights, while independence of the judiciary, legal certainty, proportionality, enhanced responsibility for the State's actions and omissions are institutional guarantees and fundamental principles in resolving conflicts that may arise.[29] In fact, after the dissolution of the former USSR and Yugoslavia, enlargement of the Council of Europe and the EU swept Eastern Europe, and new democratic governments have been established in the region. The principles, mechanisms and "acquis" in human rights remarked upon by Vice-President Nußberger have been applied promptly in Eastern Europe even if some of these "acquis" face persistent objections or are disregarded by the domestic authorities accustomed to old systems.

However, the landscape in the E + SE Asian region is considerably different from that of Europe. In this region, there still remains the cold war legacy on the Korean Peninsula and between mainland CHN and Taiwan. Though the socialist regimes in the USSR and other East European countries broke down, CHN keeps its socialist regime and has accomplished enormous economic growth. It now has become one of the super-powers in the world and is insisting on its "historic title" over a wide area of the South China Sea. On the other hand, several countries on the Indochina Peninsula have incorporated market economies and promoted foreign investment by introducing partially western economic, legal, and administrative systems with the assistance and support of JPN, EU, US, CHN, etc. Furthermore, the enlarged ASEAN has started to promote regional integration consisting of an ASEAN Political-Security

[28] Angelika Nußberger, The European Union and the Council of Europe as Legal Area of Freedom, Fundamental Rights and Rule of Law, in this book, pp. 4–5.

[29] *Ibid.*, pp. 5–11.

Community, ASEAN Economic Community, and ASEAN Socio-Cultural Community[30] based on its experience of rapid economic growth and financial crisis in the region under the influence of economic globalization and its potential human and natural resources.

Under the complicated circumstances of the region just mentioned, the human rights situation in this region differs from Europe's mainly in the following points. First, since E + SE Asian countries have no regional human rights conventions such as the European Convention of Human Rights (ECHR) protecting fundamental human rights and freedoms, and the ICESCR and ICCPR do not cover all countries in this region, substantive rights set forth in the UDHR have not been fully guaranteed to all people in this region by legally binding treaties. In certain countries, institutional guarantees such as independence of the judiciary, legal certainty, proportionality, and enhanced responsibility for the State's actions and omissions are not fully arranged. As to institutionalization and judicialization by which international judges watch over the implementation of human rights and rule of law, neither regional human rights courts nor other monitoring bodies exist, and only a few States accept individual communications procedures. Though ASEAN Member States established AICHR, it is constituted by the government representatives of the Member States and has no competence to consider individual petitions. Therefore, the institutional remedies most people in this region can personally make use of are limited to mainly local remedies set forth by the constitutional law of each country. International review remains indirect and partial in that such review of human rights situations and implementation of human rights conventions are performed in many countries in the region only through UPRs, special procedures, and consideration of State report's procedures under the UN human rights conventions concerned. It would be useful to take note of which States of the region have taken what stance with regard to international human rights in order to consider the challenges of this region for the better implementation of the UN human rights protection processes.

What has brought about this difference? It may be of use to look at against what backgrounds and particularities certain E + SE Asian countries insist on in dealing with human rights protection.

3.2 National Particularities or Historical, Cultural, and Religious Backgrounds Invoked by East and Southeast Asian Countries and Their Alleged Effects

First, the "East and West" ideological divide still remains in E + SE Asia, though each socialist or former socialist country looks to take its own path. For example, CHN, the sole permanent member of the UN Security Council and the biggest power in this region, now takes the following stance based on its own socialist principle.

---

[30] See, https://asean.org/asean-political-security-community/; https://asean.org/asean-economic-community/; https://asean.org/asean-socio-cultural/.

> [CHN] respects *the principle of universality of human rights*, and is of the view that all countries have a duty to take measures, commensurate with their national conditions, […]. The Chinese Government is working to explore paths for human rights development, establishing a robust system of human rights safeguards, and continuously enriching the theory of human rights, all *within the framework of socialism with Chinese characteristics*. It strongly advocates a scientific outlook on development, emphasizes "putting people first," and *takes the furtherance and protection of the right to subsistence and the right to development as first principles*. [emphasis added].[31]

CHN accepts the principle of universality of human rights including civil and political rights, but within the framework of its own brand of socialism. CHN insists that it takes "national conditions as the foundation," "the people as the centre," "development as the priority," "the rule of law as the criterion," and "openness as the motivator."[32] Thus, CHN has given priority to the right to development and subsistence not solely because of its socialist principles but also because of its practical urgent economic and social necessity. Within this framework, CHN pledges to uphold the principle of "the people's sovereignty," develop "socialist consultative democracy," and construct a nation, government, and society under "the rule of law."[33] In 2013 its report stated that CHN was still a developing country and the number of potential recipients of poverty relief was 100 million people. But in 2018 CHN's delegation mentioned that nearly 1.4 billion people had been lifted out of poverty and were able to lead a moderately prosperous life.[34] On this basis, its report of 2018 insists that: "There is no universal road for the development of human rights in the world. As an important element in the economic and social development of each country, the cause of human rights must be promoted on the basis of the national conditions and the needs of the people of the country, and cannot be defined on the basis of a single authority," and "[CHN] advocates international human rights exchanges and cooperation on the basis of equality and mutual respect, attaches increasing importance to the economic, social and cultural rights and the right to development that are concern to developing countries, and promotes the comprehensive development of human rights of all kinds."[35]

Alternatively, in conjunction with its One Belt-One Road initiatives, CHN may advocate new campaigns for promoting human rights cooperation in the field of economic, social, and cultural rights and the right to sustainable development based on a sort of regional cultural relativism. On the other hand, CHN has refused to accept the recommendations of the Committee on the Elimination of Racial Discrimination (CERD) on Xinjian for the reason that CHN firmly opposes interference in its

[31] UPR national rep. (CHN, 2nd, 2013), A/HRC/WG.6/17/CHN/1, para. 4; HRC Rep. 25th session (2014), supra note 20, paras. 844–845. See also UPR national rep. (CHN, 1st, 2008), A/HRC/WG.6/4/CHN/1, para. 6–7. HRC Rep. 25th session (2014), A/HRC/25/10/Add.1, paras. 844–845.

[32] UPR national rep. (CHN, 3rd, 2018), A/HRC/WG.6/31/CHN, paras. 5–9.

[33] *Ibid.*, paras. 6 & 8.

[34] UPR national rep. (CHN, 2nd, 2013), supra note 28, paras. 90–91 and 93; A/HRC/40/6 (2018), paras. 9–10.

[35] UPR national rep. (CHN, 3rd, 2018), supra note 29, para. 4 & 10.

sovereignty and internal affairs under any pretext.[36] It has also refused recommendations requesting abolishment of arbitrary detention in internment camps of Uighurs and other Muslim groups in Xinjiang or to cease the practice of "residential surveillance at a designated location" with regard to human rights defenders by arguing that in Xinjiang Uygur Autonomous Region, although efforts are made to fight terrorist extremism in accordance with law, human rights are seriously protected, and that CHN is a country under the rule of law with judicial organs that operate in accordance with laws and regulations.[37] Furthermore, the National Security Law adopted in June 2020 for Hong Kong raises another issues of compatibility with its obligations applicable to the Hong Kong Special Administrative Region under ICCPR, and so on.

The stance on human rights of socialist or former socialist countries in this region may differ from country to country. For example, VNM, while it had regarded the rights to independence and freedom and the right to self-determination as the most sacred, introduced a market economy as a transitional economic country and became a member of ASEAN. VNM shared, with other SE Asian countries, the idea that "the exercise of human rights is always linked to the history and traditions and the level of socio-economic development of a country," and remarked that "[a]s a country characterized by ethnic and religious diversity and a developing economy with a low starting point having to overcome severe consequences of wars, the protection and exercise of human rights in [VNM] have concrete priorities in accordance with the country's situation: poverty reduction, healthcare and education programmes are the focus of the State [...]."[38] At the same time it remarked that "[i]ts highest priority in this area is to enhance the rule-of-law and legal reform aiming at consolidating the institutional, legal and policy foundation for the protection and promotion of human rights. [It] will also enhance administrative reform, [...], promote democracy, reinforce the rule-of-law, and strengthen institutions for the protection of human rights, including further, thorough deliberation of the possible establishment of a National Human Rights Institution."[39] But with regard to certain recommendations from the US and European countries to the effect that it should repeal or amend its Penal Code, as well as laws on religion and cyber-security, or restrictions on freedom of expression by reason of national security, VNM rejected them by explaining that "their

[36] A/HRC/40/6 (2018), paras. 28.22 & 28.27, (recommendations by UK & Denmark); A/HRC/40/6/Add.1, para. 2, 28.22 & 28.27 (reply by CHN).

[37] A/HRC/40/6 (2018), paras. 28.175 thru 177 (recommendations by Australia, Switzerland, & US); A/HRC/40/6/Add.1, para. 2, 28.175 thru 28.177 (reply by CHN). CHN has also refused to establish an independent national human rights institution in accordance with the Paris Principles since many government agencies in China has already assume similar responsibilities. A/HRC/40/6 (2018), paras. 28.66 (recommendations by Liechtenstein, Poland, Togo, Uruguay, Seychelles, Mali); A/HRC/40/6/Add.1, para. 2, 28.66 (reply by CHN). See also, Wim Muller, Chinese practice in UN treaty monitoring bodies: principled sovereignty and slow appreciation, H. Nasu and B. Saul eds., Human Rights in the Asia–Pacific Region: Towards Institution Building (Routledge, 2013), pp. 87–104.

[38] UPR national rep. (VNM, 1st, 2009), A/HRC/WG.6/5/VNM/1, paras. 6, 11–12, and 61–63. See also UPR national rep. (VNM, 2nd, 2013), A/HRC/WG.6/18/VNM/1, paras. 75–85.

[39] UPR national rep. (VNM, 3rd, 2018), A/HRC/WG.6/32/VNM/1, para. 97.

drafts had been consulted extensively with the public" and "[a]s possible revision of these laws has yet been planned, [it] finds these recommendations impractical for the moment and does not accept them."[40]

The situation of DPRK is utterly different. Though it professed itself that it applied the *Juche* idea of "The people are my God," and would provide people with an affluent and cultural living by channeling all its efforts into economic construction, it insisted that major obstacles to its efforts for the protection and promotion of human rights were "the UN Security Council sanctions which [run] counter to human rights and the brutal unilateral sanctions of some countries" as well as "anti-DPRK 'human rights resolutions' at the UN Human Rights Council and the UN General Assembly," and therefore it rejected 63 recommendations out of 262 outright, arguing that they "severely distorted the human rights situation of the DPRK based on false information fabricated by the hostile forces and sought ulterior political purposes."[41] Among such recommendations were those requesting full cooperation with the UN human rights mechanisms including the Special Rapporteur on the situation of DPRK, eliminating discrimination based on the *songbun* (ancestral registry) system, ending summary execution, torture, or forced labor or deprivation of liberty in political prison camps, immediate return of abductees, closing of political prisoner camps, and so on.[42] So long as DPRK disregards the recommendations concerning human rights made by various UN organs, it will be very difficult to find a common basis for a genuine constructive dialogue concerning comprehensive human rights protection.

Second, the influence of a "contextual approach" advocated by leaders of the Asian values school in the early and mid-1990s seems to remain strong in some original member countries of ASEAN, according to which human rights as a natural endowment beyond the reach of government discretion, while universally valid in the world of theory, is qualified in their practical application by culture and contingency, and dependent on a society's culture and stage of development, so that each country may invoke its local culture to decide for itself which human rights were to be applicable, and to what extent.[43] This kind of argument also provides another reason in favor of the principle of non-intervention. For example, MYS, once a flag-bearer of the Asian way, took the stance in its 1st UPR that "[It] would like to accentuate its human rights values which take into account the history of the country as well as the religious, social and cultural diversities of its communities. *This is to ensure that the respect for social harmony is preserved and protected.* The practices of human rights in [MYS] are reflections of *a wider Asian value system where welfare and collective well-being of the community are more significant compared to individual rights*

[40] A/HRC/41/7 (2019), such paras. as para. 38, 38.167, 38.193, 38.204, 38.208; A/HRC/41/7/Add.1 (2019), para. 11.

[41] UPR national rep. (DPRK, 3rd, 2019), A/HRC/WG.6/33/PRK, paras. 85–86, 89, 91; A/HCR/42/10/Add.1 (2019), para. 3.

[42] A/HRC/42/10 (2019), para. 127, 127.1 thru 127.63.

[43] See, Li-ann Thio, supra note 11, p. 22; John D. Ciorciari, supra note 18, pp. 702–703. See also L. Avonius & D. Kingsbury eds., Human Rights in Asia: Reassessment of the Asian Values Debate (Palgrave Macmillan, 2008); H. Nasu & B. Saul eds., Human Rights in the Asia–Pacific Region: Towards Institution Building (Routledge, 2011).

(emphasis added)."[44] The Federal Constitution recognizes the special position of the *Bumiputra* (native sons of the soil) and natives of the States of Sabah and Sarawak, and while its article 3 declares Islam as the religion of the Federation, it also provides that other religions are entitled to be practiced in peace and harmony in any part of the Federation. Therefore MYS emphasizes that "key values embedded in the Federal Constitution among which included moderation, tolerance, understanding and acceptance" continue to be respected in the application of human rights.[45] In the 3rd UPR, while MYS expressed its positive stance to human rights protection by reaffirming its commitment to ratify all remaining international human rights instruments, it also stressed the necessity to reconcile those standards with long-standing domestic laws, traditions and circumstances as well as philosophy reflected in the Constitution, including issues of jurisdiction between the Civil and Sharia Courts and religious propagation among persons professing Islam.[46]

Another bearer of the Asian Way was SGP, but its secularism seems meticulous. SGP mentions as follows:

> We take a practical, not an ideological approach to the realisation of human rights. Human rights exist in specific cultural, social, economic and historical contexts. [...] Stability, security, and social harmony are the key prerequisites for economic growth, which enables the Government to care for and protect Singaporeans. For [SGP], our immediate priority after independence was to scrupulously manage our racial and religious differences, while steadily forging a nation out of immigrants. This was against the backdrop of religious and racial riots in the 1950s and 1960s, which were searing events in Singapore's history. For this reason, *maintaining racial and religious harmony has been the Government's top priority ever since*. We did this by ensuring and upholding *the core principles of secularism, meritocracy and multi-racialism to ensure equal standing and opportunities for all citizens* (emphasis added).[47]

Based on this idea, SGP has refused recommendations requesting the review of laws such as the Internal Security Act, Newspaper and Printing Press Act, Public Order Act, and Public Entertainment and Meeting Act by the firm reason that its laws allow its citizens to enjoy the rights of freedom of expression and peaceful assembly, while protecting the larger public interests of preserving public order and security.

Third, this region consists of religiously and ethnically different types of countries. For example, IDN is a country with the world's largest Muslim population; nearly 90% of its population are Muslims. But, IDN has recognized six official religions under the "the principle of religious freedom and tolerance" set forth in its State philosophy called *Pancasila* (five principles) and its 1945 Constitution.[48] After the fall of the New Order under Suharto's presidency in 1998, a series of measures

---

[44] UPR national rep. (MYS, 1st, 2008), A/HRC/WG.6/4/MYS/1/Rev.1, para. 114.

[45] UPR national rep. (MYS, 2nd, 2013), A/HRC/WG.6/17/MYS/1, paras. 50–51. See also UPR WG rep. add (MYS, 2nd, 2014), A/HRC/25/10/Add.1, paras. 5 and 9; and HRC Rep. 25th session (2014), U.N. Doc. A/HRC/25/2, para. 675.

[46] A/HRC/40/Add.1 (2019), p. 3, sub-title 1, and p. 4, sub-title 1.

[47] UPR national rep. (SGP, 2nd, 2015), A/HRC/WG.6/24/SGP/1, paras. 4–6. See also UPR national rep. (SGP, 1st, 2011), A/HRC/WG.6/11/SGP/1, paras. 4–9.

[48] A/69/375 (2014), para. 10; CCPR/C/IDN/1 (2012), para. 247.

were taken, according to IDN's national reports, including successive constitutional amendments from 1999 thru 2002 in order to strengthen the democratization process as well as respect for human rights and the rule of law.[49] The government remarked in the 2nd UPR that "[w]ith vastly diversified societies in terms of religious as well as ethnic groups like [IDN], the Government tirelessly promotes religious tolerance and harmony within country, including by empowering moderates," and mentions now that "[d]ue to [IDN's] vast and unique geological condition and demographic aspects, including its ethnic-cultural and local language varieties as well as its policies of decentralization and Regional Autonomy, the implementation of the global human rights norms in [IDN] entails particular measures and a certain degree of consideration for the local context."[50] While IDN has still refused to accept recommendations to undertake a thorough investigation into past human rights abuses, repeal or revise national laws and regulations that allow discrimination based on religion, sexual orientation, and gender identity, or to abolish the death penalty, it has ratified or acceded to eight core UN human rights conventions and two protocols and expresses its desire "to continue ensuring the promotion and protection of human rights for all in the country" as one of the core countries supporting AICHR.[51] Similarly, with respect to MMR, while nearly 90 percent of its population practice Theravada Buddhism, article 34 of the MMR's Constitution guarantees every citizen's right to freely profess and practice religion subject to provisions of the Constitution.[52] Though many countries including Malaysia recommended that MMR put an end to all acts of discrimination, violence, and other human rights violations against Rohingyas and other Muslims, in MMR's 2nd UPR, MMR categorically rejected all those recommendations.[53] Moreover, the report of the independent international fact-finding mission on MMR mandated by the HRC concluded in 2019 that "[MMR] has been tainted by the gravest crimes under international law committed against the Rohingya and other ethnic groups, a plethora of unresolved and deeply entrenched conflicts, and a weak and deteriorating record on the protection of fundamental freedoms. Accountability remains elusive. The military is out of control."[54]

PHI is also a country of diverse cultures with its multi-linguistic, multiethnic, and dispersed population, and certain Islamic groups in Mindanao have sought secession. Though PHI had experienced significant human rights abuses for a long time under the martial law of President Marcos, after his dictatorship, the 1987 Constitution, which reflected fundamental rights provided for in the UDHR was established, and

---

[49] UPR national rep. (IDN, 1st, 2008), A/HRC/WG.6/1/IDN/1, para.7; UPR national rep. (IDN, 2nd, 2012), A/HRC/WG.6/13/IDN/1, paras. 124–130; (IDN, 3rd, 2017), A/HRC/WG.6/27/IDN/1, paras. 6–14.

[50] A/HRC/WG.6/13/IDN/1, para. 60; A/HRC/WG.6/27/IDN/1, para. 177.

[51] A/HRC/36/7 (2017), para. 141, 141.16–17, 141.26–33, 141.36, 141.42–51, 141.53, 141.57, 141.59, 141.62, 141.64–75; A/HRC/37/7/Sdd.1; A/HRC/WG.6/27/IDN/1, paras. 11, 178.

[52] UPR national rep. (MMR, 2nd, 2015), A/HRC/WG.6/23/MMR/1, para. 144; A/HRC/31/13/Add.1 (2016), para. 14.

[53] A/HRC/31/13, para. 145, 145.39–66.

[54] A/HRC/42/50 (2019), para. 114. See also, Report of the detailed findings of the Independent Fact-Finding Mission on Myanmar, A/HRC/39/CRP.2, pp. 421–432.

independent institutions such as the Commission on Human Rights and the Office of Ombudsman for the protection of human rights were created. PHI is one of the first countries to ratify UN core human rights conventions; to date, it has ratified eight UN human rights conventions and four protocols and also accepted the individual communications procedures under ICCPR-OP and OP-CEDAW.[55] But, after 2016, while PHI puts priority to improve the welfare of poor people in the areas of health, education, adequate food and water, housing, and environmental preservation on the one hand, it pursues a campaign of zero tolerance against drugs with the slogan of "war against drugs" under Duterte's presidency, on the other. It is widely reported that the PHI authority has taken strong measures such as extra-judicial killings, enforced disappearances, or torture in order to "preserve the lives of the Filipino people and protect the country from turning into a narco-State."[56] Though many States recommended that PHI to put an end to or eradicate extrajudicial or summary executions, enforced disappearances, and torture, and prosecute the perpetrators of these acts, and also requested PHI to provide protection to journalists and human rights defenders, PHI refused to accept such recommendations by stating that there was no State policy promoting, sanctioning, or encouraging extrajudicial killings, as all law enforcement operations in pursuit of the anti-drug campaign were conducted within the boundaries of the law.[57]

Fourth, in certain countries in this region, civilian control of military force is not fully established yet. For example, in MMR, the Military, (called the "Tatmadaw") maintains strong power over MMR's government even after the National League for Democracy (NLD) won the majority in the 2015 election and NLD's government was established. The 2019 report of the Independent International Fact-Finding Mission on MMR mentioned: "Essential security sector reform has not even been discussed. The Tatmadaw retains an unrelenting grip on the country's political and economic life, permeating all sectors of [MMR] society. Without the transformation of the Tatmadaw into a modern, professional national defence force and a complete overhaul of the Constitution to ensure civilian oversight and control, genuine democratization is impossible."[58] Therefore, it recommended to the government of MMR, among others, to re-structure the Tatmadaw and to remove it from MMR's political life, as well as to ensure full compliance with international human rights law and international humanitarian law, and to end impunity and ensure full accountability for their violations especially by the Tatmadaw.[59] In THA, two coups d'état occurred in 2006 and 2014, and under the support of military government the Constitution of 2017 was established. In 2017 the Human Rights Committee recommended, among other things, that: (1) THA should revoke its derogations from articles 12(1), 14(5),

[55] A/HRC/8/28 (2008), paras. 5–12; see also UPR national rep. (PHI, 1st, 2008), A/HRC/WG.6/1/PHI/1, paras. 6–22. A/HRC/21/12 (2012), paras. 6–32.

[56] UPR national rep. (PHI, 3rd, 2017), A/HRC/WG.6/27/PHI/1, paras. 3–5; see also A/HRC/36/12 (2017), paras. 5–13 & 122–132.

[57] A/HRC/36/12, para. 132.

[58] A/HRC/42/50 (2019), paras. 116–117, see also A.HRC/39/CRP.2, paras. 81–83.

[59] *Ibid.*, paras. 1678–1682.

21, and 29, which did not comply with the rationale and the scope of article 4; (2) prompt, impartial and thorough investigations should be carried out into all allegations and complaints concerning the unlawful and excessive use of force by law enforcement officials and the military, including torture, enforced disappearances, and extrajudicial killings, including in the context of the southern border provinces; (3) THA should immediately release all victims of arbitrary detention [including detention for "attitude adjustment"] and provide them with full reparation; and (4) all trials before military courts should be exceptional and take place under conditions that genuinely afford the full guarantees stipulated in article 14.[60]

KOR, according to its national report, rose from the ashes of war and transformed itself from an authoritarian regime of the past to a democratic nation in a short time and has achieved economic development as one of the Asian newly industrializing countries. At the same time, KOR mentions that "protecting human rights is not a political option but rather a responsibility and a duty which is inherently linked with the very "raison d'être" of the nation," and has become a State party to seven core UN human rights conventions and two protocols and accepted individual communications procedures under ICCPR-OP, OP-CEDAW and article 22 of CAT. KOR also established its national human rights institution (the National Human Rights Commission of Korea). As to KOR there are no comments and recommendations which suggest serious human rights violations in the country. Though certain States recommended that KOR review its National Security Act (NSA), and release individuals imprisoned solely on the basis of their conscientious objection to military service, the Government of KOR replied that "[t]he purpose of the NSA is to safeguard basic order of liberal democracy of [KOR], which is under unique security conditions as a divided nation. The Government adheres to the strict interpretation and application of the Act," and that "[t]he unique security landscape of the Korean Peninsula and the importance of ensuring the equity of military service demand an in-depth discussion based on public consensus in introducing alternative service for [conscientious objectors]."[61]

Finally, JPN is a country with one of the most developed economies in this region, and is politically very stable based on its separation of legislative, executive, and judicial powers and parliamentary democracy as well as the rule of law. JPN's national report mentioned: "Upholding the high standards of human rights enshrined and guaranteed in its Constitution, [JPN] has consolidated its democratic political system and has developed policies for protection and promotion of human rights and fundamental freedoms as universal value".[62] As a consequence, there have been no flagrant and systematic violations or suppression of rights to physical and spiritual freedoms at least after its Constitution entered into force. Certainly, this does not mean there are no violations of human rights or no defects to be improved in JPN. While Japan has

[60] CCPR/C/THA/CO/2 (2017), paras. 5–6, 21–22, 25–26, 31–32, 35–36.

[61] UPR national rep. (KOR, 1st, 2008), A/HRC/WG.6/2/KOR/1, para. 1; A/HRC/37/11 (2017), para. 128, para. 132, 132.25, 132.94–132.132.106, 132.109–132.111; A/HRC/37/11/Add.1 (2018), paras. 32–33.

[62] UPR national rep. (JPN, 3rd, 2017), A/HRC/WG.6/28/JPN/1, para. 1.

already ratified or acceded to eight UN core human rights conventions and two of their protocols, it has not accepted the individual communications procedure at all and has failed to establish a national human rights institution based on the Paris Principles[63] or a national preventive mechanism required by the CAT-OP. Substantively, many countries recommend that JPN abolish or suspend the death penalty, address hate speech, combat trafficking in persons (especially in women and children) with strict punishment, etc.[64] JPN has refused to abolish or suspend the death penalty on the ground that "each sovereign country should be allowed to make decisions on the issue of the death penalty independently. Domestic public opinion, the existence of extremely vicious crimes, and other factors made it inappropriate to abolish the death penalty. A moratorium was also inappropriate, since the final judgment must be executed impartially and thoroughly under the rule of law."[65] With regard to its contribution to the international community, the Government of JPN stated, "[it] has held regular dialogues and consultations on human rights with the governments of more than 10 countries and the regional economic integration organization, including Myanmar, Cambodia, Iran and the EU; [it] will continue to hold these dialogues on human rights with various countries, and contribute to each country's efforts to solve human rights issues by sharing best practices and other means" in addition to its contributions to international organizations and other multilateral cooperation and assistance scheme according to the Development Cooperation Charter established in 2015.[66]

A brief sketch of the human rights situation in E + SE Asian countries as well as their basic stances towards UN human rights process seen through the UPR shows that, contrary to Europe, E + SE Asia does not have a narrative about "a legal area of freedom, human rights and rule of law," because no groups of States within this region have ever succeeded in constructing an effective institution for the protection of human rights and rule of law. To sum up, from the end of WWII to the present, an ideological divide between capitalist and socialist countries continues and brings about tensions on the Korean Peninsula and in the Taiwan Strait but also affects the internal politics of certain countries in the region. In addition, CHN's claim over the South China Sea amplifies tensions not only between China and ASEAN member States but also China and the US, JPN, and India. Furthermore, in some countries in this region the vast majority of people are Muslims and in other Buddhists constitute the overwhelming majority, and many countries consist of diverse communities of religious, social, and/or cultural groups, so that those countries have considered social harmony among communities as a top priority and tend to adhere strongly to the principle of territorial integrity and non-intervention as was expressed in both the ASEAN Charter and AHRD. Therefore, a contextual approach to universal human

---

[63] As to JPN position on this issue, see A/HRC/WG.6/28/JPN/1, paras. 72–75; A/HRC/37/15 (2018), para. 149.

[64] A/HRC/37/15 (2018), para.161, 161.4–161.8, 161.84–161.85, 161.95–161.110, 161.116–161.124,

[65] *Ibid.*, para. 147. See also A/HRC/37/15/Add.1 (2018), replies to 161.99, 161.107 and 161.108.

[66] UPR national rep. (JPN, 3rd, 2017), A/HRC/WG.6/28/JPN/1, paras. 95–100.

rights is still strong particularly in ASEAN member countries. Moreover, civilian control over national military forces has not yet been firmly established in certain countries.

Although most E + SE Asian countries invoke the concepts of human rights, rule of law, and democracy, their perceptions of the contents of these concepts differ considerably. For example, liberal democracy, parliamentary democracy based on separation of legislative, administrative, and judicial powers, and socialist consultative democracy are different things. The concept of rule of law looks sometimes misused one-sidedly and arbitrarily by authoritarian State authorities without judicial review to mean that any rule of criminal law whatsoever may be strictly applied. Under these circumstances, E + SE Asian countries have not been able to institute an effective legal mechanism on the basis of which an "acquis" in human rights and rule of law is created, although a small bud thereof is in operation in ASEAN countries.

Nevertheless, globalization of economy and information has brought about not only regional and worldwide movement of products, service, investment, and information, but also migration of populations on a large scale. Rapid industrialization and economic growth in several E + SE Asian countries as well as rapid aging of population and the structural change of a population pyramid in JPN, KOR and CHN also accelerates the migration of people in this region, especially including migrant workers and their families. As synergistic effects between the migration of people and the economic and their social integration were one of the main thrusts for the establishment of ASEAN and its enlargement, new developments in population migration accompanying the movement of commodities, capital, and services will probably call for a new stage of human rights protection and rule of law. What sort of design for the protection of human rights could we expect?

4 Potential of East and Southeast Asian Countries to Institutionalize a Legal Area of Freedom, Fundamental Rights, and Rule of Law: Tentative Concluding Remarks

Vice-President Nußberger asked whether or not the European model is inspiring for Asian countries if they want to coordinate their efforts in order to create a similar institutionalized system. Even if the question is limited geographically to E + SE Asian countries, it is a difficult question. Certainly, just as the European Convention on Human Rights (ECHR) was a model for the American Convention of Human Rights (ACHR) and the African Charter on Human and Peoples' Rights (ACHPR), ECHR would surely become one of the models to be followed if E + SE Asian countries should choose to conclude some kinds of regional human rights conventions. The fact that case law of the European Court of Human Rights (ECtHR) has often been invoked in order to make clear or develop the contents of human rights in certain Asian countries including Japan shows the potentially influential power of the European "acquis" in human rights and rule of law.

However, I agree with the Vice-President's remark that "it is helpful not to have utopian visions, but to see reality as it is."[67] As was mentioned in Sect. 3, it would be unrealistic to try to establish a regional human rights court like the ECtHR, given the fact that no regional convention protecting human rights and fundamental freedoms exists yet in this region, and only a few States have accepted the individual communications procedures of the UN human rights conventions.

On the other hand, it should not be overlooked that all or almost E + SE Asian countries are now State parties to CEDAW, CRC, OP-CRC-AC, OP-CRC-SC, and CRPD, and eleven or twelve among sixteen countries have become State parties to ICERD, ICESCR, ICCPR, and CAT. Since most countries in this region recognize human rights set forth in the seven core conventions and two protocols mentioned above (plus ICED to suppress impunity for the most heinous crimes) as universal by consenting to be bound, this region should have a stable and firm foundation for the protection of human rights, and for giving substantial legal basis to "the duty of States, regardless of their political, economic and cultural system, to [...] protect all human rights and fundamental freedoms (Vienna declaration, part I, para.5)." Therefore, further efforts should be made, among others, to invite States that have not joined ICERD, ICESCR, ICCPR, CAT, and ICED to become their parties as soon as possible.

Second, if the international or regional institutions are to play only a subsidiary role, more efforts should be made to strengthen the domestic institutions available to all persons and to give effective remedies to the alleged victims. In this connection, guarantee of a fair trial before independent national courts as well as the establishment of national human rights institutions according to the Paris Principles are matters of special importance in this region. In the UPR process and in the consideration of State reports, more attention should be given to these issues.

Third, acceptance of individual communications procedures of the core UN human rights conventions are essential for the real improvement of the human rights situation in this region. In this connection, Japan should create national human rights institutions and accept individual communication procedures including that of ICCPR-OP as soon as possible. At the same time, Japan should continue its legal technical assistance to countries with transitional economies in this region to help them construct legal infrastructures for the better protection of human rights. If the countries in this region could enhance their capability to promote and protect human rights, the human rights situation in this region would improve significantly and it would provide this region with the foundation to construct regional institutions for the protection of human rights.

We should not forget that in this region there are various political and military tensions which may cause human rights abuses. In addition to the confrontations between PRK and KOR, and CHN and Taiwan, which continue from the period of the Cold War, new conflicts between some ASEAN States and CHN in the South China Sea have emerged after CHN's unilateral invocation of its "historical title" over the islands and ocean. Furthermore, serious violations of human rights have been reported

[67] A. Nußberger, *supra* note 28, p. 14.

and taken up in various forums including the UN human rights process. Among those are CHN's assimilation policy in Tibet and Uyghur areas; the enactment of the new national security law for Hong Kong; human rights violations committed after THA's coups d'état in 2006 and 2014 under the declarations of public emergency; systematic and gross violations in PRK reported by the commission of inquiry on human rights in PRK; serious violations against the Rohingya in MMR, and so on. Flagrant violations of human rights should not be permitted irrespective of any political, economic, religious, or cultural system. Even in times of public emergency threatening the life of a nation, there are fundamental rights and freedoms from which States are not allowed to derogate. It seems that governments in this region have the tendency to hesitate to take up such serious violations straightforwardly due to the principle of non-intervention, so long as such violations affect only the rights of nationals of the responsible State. In order to prevent and stop flagrant violations of human rights, it is necessary for States, as well as civil societies including human rights NGOs, to make efforts to unite and streamline all outcomes, evaluations, and recommendations into a strong call for ending flagrant violations of fundamental human rights. Considering the situation of human rights in the E + SE Asian region and its surrounding circumstances, regional human rights mechanisms which would have close connection and synergistic effects with UN human rights protection mechanisms are needed more than ever.

Peacekeeping, Protection of Human Rights, Democracy and the Rule of Law in Europe—Problems, Future Prospects and an International Role Model

Rupert Scholz

1 Presentation Kyoto, February 2019

Since the end of the Second World War and after centuries of wars within Europe, violence and conflict, Europe has developed into a zone of peace, democracy and the rule of law—first in Western Europe and after the end of the East–West conflict in the early 1990s also in the Eastern European states. From the insight that this centuries-long catastrophic history must not be repeated in Europe, the will and readiness to literally rewrite Europe—to rewrite it as a zone of peace, democracy and the rule of law—grew. These fundamental values became the universally accepted common structural principle for the further development of Europe and created the willingness to create common institutions for securing peace, democracy and the rule of law also in a supranational respect. This began at the end of the 1940s with the Universal Declaration of Human Rights of 1948 and then on a European basis with the European Convention on Human Rights (ECHR), which continued in the course of the 1950s with the conclusion of the two universal pacts IPBPR (International Covenant on Civil and Political Rights of 16.12.1966) and the IPWSKR (International Covenant on Economic, Social and Cultural Rights of 16.12.1966). The basis of this development was the Council of Europe and its Statute of 05.05.1949. Later, the ECHR was joined by the ECHR, which, as a supranational court, monitors the observance of European human rights in accordance with the ECHR and in recent years has become increasingly important in terms of legal policy. Members of the Council of Europe are 47 European states, also far beyond the member states of the European Union—for example also the Russian Federation, Switzerland, Turkey and Ukraine, even Azerbaijan. From a geographical point of view, the territory of the Council of Europe does not only include the core countries of Europe, but also, especially in eastern terms, countries which, although they may still belong to Europe

R. Scholz (✉)
LMU München, Munich, Germany
e-mail: Rupert.Scholz@jura.uni-muenchen.de

M. Deguchi and K. Yakushiji (eds.), *Europe and Asia as a Legal Area for Fundamental Rights*, https://doi.org/10.1007/978-981-19-7542-4_3

geographically, have relatively little in common with Europe in the aforementioned core sense. This, however, does not change the fact that the common creed of values exists and functions well to a large extent.

Such a common commitment to values, i.e. the commitment to peace, democracy, human rights and the rule of law, is one of the foundations of every international peace order, although it must be differentiated in terms of development. Such a shared commitment to values is, however, still relatively new in the history of international relations—irrespective of the early agreements and obligations within the framework of the UN. Traditionally, all international relations have been based on the existence and sovereignty of individual nation states, and this is still the case today. There are still no confederations of states or federal states with an international quality, or only in modest approaches. However, this is not harmful, since the nation states themselves are a symbol of all national and social identity and thus still guarantee the most important prerequisite of social self-determination and state existence. In today's increasingly globalised world, the political and legal significance of nation states is increasingly receding. There is a growing need and willingness for more international interdependence, cooperation and joint supranational institutionalisation. However, the ways to achieve this are as diverse as they are different. As a rule, such developments begin with the identification of common **interests**, especially in the economic sphere (development of free trade zones, customs unions, etc.). In other words: At the beginning of all developments to be examined here are common interests or interests identified as common, i.e. above all economic interest communities. As a rule, such common interests also and initially give rise to a willingness to **secure mutual peace**. The readiness for democracy, the rule of law and the protection of human rights is by no means automatic. This will only succeed if the above-mentioned communities of interests also develop into communities of **values** and, consequently, **communities of rights**, if a common commitment to the fundamental values of democracy, the rule of law and human rights arises, if there is a willingness to assert these fundamental values in one's own (nation-state) sphere and, in a second or further phase of development, to take them on board internationally or to guarantee them to one another internationally. The decisive factor here is first and foremost domestic development in the area of the individual nation states themselves. Here, the corresponding basic values must be recognised and guaranteed in the respective societies and, via these, first of all in the national constitutions. In other words: At the beginning of the international and supranational guarantee of democracy, the rule of law and human rights stands the development of **civil societies**, which are to be initiated nationally in each case and then also to be guaranteed, which constitute themselves on the basis of the aforementioned common confession of values and mutually recognize each other in the next development phase.

If one follows the path of individual states from the (mere) community of interests via the common community of values to the (supranational) community of institutions, the European Union is an outstanding example of this and unique in the world to date. The European Union began as an economic community (customs union, internal market—EEC) and today has grown together into a largely complete political and value-bound union. Details can be found in the current version of the TEU.

It is committed to peace, the rule of law, democracy and the protection of human rights (Art. 2 et seq., 9 et seq. TEU). Supranational institutions have been created through the joint institutions of the European Council, Council, European Commission, European Parliament and European Court of Justice, which are based on the corresponding renunciations of sovereign status of the 28 and—after the withdrawal of Great Britain (Brexit)—27 member states. The European Union is still based on the individual member states and their national sovereignty. The supranational sovereign rights of the European Parliament, the European Commission, the European Court of Justice and the European Council as well as the Council are all based on corresponding acts of delegation by the member states, which in this respect have waived their sovereignty and regulatory powers in favour of the European Union and its organs. However, this does not alter the fact that the sovereign rights of the European Union are not of an autonomous nature; they are all (only) derived. In this sense, the principle of limited empowerment applies. The organs of the European Union have their own sovereign powers or competences only to the extent that they have been transferred to them by the member states by virtue of international treaties (TEU) (Art. 4 TEU). However, the common recognition of values is supra-nationally binding—from the TEU to the European Charter of Fundamental Rights.

The European Union is neither a (mere) confederation of states nor an independent confederation. The degree of integration goes far beyond the confederation and the confederation lacks its own (supranational) sovereignty or autonomy. In this sense, the construction of the European Union is historically unique. The German Federal Constitutional Court has coined the term "association of states" for this purpose, which has since found its way into the general, international language of definition. The basis of the European Union remains the nationally constituted member states and their national sovereignty. In this sense, the TEU also expressly states that the national identity of the member states must or must be preserved (Art. 3 TEU). Only the basic values of peacekeeping, democracy, the rule of law and the protection of human rights are of common or common identity. However, these fundamental values are also of national quality, i.e. they are judged according to the individual constitutional systems of the member states. However, these national constitutional systems must adhere to the basic values of the EU Treaty in their common understanding of fundamental values. If this is not the case, the European Union will also have sanctions at its disposal, as is currently the case, for example, in the relationship between the European Commission and the European Parliament on the one hand and states such as Hungary and Poland on the other, where differences arise over the constitutional guarantee of a judiciary that is also independent in the national sphere (cf. Art. 7 TEU). An almost complete measure of commonality or supranational-overlapping identity can only be found in the area of the protection of human rights. Here, too, the national constitutional systems are initially decisive—including the respective jurisdictions, whereby the German Federal Constitutional Court has a special status. However, a completely identical protection of fundamental rights also exists supranationally via the ECHR and its Court of Justice, the ECHR. In addition, there is the EU Charter of Fundamental Rights, which is binding for all sovereign acts of the organs of the European Union as well as for their implementation in the respective national areas (Art. 51 f. GR-Ch.). In this respect, the European Court of Justice watches over the latter with unrestricted binding force.

On the one hand, the TEU is committed to the national identity of the member states and thus (at the same time) to diversity and difference beyond the common basic values or the corresponding community of values. On the other hand, the larger the European Union becomes, i.e. the more the number of member states grows, the more often problems arise and individual conflict potentials open up. The fundamental programme of parallel "deepening" and "widening", which had long been announced for the development of the European Union, is now proving to be problematic. For the larger the number of member states, the more different views and different constitutional structures open up, which must be respected from the point of view of national diversity, but which, on the other hand, can also question the common good of integration at one point or another. The answer to this cannot be simple "deepening", for this means nothing other than further centralisation at the EU level with ever more extensive, ever more extensive competences and sovereign powers of the organs of the European Union. It is precisely these centralisation tendencies that have led in many ways to the acceptance of the European Union in the societies of the member states not growing, but rather diminishing. The answer that is actually decisive, on the other hand, can already be found in the TEU itself with its commitment to the principle of subsidiarity (Art. 5 TEU). Subsidiarity means that the institutions of the European Union may only have competences and their own sovereign powers where the corresponding regulatory concerns cannot be adequately regulated at national level. In other words: In many areas, the principle of decentralisation before centralisation actually applies. In the history of the European Union, however, this very principle has all too often been disregarded; as a rule, the tendencies towards growing centralisation have dominated—unfortunately also supported in many ways by the case law of the European Court of Justice. What is needed here is real change and definitive reforms. The decisive warning signal should be the Brexit. Because behind the Brexit or the corresponding referendum in Great Britain stood and stands above all the growing displeasure about an all too centralistically constituted and all too centralistically acting European Union.

There are other reform requirements within the euro zone that can certainly be described as fundamental. The relevant European treaties have committed the member states of the euro zone to monetary stability—up to and above all to corresponding limits for their national debt. However, all of this has worked less and less in recent years. Member states such as Greece, Spain, Portugal, Ireland and now above all Italy have violated these regulations and common stability rules excessively—with the consequence that the European Central Bank in particular has had to intervene more and more intensively and with more and more overruns of its own competences. The euro zone suffers above all from the differing financial and economic strengths of the respective member states. Real monetary stability presupposes a corresponding degree of reasonably equivalent stability; and this does not currently exist or still does not exist—with the consequence that above all the financially better-off states, above all Germany, have repeatedly had to help out with many billions in favour of the weaker nations. This, too, cannot continue in the long term if the euro is to remain an effectively functioning common currency.

To sum up all this, on the one hand it can be said that the European Union as a whole is a successful integration model, but that many problems and reform needs also arise within this integration model. All this, however, does not change the fact that the development of the European Union has become a model for a world that is increasingly characterised by globalisation and the withdrawal of national sovereignty. The path taken by the European Union—from the (mere) community of interests to the community of values, the community of law and the institutional community of competence—has certainly proved to be exemplary and directional.

This exemplary function of the European Union and the European integration process can now be observed and understood worldwide. This begins with the supranational transformative constitutionalism in America, where the American Convention for the Protection of Human Rights came into force on 18.07.1978 and where the Inter-American Court of Justice for the Protection of Human Rights is now also institutionally active. The same applies to the Asian region. This begins with the Asia–Pacific Economic Community (APEC), which has constituted a form of economic community of interest (free trade zone, etc.) for a number of Asian and Pacific states. However, APEC has not yet moved beyond this community of interests, and from my point of view there are few reasons why this will change in the foreseeable future. Even the fundamental, not only economic, but also political conflicts of interest between the two world powers, the USA and China, are unlikely to permit further developments of an integrative nature. The opposite is true for ASEAN. The 10 Southeast Asian states have been cooperating for over 50 years. A common internal market has existed since 2015, regardless of the different political systems in the individual member states. Above all, congruent or stable democratic structures do not yet exist. In addition to democratically constituted member states, there are also dictatorships or militarily controlled systems. Economic, political and social cooperation began and later also issues of security, peacekeeping, culture and environmental protection were addressed. Already in 2009, the goal of a common economic area was propagated similar to that of the European Union. It is based on the ASEAN Charter, which is expressly committed to democracy, the rule of law, the protection of human rights and peacekeeping (Art. 1 et seq.). At the same time, the ASEAN Charter also includes a whole series of already institutional forms of integration: from the ASEAN Summit to the ASEAN Coordinating Council, the ASEAN Community Councils, the ASEAN Sectoral Ministerial Bodies and the Committee of Permanent Representatives (Art. 7 ff.). Last but not least, the ASEAN Human Rights Body should also be mentioned (Art. 14). All this reveals similar development trajectories to those of the European Union. It all began with the economic community, which was initiated primarily from an economic and economic policy point of view. Later, certain commitments to values were added and the whole thing led to legal or institutional forms of regulation. However, all of this is expressly subject to the strict reservation of the national sovereignty of the individual member states, which can easily be explained by the massively different political systems of the member states mentioned. Accordingly, the aforementioned institutional regulations have so far hardly had any truly fundamental or even radical competences of supranational quality. However, this does not change the fact that ASEAN is associated with many hopes and realistic prospects for the future; prospects which are reminiscent of those in the European Union and for which the European Union with its development and perspectives will continue to be and remain a real role model in the future.

The ASEAN Charter already achieves and implements a high degree of cross-cutting common values. This applies above all to the fundamental values of peace-keeping and the protection of human rights. However, the step towards an institutionally secured legal community has not yet been fully achieved in these areas either. The ASEAN Human Rights Body also has at best an expert function. But it could—and in my view should—also be developed into an institutional and judicial body. The commitment of the ASEAN Charter to the protection of human rights could—and should—first be developed into a genuine and binding catalogue of fundamental rights in line with the model of the ECHR, and subsequently the ASEAN Human Rights Body should also be developed into a judicial body in line with the model of the European Court of Human Rights. The fact that the member states of ASEAN still have very different political systems or build on such differences should not be an obstacle to this. Political system differences do not, in principle, prevent a common commitment to human rights and should therefore not stand in the way of a corresponding judicial-supranational instance. In this sense, I see the future of ASEAN above all in the model of the ECHR and the ECHR. The next step, following the example of the European Union in creating supranational institutions in a comprehensive manner, is still very far-reaching. In this respect, the differences in the political systems of the ASEAN member states are indeed proving to be all too obstructive.

We live in an increasingly globalised world and this world needs international cooperation, international integration and—as a consequence—supranational cooperation, supranational mergers and supranational value identities. All this to protect peace, democracy, the rule of law and human rights.

2 Comment on the Speech of Prof. Scholz

Toru Mori

Prof. Scholz, thank you for your excellent speech. I summarize it in English at first and add some comments.

Prof. Scholz has spoken about the development of Europe as the zone of peace, democracy, human rights and rule of law. He acknowledges at first that the basis of all international cooperation lies in the sovereign states, and it's not a bad thing. The

T. Mori
Kyoto University, Kyoto, Japan
e-mail: mouri@law.kyoto-u.ac.jp

nation states still guarantee the possibility of the social self–determination. As the globalization has been developing, however, they need to be ready to cooperate each other, as we know. Prof. Scholz shows the typical steps of the deepening process of international cooperation. It begins with the recognition of common economic interests. Then comes the readiness to guarantee the security each other. In contrast, the common commitment to democracy, rule of law and human rights does not come into being until a community sharing the same values develops between the states. Here the commitment to these values in each state plays the decisive role.

Prof. Scholz emphasizes the uniqueness of the highly developed integration of the European Union, but at the same time he calls our attention to the fact that the authority of the EU is not original but derived from the member states. It commits also to guarding their national identities. Almost the same guarantee has been realized only in the field of the human rights. As the EU has been growing, the conflicts between the member states have been increasing. He criticizes the tendency of the centralization in the EU and emphasizes the importance of the subsidiarity principle.

Then Prof. Scholz asks if in other areas, especially in Asia, integrations like the EU have a chance to be realized. He takes up the ASEAN. Its charter includes the commitment to democracy, peace, rule of law and human rights, though the integration still stays at a low level. He suggests that the ASEAN Human Body could develop to a kind of international court to guarantee the human rights. He says that this development might be realized even if the political systems of its member states remain very different.

I agree with Prof. Scholz's idea of the step-by-step development of international cooperation between states and his acknowledgment of the difficulty of building a regional community sharing the same values. The EU has learned the necessity to rely on democracy and human rights from the huge harm of the wars, from the religious wars to the Second World War. The uniqueness of the EU has its origin in this history, which cannot and should not be repeated in other areas. Then we can realize that outside of Europe deepening the regional integration is very difficult.

Prof. Scholz finds the integration in the EU has gone too far slighting the national identities of the member states. At the same time, he seems to think the achievement of the same level protection of the human rights with the help of the European courts is a fruitful success. Therefore, perhaps, he can expect the development of the human rights protection in the ASEAN without removing the differences of the political systems of its member countries. I wonder if this separation of human rights from other political values is persuasive and can be realized.

It is true that at a primitive level the human rights should be and can be guaranteed independently of the types of political regimes. The ban on the torture is such an example. When we strive to ensure the various human rights up to higher levels, however, they must be dependent to the structure of political systems. The right to access to fair legal process cannot be guaranteed without the system of independent courts. The freedom of expression is easily suppressed in the countries where the principles of democracy are not accepted. The development of the human rights in Europe has been enabled by the common commitment of the member states to democracy and separation of powers, although they have different political systems concretely. The waver of the basic political structure in some countries in Europe means therefore also some danger to the protection of human rights there. This necessary connection between political values might explain the tendency of the centralization of the EU which cannot be stopped even if most citizens and politicians object to it in principle.

Prof. Scholz recognizes that the support to the human rights belongs to the cultural achievements which are generated at first in the nation states. The readiness to accept a high-level protection of human rights is then dependent to the cultural and political situations of each country. Perhaps it is difficult to develop a system of international legal guarantee of human rights without the shared commitment to the political values.

This does not deny the significance of the influences of international institutions on the situations of human rights in nation states. Their stimuli have been playing an important role to improve the situations of human rights in many countries including Japan. The integration of Europe as "Werte- und Rechtsgemeinschaft" (community of values and law) is truly a model also for Asian people.

BREXIT and the European Convention on Human Rights

Tim Eicke

1 Introduction

I am very grateful to have been invited to address this distinguished audience tonight on the topic of "BREXIT and the European Convention on Human Rights". However, before I do so, it is important to note the following:

a. What is commonly referred to as Brexit is an intensely political issue and process which at present moves at an incredible speed with changes to both the legal and political parameters potentially taking place on a daily basis. After all, the intended date of withdrawal is now merely a few weeks if not days away;
b. While judges are, in any event, naturally and understandably reluctant to enter into the political arena, this is even truer in the highly charged political nature of some of the issues raised by Brexit and the process itself and, if the judge asked to speak is the current judge at the European Court of Human Rights elected in respect of the UK.

That said, there are a number of issues of law arising in the context of the potential relationship between Brexit and the European Convention which I will endeavour to describe without, however, seeking to judge the merits or demerits of any of them. The purpose of this talk is, therefore, purely to provide you with the relevant context and information but—as I said—without in any way seeking to form a judgment or express a view on the fact of Brexit, the process of Brexit or any of the issues raised by that process.

T. Eicke (✉)
European Court of Human Rights, Strasbourg, France
e-mail: Tim.Eicke@echr.coe.int

M. Deguchi and K. Yakushiji (eds.), *Europe and Asia as a Legal Area for Fundamental Rights*, https://doi.org/10.1007/978-981-19-7542-4_4

2 Defining Brexit

The term "Brexit"—as the OED confirms—refers to "the (proposed) withdrawal of the United Kingdom from the European Union, and the political process associated with it".

As both the UK Prime Minister as well as a former Foreign Secretary and leading Brexit campaigner said, it is about "leaving the European Union [but not] leaving Europe".

3 The ECHR and the EU

Of course, the European Union and the Council of Europe, of which the European Convention and Court of Human Rights are perhaps the most significant achievements, are two separate and distinct entities.

While there may be some superficial similarities between the two organisations—e.g. the EU uses the same flag and the same hymn as the Council of Europe—the distinctions are clear:

a. The Council of Europe is an international organisation set up in 1949 to promote democracy and protect human rights and the rule of law in Europe. Based in Strasbourg, France, it now comprises 47 countries of Europe (in excess of 800 million citizens). In 1950 it adopted the European Convention on Human Rights, which entered into force in 1953. The UK was one of the original parties to the Council of Europe and the European Convention on Human Rights. The Convention provided for a Court—the European Court of Human Rights ("ECtHR")—which is charged, on application by affected individuals or another State, to "ensure the observance of the engagements undertaken by the High Contracting Parties in the Convention and the Protocols thereto" (Article 19). Judgments of the Court are "binding" on the Respondent State in any proceedings as a matter of international law (only).
b. By contrast, the European Union (as it is today known) was set up in stages between 1951 and 1957. The UK was not one of the original parties but only joined in 1973. The EU currently (still) has 28 members who have delegated (or pooled) some of their sovereignty on specific matters of joint interest. Since 1 December 2009, the EU has its own Charter of Fundamental Rights which protects enumerated rights and is applicable "to the Member States only when they are implementing Union law".[1] The EU Treaties also provide for a court, the Court of Justice of the European Union. Based in Luxembourg, this supranational court ensures compliance with the law in the interpretation and application of the Treaties underlying the European Union as well as the extensive secondary

[1] Article 51(1).

legislation adopted by the EU. Unlike judgments of the ECtHR, its judgments—just as any directly effective EU law—have direct effect in domestic law (to be enforced by the domestic courts) and take primacy over conflicting domestic law, including, where relevant, constitutional norms.

However, it is perhaps important to note that it has been an unfortunate aspect of the UK's relationship with both European institutions that there has always been and remains a lack of a clear understanding of that distinction in UK public discourse. The most recent example of this is a BBC interview of 13 January 2019, in which the leader of the Opposition, Jeremy Corbyn MP, set out the Labour Party's position as follows:

> On human rights issues I have made it very clear all the way through that we [Labour] would maintain our support and membership for the European Convention on Human Rights, the European Court of Human Rights, which is only in part an EU institution.[2]

There is, however, also some overlap or interaction between the two institutions. As such, all current members of the EU are also parties to the Convention on Human Rights; though the EU itself is currently not a party. As a result, the law of the Convention plays an important part in EU law. Article 6 of the Treaty on European Union provides both that:

a. "the Union shall accede to the European Convention for the Protection of Human Rights and Individual Freedoms …"; and
b. "Fundamental rights, as guaranteed by the European Convention for the Protection of Human Rights and Individual Freedoms … shall constitute general principles of the Union's law".

By contrast, while the European Court of Human Rights may have regard to developments in EU law when considering whether there has been a violation of any of the provisions of the Convention, EU law does not form any part of Convention law. It is treated either as relevant domestic law of the respondent State (where that state is an EU member) or as potentially relevant international law (where the respondent state is not an EU member).

Where a State is alleged to have been in breach of the Convention when implementing EU law, the Court has consistently[3] applied a rebuttable presumption that the EU:

> … protects fundamental rights, as regards both the substantive guarantees offered and the mechanisms controlling their observance, in a manner which can be considered at least equivalent – that is to say not identical but 'comparable' – to that for which the Convention provides (…). If such equivalent protection is considered to be provided by the organisation, the presumption will be that a State has not departed from the requirements of the Convention when it does no more than implement legal obligations flowing from its membership of the organisation.

[2] https://www.legalcheek.com/2019/01/human-rights-barristers-tweet-flagging-corbyn-echr-clanger-goes-viral/.

[3] *Avotiņš v. Latvia* [GC], no. 17502/07, § 101, 23 May 2016.

> … In addition, any such presumption can be rebutted if, in the circumstances of a particular case, it is considered that the protection of Convention rights was manifestly deficient. In such cases, the interest of international cooperation would be outweighed by the Convention's role as a 'constitutional instrument of European public order' in the field of human rights.[4]

Enough by way of background. Let us now turn to look in a little more detail at "Brexit".

4 The UK Position—Referendum and Beyond

On Thursday 23 June 2016 the United Kingdom held a referendum on the—apparently simple—question[5]: "Should the United Kingdom remain a member of the European Union or leave the European Union?".

Statute also specified the two possible—equally simple—answers[6]:

a. "Remain a member of the European Union"; or
b. "Leave the European Union".

As you will all know, the outcome was that, on a voter turn-out of 71.8%, with more than 30 million people voting:

a. 48.1% for "Remain".
b. 51.9% for "Leave".[7]

Following that decision, on 29 March 2017, the UK government gave notice of its intention to withdraw from the European Union under Article 50(2) of the Treaty on European Union ("TEU"), a provision also added by the Lisbon Treaty. This first invocation of this procedure had been expressly authorised by Parliament in the form of the European Union (Notification of Withdrawal) Act 2017.[8]

By virtue of Article 50(3) TEU, absent the prior entry into force of a Withdrawal Agreement, as a matter of EU and public international law the EU Treaties will, therefore cease to apply to the UK two years later, namely—applying EU law rules

---

[4] Ibid.

[5] Section 1(4) of the European Union Referendum Act 2015.

[6] Section 1(5).

[7] With London (59.9%), Scotland (62%), Northern Ireland (55.8%) and Gibraltar (95.9%) voting for "remain" and the remaining regions and country (Wales) voting for "leave": the vote for "leave" in Wales was 52.5% and the highest vote for "leave" elsewhere in England was 59.3% in the West Midlands.

[8] The European Parliament's Briefing "Article 50 TEU: Withdrawal of a Member State from the EU" of February 2016 (http://www.europarl.europa.eu/RegData/etudes/BRIE/2016/577971/EPRS_BRI(2016)577971_EN.pdf) refers the *travaux preparatoires* of Article 50 to make clear that "That the introduction of the withdrawal clause was a compromise necessary in order to reach agreement on the Constitutional Treaty is clear from the comments attached to the draft provision (Article I-59) saying that it was a 'political signal to anyone inclined to argue that the Union is a rigid entity which it is impossible to leave'".

on the calculation of time limits—on the stroke of midnight Brussels Time (or 11 pm UK time) on 29 March 2019.

The UK Parliament also enshrined this date into UK domestic law as "exit day".[9]

The notification letter to the President of the Council of Ministers of 29 March 2017[10] goes on to express the wish of the UK government to seek to agree a "deep and special partnership" between the UK and the EU and sets out some of the UK's "proposed principles for our discussions". These included *inter alia* that:

> **We should continue to work together to advance and protect our shared European values. ....**[11]

On 30 March that year, the UK Government published its White Paper entitled "Legislating for the United Kingdom's withdrawal from the European Union".[12] This was to set out the UK's intention in relation to converting "the body of European Union legislation"[13] into domestic law with effect from "exit day" by means of what was then referred to as the "Great Repeal Bill". Importantly, that White Paper made clear that the ECHR is:

> An international convention, ratified by the United Kingdom and incorporated into UK law in the Human Rights Act 1998. ... All member states are parties to the Convention. The Convention is a Council of Europe Convention, which is a different organisation from the EU. ....[14]

The White Paper further made clear that the EU Charter would "not be converted into UK law by the Great Repeal Bill"[15] but that:

> The ECHR is an instrument of the Council of Europe, not of the EU. The UK's withdrawal from the EU will not change the UK's participation in the ECHR and there are no plans to withdraw from the ECHR.[16]

Shortly thereafter, on 18 April 2017, the Prime Minister called a General Election to take place on 8 June 2017 which resulted in a Conservative government without an overall majority. While the election and its outcome may have had an impact on the politics of Brexit, it did not affect the UK's legal situation or the operation of either Article 50 TEU.

The negotiations between the UK and the EU continued throughout this period:

---

[9] Section 20 of the European Union (Withdrawal) Act 2018 defines "exit day" as meaning "29 March 2019 at 11.00 p.m."

[10] https://assets.publishing.service.gov.uk/government/uploads/system/uploads/attachment_data/file/604079/Prime_Ministers_letter_to_European_Council_President_Donald_Tusk.pdf.

[11] Paragraph vii, bold in original.

[12] Cm 9446; https://assets.publishing.service.gov.uk/government/uploads/system/uploads/attachment_data/file/604516/Great_repeal_bill_white_paper_accessible.pdf.

[13] Referred to as the "EU 'acquis'".

[14] Glossary, underlined emphasis added.

[15] Paragraph 2.23.

[16] Paragraph 2.22, underlined emphasis added.

a. On 8 December 2017, the UK and the EU published a Joint Report on progress in the first phase of the negotiations.[17]
b. Following further negotiations, on 19 March 2018, they published draft elements of a Withdrawal Agreement setting out an agreed legal text for significant number of articles.[18]
c. On 19 June 2018, they published a Joint Statement setting out the further progress made in negotiations since March[19]; and
d. On 14 November 2018, the UK and the EU published their Draft Withdrawal Agreement which was to be put before the EU leaders for their approval.[20]

At a special meeting of the European Council on 25 November 2018, after some 20 months of negotiations, all EU leaders, including the UK Prime Minister, endorsed the proposed Withdrawal Agreement in the terms put before them.[21]

None of these documents,[22] however, make any reference to the European Convention on Human Rights.[23]

---

[17] https://www.gov.uk/government/publications/joint-report-on-progress-during-phase-1-of-negotiations-under-article-50-teu-on-the-uks-orderly-withdrawal-from-the-eu.

[18] https://www.gov.uk/government/uploads/system/uploads/attachment_data/file/691366/20180319_DRAFT_WITHDRAWAL_AGREEMENT.pdf.

[19] https://assets.publishing.service.gov.uk/government/uploads/system/uploads/attachment_data/file/717697/Joint_Statement_-_19_June_2018.pdf.

[20] https://assets.publishing.service.gov.uk/government/uploads/system/uploads/attachment_data/file/756374/14_November_Draft_Agreement_on_the_Withdrawal_of_the_United_Kingdom_of_Great_Britain_and_Northern_Ireland_from_the_European_Union.pdf.

[21] https://www.gov.uk/government/publications/withdrawal-agreement-and-political-declaration.

[22] Including the Withdrawal Agreement, which runs to some 599 pages, including 185 Articles plus numerous Protocols.

[23] According to the UK Government's "Explainer" (https://assets.publishing.service.gov.uk/government/uploads/system/uploads/attachment_data/file/759020/14_November_Explainer_for_the_agreement_on_the_withdrawal_of_the_United_Kingdom_of_Great_Britain_and_Northern_Ireland_from_the_European_Union.pdf), the Withdrawal Agreement is intended to provide for:

a. a deal on citizens' rights that protects the rights of EU citizens in the UK and UK nationals in the EU, ensuring they can continue contributing to their communities and live their lives broadly as now;
b. separation provisions that wind down certain arrangements (for example cooperation on civil court cases still ongoing at the end of the implementation period) under the current EU legal order to ensure an orderly withdrawal and smooth transition to the future relationship, noting that the majority of these provisions could be superseded by the agreement on the future relationship;
c. a time-limited implementation period that provides certainty to businesses and individuals and ensures they only have to adjust to one set of changes in line with the future relationship with the EU;
d. arrangements on the financial settlement that represent a fair settlement of the UK's rights and obligations as a departing Member State, in accordance with its legal commitments and in the spirit of the UK's continuing partnership with the EU;
e. governance arrangements that provide legal certainty and clarity to citizens, businesses and organisations and respect the autonomy and integrity of both the UK's and the EU's legal orders;
f. the unique circumstances in Northern Ireland, including the continuation of the Common Travel Area arrangements, the ongoing protection of rights of individuals in Northern Ireland, and

That said, in parallel the UK and the EU had also negotiated a Political Declaration on the future relationship between them, resulting in:

a. "Outline of the Political Declaration setting out the Framework for the future relationship between the European Union and the United Kingdom" of 14 November 2018; and
b. A final version of the Political Declaration as endorsed at the special meeting of the European Council on 25 November 2018.[24]

Both of these do make express reference to the ECHR, though in slightly different terms;

a. The 14 November Outline of the Political Declaration does so in the following terms:
   i. in its first paragraph identifies the "basis of cooperation" between the UK and the EU as including:

      > … Reaffirmation of the United Kingdom's commitment to the European Convention on Human Rights (ECHR), ….[25]

   ii. under the heading "Law Enforcement and Judicial Cooperation in Criminal Matters" it includes:

      > … continued adherence to the ECHR and its system of enforcement, ….

b. The final (so far) Political declaration of 25 November 2018, under the same two headings, refers to a:

   > … the United Kingdom's continued commitment to respect the framework of the European Convention on Human Rights ….[26]

   > … continued adherence and giving effect to the ECHR, ….[27]

---

guarantees that, even in the unlikely event that our future relationship with the EU is not in place by the end of the implementation period, there will be no hard border between Northern Ireland and Ireland or a splitting of the UK customs territory;

g. maintaining the UK's international commitments in respect of the Sovereign Base Areas (SBAs), protecting the interests of Cypriots living and working in the SBAs and ensuring the continued effective operation of the SBAs for military purposes; and
h. a Protocol on Gibraltar which will form part of a wider package of agreements that address issues of importance to citizens and businesses in Spain and Gibraltar and reflect the parties' desire to work together in support of the shared prosperity and security of the area.

[24] https://assets.publishing.service.gov.uk/government/uploads/system/uploads/attachment_data/file/759021/25_November_Political_Declaration_setting_out_the_framework_for_the_future_relationship_between_the_European_Union_and_the_United_Kingdom__.pdf.

[25] Underlined emphasis added.

[26] Ibid., paragraph 7, underlined emphasis added.

[27] Ibid., paragraph 83, underlined emphasis added.

5 Why the Question About the Relationship Between the ECHR and Brexit

It might well be asked why, in light of the position expressed by the UK government in its March 2017 White Paper and the text of the draft Political Declaration as endorsed by all the EU leader on 25 November 2018, a question arises about the relationship between Brexit and the ECHR: is the position not absolutely clear?

There seem to me, however, to be two questions where Brexit, in its widest sense, may be said to have potential impact on or at least come into contact with the ECHR:

a. The first is in relation to the question—often discussed by NGOs and human rights advocates in the UK—whether, after exit day, the UK will, in fact, wish to remain a party to the European Convention on Human Rights and, therefore, subject to the jurisdiction of the European Court of Human Rights; and
b. Secondly: are there any possible challenges against Brexit or arising from Brexit which may be brought before the European Court of Human Rights?

In relation to the first, it is, of course, not for me—as a serving judge on the European Court of Human Rights-to second guess the intentions of the UK government; and I am not suggesting in any way that the UK's clear statements of its continued adherence to the ECHR post-Brexit are anything other than clear commitments to that effect.

That said—and here we have to venture a little into the political context or *hinterland* of Brexit—there appears to be some anxiety including amongst some observers that the position may not be as secure as it may seem. This suspicion appears to be based on three key events:

a. A speech made by the Theresa May (then the Home Secretary), campaigning for "remain" in April 2016, in which she stated that[28]:

> … the case for remaining a signatory of the European Convention on Human Rights - which means Britain is subject to the jurisdiction of the European Court of Human Rights - is not clear. ….
>
> …. So regardless of the EU referendum, my view is this. If we want to reform human rights laws in this country, it isn't the EU we should leave but the ECHR and the jurisdiction of its court.

b. The Conservative Party Manifesto for the 2017 General Election which[29] stated:

> We will not bring the European Union's Charter of Fundamental Rights into UK law. We will not repeal or replace the Human Rights Act while the process of Brexit is underway but we will consider our human rights legal framework when the process of leaving the EU concludes. We will remain signatories to the European Convention on Human Rights for the duration of the next parliament.

[28] https://www.gov.uk/government/speeches/home-secretarys-speech-on-the-uk-eu-and-our-place-in-the-world.

[29] https://s3.eu-west-2.amazonaws.com/conservative-party-manifestos/Forward+Together+-+Our+Plan+for+a+Stronger+Britain+and+a+More+Prosperous....pdf, p. 37.

c. The—slight—change in wording we identified earlier between the draft Political Declaration of 14 November 2018 and that of the text finally agreed on 25 November 2018.

That difference in language led Lord Boswell, the Chairman of the House of Lords European Union Committee, to write to the Justice Secretary on 19 December 2018, asking[30]:

> What accounts for these drafting changes, and what do they mean in practice? Does the Government intend to bring forward plans to break the formal link between the UK courts and the European Court of Human Rights after Brexit?

The reply came by letter, dated 4 January 2019[31]:

> This difference in wording does not represent a change in the UK's position on the ECHR. The UK is a founding member of the Council of Europe and one of the first countries to ratify the Convention, which I can assure you and your committee the UK has no plans to withdraw from.

Whatever the political landscape may be in light of these various declarations and statements, some further indication can be derived from two recent cases before the Court of Justice in the context of potentially important areas of future cooperation between the UK and the EU.

The first is a case, which arose in the context of cooperation in relation to criminal justice and law enforcement, called *R O*.[32] The applicant in that case, RO, was the subject of two European arrest warrants issued by the courts of the United Kingdom. He sought to object to his surrender to the United Kingdom on the basis of, *inter alia*, the withdrawal of the UK from the European Union and Article 3 of the ECHR (the prohibition of torture, inhuman or degrading treatment or punishment). The Irish High Court stayed its proceedings and asked the Court of Justice for a preliminary ruling.

Following a hearing at which the UK government was also represented, the Court of Justice ultimately stated that[33]:

> …, it must be observed that, in this case, the issuing Member State, namely the United Kingdom, is party to the ECHR and, as stated by that Member State at the hearing before the Court, it has incorporated the provisions of Article 3 of the ECHR into its national law. Since its continuing participation in that convention is in no way linked to its being a member of the European Union, the decision of that Member State to withdraw from the Union has no effect on its obligation to have due regard to Article 3 of the ECHR, to which Article 4 of the Charter corresponds….
>
> …

[30] https://www.parliament.uk/documents/lords-committees/eu-justice-subcommittee/CWM/LBtoDG-ECHR-PoliticalDeclaration191218.pdf.

[31] https://www.parliament.uk/documents/lords-committees/eu-justice-subcommittee/CWM/EAtoLB-PolDeclationReferencetoECHR040119.pdf.

[32] Case C-327/18 PPU, Judgment of 19 September 2018, ECLI:EU:C:2018:733.

[33] At §§ 50–52 and 61 of its judgment.

> Consequently, [...], in a case such as that in the main proceedings, in order to decide whether a European arrest warrant should be executed, it is essential that, when that decision is to be taken, the executing judicial authority is able to presume that, with respect to the person who is to be surrendered, the issuing Member State will apply the substantive content of the rights derived from the Framework Decision that are applicable in the period subsequent to the surrender, after the withdrawal of that Member State from the European Union. Such a presumption can be made if the national law of the issuing Member State incorporates the substantive content of those rights, particularly because of the continuing participation of that Member State in international conventions, such as the European Convention on Extradition of 13 December 1957 and the ECHR, even after the withdrawal of that Member State from the European Union. Only if there is concrete evidence to the contrary can the judicial authorities of a Member State refuse to execute the European arrest warrant. (emphasis added)

This, of course, mirrors the approach taken by the ECHR e.g. in *Stapleton v. Ireland* (dec.), no. 56588/07, § 26, ECHR 2010.

A similar question was decided, in the context of the EU's common asylum policy, on 23 January 2019 in the case of *M.A., S.A., A.Z.*.[34] In that case, the question arose as to the impact of the anticipated withdrawal of the UK from the EU on the ability of the Irish authorities to return the applicant asylum seekers to the UK. In its judgment, the Court of Justice noted (in §§ 83 -85) that:

> [...], since the Member States are parties to the Geneva Convention and the 1967 Protocol, as well as to the ECHR, two international agreements upon which that Common European Asylum System is based, the continuing participation of a Member State in those conventions and that protocol is not linked to its being a member of the European Union. It follows that a Member State's decision to withdraw from the European Union has no bearing on its obligations to respect the Geneva Convention and the 1967 Protocol, including the principle of non-refoulement, and Article 3 ECHR.

It appears, therefore, that the Court of Justice has not only suggested that future or continuing cooperation in relation to these policy areas are likely to be conditional on the UK's the continuing participation in international conventions, such as the European Convention on Human Rights; in *R O* it has also recorded the positive submission on behalf of the UK government before that Court that the continued protection of those rights could and should be assumed because "it has incorporated the provisions of Article 3 of the ECHR into its national law".

Now in relation to the second potential interface between the European Court on Human Rights and Brexit, namely litigation before the former in relation to the latter, let me start by saying that—when I last checked—there were no Brexit related cases currently pending before the Court and, in any event, in order to be admissible any of these cases would have to have been advanced before the UK courts first in order to satisfy the requirement under Article 35(1) of the Convention that the Court "may only deal with the matter after all domestic remedies have been exhausted, according to the generally recognised rules of international law".

That said, academia and other human rights commentators have, in the course of the last 2.5 years identified and discussed a number of possible causes of action before the European Court. What I want to do in the next few minutes is just to

---

[34] Case C-661/17, ECLI:EU:C:2019:53.

identify two of these for you without, however, in any way seeking to comment on their individual merits. You will appreciate that it would be highly inappropriate for me, as the sitting judge elected in respect of the United Kingdom, to seek to discuss or anticipate the merits or demerits of any actions which may yet be brought before my court and on which, under the terms of Article 26 § 4 of the Convention, I would be required to sit *ex officio* as the national judge as part of the relevant composition of the Court:

Perhaps the most likely is that identified by the Joint Committee on Human Rights of the UK Parliament in its Report "The human rights implications of Brexit" of 19 December 2016[35] which relates to the right to respect for private and family life under Article 8 of the Convention. Having heard detailed evidence in the course of its enquiry, the Joint Committee concluded *inter alia* that, in summary[36]:

> One of the most immediate and pressing concerns arising from Brexit relates to the residence rights of EU nationals currently in the UK and UK nationals in the EU. It is estimated that there are currently 2.9 million EU nationals resident in the UK. Just under 1.2 million UK nationals are thought to live in the 27 other EU Member States.
>
> ...
>
> The actual position of such individuals is legally complicated and will depend on length of residence and other factors. The picture for both UK and EU citizens remains far from clear at this stage. For example, the House of Lords EU Justice Sub-Committee has received compelling evidence to the effect that some EU nationals who have been in the UK for over five years will not currently meet the criteria for permanent residence in circumstances where they have not effectively been exercising their Treaty rights whilst resident in the UK.
>
> The rights of EU and UK nationals may be protected under Article 8 of the ECHR, but these rights are in no way absolute and do not provide the same protections as offered by EU law. Notably, interferences with Article 8 rights can be justified in certain circumstances where they would not be under current EU law.
>
> However, although ECHR rights can be restricted, it would not be possible for the UK Government to establish a bright-line rule that would allow the deportation of EU nationals merely on the grounds that they had only been resident for a fixed period of time. Other factors, such as family connections and the residence rights of any children, would certainly be relevant and each case would have to be considered on its own facts. In the unlikely event that the Government sought to deport EU nationals, there could be the potential for significant, expensive and lengthy litigation leading to considerable legal uncertainty for a prolonged period of time. These cases would also have the potential to clog-up and overwhelm the court system.

The second, more fundamental, is set out in an article in Prospect magazine of 11 October 2018 entitled "The Brexit withdrawal agreement may violate the European Convention on Human Rights"[37] and is based on the judgment in *Matthews v. the United Kingdom* [GC], no. 24833/94, ECHR 1999-I, in which the Court found a violation of Article 3 of the First Protocol to the European Convention on Human

---

[35] HL PAPER 88, HC 695; https://publications.parliament.uk/pa/jt201617/jtselect/jtrights/695/695.pdf.

[36] Ibid., pp. 4–5 (headings omitted).

[37] https://www.prospectmagazine.co.uk/politics/the-brexit-withdrawal-agreement-may-violate-the-european-convention-on-human-rights.

Rights, (the duty to hold free elections at reasonable intervals by secret ballot) on the basis that Mrs Matthews, like all residents of Gibraltar, was denied the right to vote for the European Parliament. This leads the author to suggest that [to use his words]:

> The provision of the draft withdrawal agreement that deals with the post-Brexit transition lays down this fundamental rule [that] EU law will apply in the UK during the transition period more or less exactly as it does now. In particular, any new EU regulation passed by the European Parliament and Council will have direct effect in—i.e. will automatically become law in—the UK. …
>
> …
>
> [referring to Matthews] The UK will continue to be bound by EU law. But UK voters will have no right to vote for an MEP.
>
> …
>
> … even if the UK, which notoriously fails to provide for any significant constitutional restriction on the powers of its parliament, could lawfully ratify the withdrawal agreement in those circumstances, there must be some doubt as to whether the EU institutions could lawfully do so, at least without an amendment to the EU Treaties. As a result, a UK court might be invited not only to rule on the compatibility of the withdrawal agreement with Article 3 of Protocol 1, but also (if it thinks it is incompatible) to make a reference to the Court of Justice of the question whether the EU institutions have power to enter into such an agreement.

6 Conclusion

As you will all be aware and as I indicated at the outset, the nature and state of Brexit—if one can call it that—is currently in constant flux and the nature of any arrangements in place on exit day—if any—is yet to be seen. Developments both in London and in Brussels mean that the parameters of the issue I have sought to address can change from one week to another and at times possibly even on a daily if not hourly basis.

As I indicated at the outset, I have consciously not sought to judge or pre-judge any of these developments or to comment on or take a position on the merits or politics of Brexit. To do so would have been wholly inappropriate for a sitting judge at the European Court of Human Rights.

Nevertheless, I hope I have been able to give you an overview of the legal state of play in so far as it can be discerned from publicly available documents and of some of the issues potentially arising in the context of Brexit in so far as they touch or may touch the European Convention on Human Rights and the European Court of Human Rights.

Ultimately, only time will tell what form Brexit will ultimately take and whether, and if so in what form, the European Court of Human Rights may be—at least indirectly—confronted with it. But that is plainly for another day!

Until then, this is very much a question of “watch this space”.

Thank you.

The EU as a Defender of the Liberal International Order and the Rule of Law

Michael Reiterer

1 Introduction

The Liberal International Order (LIO) is a child of World War II. The "*West*"—and this has remained the Achilles heel of LIO which never got the buy-in of all despite most profited from it—built multilateral relationships and institutions to strengthen and spread liberal values such as rule of law, democracy, open markets, multilateralism and human rights. This is in stark contrast to earlier **politics of power** leading to **power politics** which had produced imperialism and colonialism, disrespect for human rights and wars culminating in WWII. Returning to the **policies of spheres of influence** and regional Great Power projects based on nationalism and protectionism would undoubtedly turn the clock back and wipe out gains in prosperity and well-being.

The LIO produced seventy years of economic growth based on openness and multilateralism, lifted billions out of poverty, relative peace through security cooperation and security architectures,[1] a surge in democracy paired with some degree of democratic solidarity. This was based on what is called "**globalisation**" either positively or negatively.

The end of another war, the Cold War, gave the LIO another temporary boost. Democracy bloomed not only in Europe after the fall of the Berlin Wall and the Iron Curtain but also in Latin America and Asia. The World Trade Organisation (WTO) was meant to cement the rule-based trading system, participatory processes like the G20 got traction and the world united first behind the Millennium and then

[1] See also: Security Architectures Under Threat, The Status of Multilateral Fora. Panorama, 02/2017.

M. Reiterer (✉)
Centre for Security, Diplomacy and Strategy, Brussels School of Governance, Vrije Universiteit Brussel, Brussels, Belgium
e-mail: Michael.Reiterer@vub.be

M. Deguchi and K. Yakushiji (eds.), *Europe and Asia as a Legal Area for Fundamental Rights*, https://doi.org/10.1007/978-981-19-7542-4_5

the Sustainable Development Goals (SDGs) in and by the United Nations. "The Arab Spring" was mistakenly perceived as democracy encroaching North Africa.

Based on the catastrophes of WWII and the holocaust which were in violation of international law and where the Nuremberg and Tokyo war tribunals attempted to exercise accountability, the need for respect for and the rule of law was embedded in the United Nations from its outset as well as in the minds of the founding fathers of the European Union.

The principle of rule of law is already enshrined in the UN-Charta. One of the aims of the UN is "*to establish conditions under which justice and respect for the obligations arising from treaties and other sources of international law can be maintained*".

Furthermore, the UN strives "*to bring about by peaceful means, and in conformity with the principles of justice and international law, adjustment or settlement of international disputes or situations which might lead to a breach of the peace*."

The principle was further developed by the UN-Secretary-General describing 2004 the **rule of law** as

> a principle of governance in which all persons, institutions and entities, public and private, including the State itself, are accountable to laws that are publicly promulgated, equally enforced and independently adjudicated, and which are consistent with international human rights norms and standards. It requires, as well, measures to ensure adherence to the principles of supremacy of law, equality before the law, accountability to the law, fairness in the application of the law, separation of powers, participation in decision-making, legal certainty, avoidance of arbitrariness and procedural and legal transparency.[2]

Work continued on the concept, the 2006 report by the SG entitled ***Uniting our strengths: Enhancing United Nations support for the rule of law***,[3] classifies the rule of law-related activities of the UN into three main "baskets"[4]:

1. "rule of law at the international level";
2. "rule of law in the context of conflict and post-conflict situations";
3. "rule of law in the context of long-term development".

2018 saw the 70th anniversary of the Universal Declaration of Human Rights which puts rule of law in its center underlining that "*... it is essential, if man is not to be compelled to have recourse, as a last resort, to rebellion against tyranny and oppression, that human rights should be protected by the rule of law...*".

The General Assembly followed up in 2012 and organised a High-level Meeting on the Rule of Law at the National and International Levels. UN Member States, non-governmental organisations and civil society committed to strengthening the

[2] Report of the Secretary-General: The rule of law and transitional justice in conflict and post-conflict societies (S/2004/616); par. 6, p. 4.

[3] UN Secretary-General, Uniting Our Strengths: Enhancing United Nations Support for the Rule of Law, Report to the General Assembly and the Security Council, 14 December 2006, par. 40–42, p. 13.

[4] André Nollkaemper, Jan Wouters and Nicolas Hachez (2008). "Accountability and the Rule of Law at International Level" (emphasis added) at https://www.mzes.uni-mannheim.de/projekte/typo3/site/fileadmin/reports/report%20Accountability%20and%20Rule%20of%20Law.pdf.

rule of law. The High-level Meeting concluded with the adoption by consensus of a Declaration of the High-level Meeting of the General Assembly on the Rule of Law at the National and International Levels[5] reaffirming the Members commitment to the rule of law and elaborating on the measures to strengthen the rule of law in its various aspects. It recognises "***that the rule of law applies to all States equally**, and to international organizations, including the United Nations and its principal organs, and that **respect for and promotion of the rule of law and justice should guide all of their activities and accord predictability and legitimacy to their actions**. [It] also recognize[s] that **all persons, institutions and entities, public and private, including the State itself, are accountable to just, fair and equitable laws** and are **entitled without any discrimination to equal protection of the law***." The cross-cutting nature of the rule of law, linking the **three pillars of the UN: peace and security, human rights and development**,[6] was recognised.

2 Rule of Law Is No Longer Limited to States

The ***Foreign Ministers of the G8***, in their declaration of 30 May 2007, acknowledge the fact that the promotion of the international rule of law would gain from not focusing too much on the international legal system *stricto sensu*, but also from taking into account other non-state regulatory initiatives and actors:

> In order to meet these challenges [i.e. the promotion of the international rule of law], we, the Foreign Ministers of the G8, undertake to promote a more coherent international approach, tying together existing initiatives and supporting the United Nations, regional organisations, states and non-state actors active in this field. We recognize the importance of encouraging and respecting local ownership and leadership in the efforts towards the promotion of the rule of law. In order to effectively promote the rule of law, **all stakeholders**, international and national, governmental and non-governmental, have to join efforts.[7]

Non-state actors such as international organisations, NGOs, multinational companies exercise a growing influence on the development and application of the rule of law i.a. when NGOs seek to hold governments and multinationals accountable.

[5] A/RES/67/1 (30 November 2012) at https://www.un.org/ruleoflaw/files/A-RES-67-1.pdf (emphasis added).

[6] These linkages between the rule of law, human rights, peace and security and development have been further elaborated in the addendum to the 2014 Report of the Secretary-General on Strengthening and coordinating United Nations rule of law activities (A/68/213/Add.1).

[7] G8 Chairman's Statement, 30 May 2007; at http://www.g7.utoronto.ca/foreign/formin070530.pdf (emphasis added).

3 The EU Promotes Rule of Law from the Outset

The founders of the EU drew inspiration and aspiration from the WWII experience. Therefore, the EU was conceived from the outset[8] as a treaty-based organisation, guaranteeing rights and formulating duties in the service of the original idea, namely banning warfare from the European continent by replacing battle fields with conference rooms, armies with diplomats or judges. The rule of law was the instrument to realise these goals.

The European Court of Justice confirmed this view in 1986:

> [T]he European Economic Community is a Community based on the rule of law, inasmuch as neither the Member States nor its institutions can avoid a review of the question whether the measures adopted by them are inconformity with the basic constitutional charter, the Treaty.[9]

The rule of law is part of the EU treaties since 1992, the Treaty of Maastricht. The principle applies internally to external relations e.g., it has become a constitutional pillar of the entire EU system. Unlike many states the content of the EU's foreign policy is determined by the Treaty of Lisbon through a list of normative objectives which aim to ensure:

> [T]hat the Union's action on the international scene be guided by the principles which have inspired its own creation, development and enlargement, and which it seeks to advance in the wider world: democracy, the rule of law, the universality and indivisibility of human rights and fundamental freedoms, respect for human dignity, the principles of equality and solidarity, and respect for the principles of the United Nations Charter and international law. (Article 21.1 TFE)

These principles are drawn from Article 2:

> The Union is founded on the values of respect for human dignity, freedom, democracy, equality, the rule of law and respect for human rights, including the rights of persons belonging to minorities. These values are common to the Member States in a society in which pluralism, non-discrimination, tolerance, justice, solidarity and equality between women and men prevail.

These ideas also apply to the corresponding common policies and actions by the EU in order to:

a. safeguard its values, fundamental interests, security, independence and integrity;
b. consolidate and support democracy, the rule of law, human rights and the principles of international law;

---

[8] Michael Reiterer (2014). "The Rule of Law in the External Relations of the European Union with a Special Focus on China", US-China Law Review, vol. 11, 2014; pp. 1279–1301.

[9] Judgment of the Court of 23 April 1986—Partie écologiste "Les Verts" v European Parliament—Action for annulment—Information campaign for the elections to the European Parliament—Case 294/83; at http://eur-lex.europa.eu/LexUriServ/LexUriServ.do?uri=CELEX:61983J0294:EN:HTML.

c. preserve peace, prevent conflicts and strengthen international security, in accordance with the purposes and principles of the United Nations Charter, with the principles of the Helsinki Final Act and with the aims of the Charter of Paris, including those relating to external borders… (Article 21.2 TFE).

4 LIO and Its Values Under Duress

This order is now under duress with nationalism and populism rising in the United States and Europe, authoritarianism reverenced by China in form of state capitalism with Chinese characteristics paired with tightening political control, a policy also followed by Putin's Russia. There are differences and nuances within the authoritarian spectrum—Vietnam may be on one end, Singapore on the other.

Acknowledging that there was no end to history, idealists were slow in realising that there is no automatic pathway to the ideals and principles the LIO stands for. Globalisation is not inherently good (or bad) if not accompanied by corrective policies; there is a need for active engagement and stirring to avoid the deepening of inequalities and to meet discontent. Otherwise LIO appears as an elite project, out of step with the expectations of the people. Furthermore, some claim that LIO was never 'liberal' nor 'international' nor an 'order' to begin with![10]

Trump's '***America First***' signals the end of liberal leadership by the US and is together with Brexit a severe challenge to the LIO, however, on a different scale and in importance. *America First* means that the main creator, promotor and supporter of the LIO is about to abandon its brain child, at least temporarily. This process of erosion has already started earlier with the Iraq War in 2003 and the Financial Crisis in 2008/2009 which spread from the US.

Irritants which impact negatively on the LIO:

- the unilateral renunciation by the US of the UN-sanctioned Iran agreement (JCPOA, spearheaded by the EU), which amounts to a de facto breach of a treaty;
- protective and punitive trade measures in violation of the WTO or its spirit in invoking national security;
- the launching of a trade policy which could turn in a world-wide trade war;
- the corresponding weakening of the WTO and its crown-jewel, the dispute settlement system;
- the US withdrawal from the Paris Agreement;
- the criticism of the partners' lack of engagement in and financing of NATO symbolising the creeping retreat from alliances built over the last decades in a hub-spokes manner;
- the reaction to the murder of a Saudi journalist in the Saudi Consulate in Turkey.

[10] Hans Kundnani (2017). "What is the Liberal International Order?". GMF, Policy Essay, no. 17, 2017; at http://www.gmfus.org/publications/what-liberal-international-order.

Furthermore, the LIO is stressed by

- the illegal annexation of the Crime by Russia, threatening the post-war order based on the Helsinki Agreement,
- the poison attacks on Russian citizens abroad (Salisbury),
- China's neglect for the UNCLOS arbitration in the South China Sea, its island building and their militarization,
- the distancing of China from the LIO institutions in setting up its own like the Asia Infrastructure Investment Ban (AIIB), but also earlier creations like the Shanghai Cooperation Organisation.

First Conclusion: Europe has to take its fate more energetically in his own hands. This insight is gaining momentum with European citizens but needs operationalisation by politicians. It remains to be seen whether this will lead to a new paradigm in European policy making if the Anglo-Saxon *weltbild* loses it European dimension and thereby traction.

> It is time Europe developed what I coined 'Weltpolitikfähigkeit' – the capacity to play our role in shaping global affairs. Europe has to become a more sovereign actor in international relations. [...] The belief that 'united we stand taller' is the very essence of what it means to be part of the European Union. (Jean-Claude Juncker, State of the European Union Address 2018)[11]

In order to maintain credibility to EU is challenged to apply these principles also internally and to stand-up to illiberal policies and populism which endanger the very principles on which the Union is built.

5 The Changing Nature of LIO

The role of LIO in the Post-Cold-War order was different from the role it played in Post-World-War II order: while the latter was built on values and institutions in the context of the bi-partisan competition between "the West" and the Soviet Union and what they stood for, the Post-Cold War order turned for some time unilateral and triumphant (Fukuyama: End of history) until new states and new actors demanded recognition and a role to play.

The G20 is just one incarnation of this process. Today LIO has to adapt to this new surrounding; forces of retention of the status quo defending vested interest and power positions are in conflict with reformists arguing the need to adapt and modernise to stay relevant. This conflict crystallises in the debate of which form of governance is appropriate today. This could also be called the **globalisation crisis of LIO** which needs to find answers on a global scale for more players in a rapidly evolving setting.

On the international scale LIO defenders have to recognise that past policies of engaging China and Russia in the belief that economic liberalism, capitalism,

---

[11] Jean-Claude Juncker: Speech at the State of the European Union Address (12 September 2018) in Strasbourg; at http://europa.eu/rapid/press-release_SPEECH-18-5808_en.htm.

participation in the relevant international organisations will automatically lead to liberalism and democracy have failed.

6 The EU on the International Scene—Leave the Chorus Line

On the international scene, the weakening of US leadership pushes Europeans from the chorus line to the first line of defence of the LIO which could lead to "**Enligthenment.2**".

This is not an easy task: Unlike in 2003 when optimism reigned—"*A Secure Europe in a Better World*"[12] was the title of the then EU Security Strategy. The LIO seemed to unfold unopposed in the wake of the Teutonic changes in Europe. However, today's return of geopolitics as well as geo-economics brings back **power politics, related zero-sum-thinking, all akin to multilateralism,**[13] **the key concept in the EU's foreign relations**. The pendulum in the debate between realists and idealists swings back to the former.

Therefore, the EU's comprehensive approach to international politics focusing on smart and soft power, rule of law and multilateralism could be seen as slightly out of date.

However, as outlined in the 2016 EU Global Strategy (EUGS)[14] there is a need for a large player like the EU not only to maintain but also to defend these values, not least to help preserving the positive elements of the LIO, a role which fits the profile of the EU. 'Defending' also means to reform and re-invigorate to adapt to today's changed circumstances.

Compared to 2003 the 2016 EUGS strengthens the **defence** component which got a strong boost within only two years of implementation of the EUGS in the form of the *Permanent Structured Cooperation.*[15] Furthermore, strong concern for **resilience** of states and societies introduces a strong element of security to mitigate threats while staying tuned to values in the interest of European citizens.

> Allow me to clarify one important point: we will not militarise the European Union. What we want is to become more autonomous and live up to our global responsibilities. (Jean-Claude Juncker, State of the European Union Address 2018)[16]

---

[12] https://europa.eu/globalstrategy/en/european-security-strategy-secure-europe-better-world.

[13] Sven Biscop (2018). "The EU and Multilateralism in an Age of Great Powers", Egmont Institute; at http://www.egmontinstitute.be/content/uploads/2018/07/The-EU-and-Mulitlateralism-in-an-age-of-great-powers-Sven_Biscop.pdf. See also Christian Echle, Patrick Rueppel, Megha Sarmah, Yeo Lay Hwee (eds.) (2018). Multilateralism in a Changing World Order. Konrad Adenauer Stiftung, Singapore: 159 p.

[14] https://europa.eu/globalstrategy/en/global-strategy-foreign-and-security-policy-european-union.

[15] https://www.pesco.europa.eu/ (accessed 20 April 2022).

[16] Jean-Claude Juncker: Speech at the State of the European Union Address (12 September 2018) in Strasbourg; at http://europa.eu/rapid/press-release_SPEECH-18-5808_en.htm. See also Daniel

As a foreign policy actor which is also a multilateral entity, the EU aims to promote consensual solutions at a global level. Not least for the sake of credibility the Treaty on European Union sets out as mentioned above that "*The Union's action on the international scene shall be guided by the principles which have inspired its own creation, development and enlargement, and which it seeks to advance in the wider world*".[17]

Consequently, the toolbox of the EU stresses cooperation in all fields of international relations, to "*promote an international system based on stronger multilateral cooperation and good global governance*" (Article 21).

As the then President of the European Commission *Jean-Claude Juncker* underlined,[18] extending majority voting to foreign policy would increase effectiveness of the EU action—more needed than ever to preserve and develop the LIO. The likelihood is however, low as changing the Treaty is a major political operation with ratification processes in all member states and the European Parliament.

The strength of the LIO is its own systemic resilience anchored in the need for cooperation as the very nature of the problems to solve (climate change, pandemics, cybersecurity…) as well as the functioning of the present order (transport, energy, production, financial networks…) need a cooperative approach.

The mode of cooperation may change back to the Westphalian model—supranationalism has only excelled to a certain degree in the EU. More bilateralism or mini-lateralism instead of multilateralism, less rule of law will roll-back some of the achievements of the ILO in setting up a more just order and focus on its functional aspects, but will not entirely replace it. The latter will only happen if the process is stirred sustainably to achieve greater resilience.

The 2019 *Münchner Sicherheitskonferenz* luckily was more than a wake-up call. Chancellor Angela Merkel not only pleaded the case of the LIO, multilateralism and cooperation in a passionate speech[19] but also made a strong rebuttal of unilateralism as a means unfit to meet today's challenges, to solve today's problems.

The German and French foreign ministers had prepared the ground in an op-ed advocating the setting up of an **alliance for multilateralism**:

> To counter this trend, like minded states must make common cause and double their efforts to promote multilateralism. France and Germany intend to lead the way. Together with our European partners, we are placing our faith in multilateral cooperation and a rules-based world order. We firmly believe that a new commitment to multilateralism, an alliance for multilateralism, is more necessary than ever if we are to stabilise the rules-based world order, to uphold its principles and to adapt it to new challenges where necessary. We therefore

Fiott (2018). "Strategic Autonomy: Towards 'European Sovereignty' in Defence?" at https://www.iss.europa.eu/sites/default/files/EUISSFiles/Brief%2012__Strategic%20Autonomy.pdf.

[17] Article 21.

[18] Jean Claude Juncker: Speech at the European Institute in Florence (11 May 2018): « Je propose donc que dorénavant nous décidions en matière de politique étrangère à majorité qualifiée. C'est faisable, parce que le Traité de Lisbonne, qui a ses vertus, contient une disposition qui permet au Conseil européen de décider à l'unanimité de décider dorénavant à majorité qualifiée dans certains domaines.» http://europa.eu/rapid/press-release_SPEECH-18-3761_fr.htm.

[19] https://www.youtube.com/watch?v=QkKaVFD-5i4.

> want to establish a global network of like-minded states which are convinced that pursuing legitimate, national interests and protecting the collective property of humankind are fully compatible, not mutually exclusive.

They also made clear that this alliance has to serve an important cause:

> We have to protect international norms, agreements and institutions when they come under pressure, or when their existence or funding is jeopardised. This includes international law as well as human rights and international humanitarian law, which are violated on a daily basis throughout the world, thus triggering conflicts. We are therefore calling for open and fair world trade. Furthermore, we will do all we can to safeguard major diplomatic successes such as the nuclear deal with Iran, the agreements on combating climate change or the arms control regimes.[20]

The LIO shares one important trait with democracy—it is far from perfect, but it is preferable to the Leviathan alternative, an international system ruled by naked self-interest and tyranny of the powerful which was at the origin of the catastrophes which gave birth to the EU and the LIO.

No need for history to repeat itself—the application of the rule of law would make an important contribution to this goal. The support of like-minded partners is Asia, in particular democracies and strategic partners like Japan, Republic of Korea and India, as well as Australia and New Zealand is essential to this end.

"*If you want to go fast, go alone. If you want to go far, go together*": As the history of the Rule of Law discussion shows, the realisation of this goal is a long march which needs many co-walkers!

7 Epilog (April 2022)

Re-reading and updating a paper written three years ago is a rare occasion for publication, but first and foremost a useful exercise for a self-test: How pertinent was the analysis at the time, would have the reader gained some insight?

The 2019 presentation predates two major events—the COVID-19 pandemic and Russia's war of aggression against the Ukraine. I join the majority of those who did not foresee them.

However, identifying the need for international cooperation as a means to strengthen the resilience of the LIO was highlighted back in 2019. The illegal annexation of the Crime by Russia was identified as a threat to the post-war order based on the Helsinki Agreements, impacting negatively on the LIO.

Unfortunately, the warning for LIO defenders was right that the policy of engaging China and Russia will not lead to more liberalism and democracy. Power politics, related zero-sum thinking, akin to multilateralism came back in form of war and cruelty against civilians to a degree outperforming the wars in the wake of the

[20] "Who, if not us?". Joint letter by the foreign ministers of Germany and France Heiko Maas and Jean-Yves Le Drian (emphasis added) Süddeutsche Zeitung (14 February 2019); at https://www.auswaertiges-amt.de/en/newsroom/news/maas-le-drian-sueddeutsche/2189696.

breaking-off of Yugoslavia. Enormous efforts will be necessary to avoid, that the Leviathan alternative, an international system ruled by naked self-interest and tyranny of the powerful which was at the origin of the catastrophes which gave birth to the EU and the LIO, becomes the new normal.

While surprised too by the outpouring of violence and disrespect for the rule of law, the EU had already embarked on a path aiming at strengthening its security policy through working for two years on its first security doctrine, the Strategic Compass.[21] With the draft focusing heavily on China, a last-minute re-write introduced measures to stand-up to Russia and tackle more vigorously the dependence on Russian energy supplies. In reply to China's assertive expansionism through the Belt and Road Initiative, the EU countered with the Connectivity[22] and Global Gateway[23] strategies; the Indo-Pacific Strategy[24] also has a strong security element.

However, the blatant breach of international law and the principles of the UN-Charta by a permanent member of the United Nations Security Council shakes the very foundations of the LIO at a moment, when it just had weathered the onslaught of former President Trump, whose return, directly or indirectly, cannot be ruled out. As I had identified in 2019, multilateralism and the rule of law were weakened, therefore the question is legitimate to ask whether the resulting weakness is lethal for the LIO. In combination with democracy receding world-wide, authoritarianism mounting—even within the EU[25] and the US—counter-actions and reform require energy and political will, politicians seem to have difficulties to foster.

Taking up the challenge, formulated also in the Joint Statement of China and Russia[26] in the wake of the opening ceremony of the 2022 Beijing Winter Olympics, in advocating a New Era and the Global Sustainable Development, needs leadership and vision to present a coherent counter-model. It also needs the conviction that the model based on the LIO is the one which reflects the values and the life-style Europeans want to pursue. The Versailles Declaration[27] was a first attempt; the ongoing

---

[21] A Strategic Compass for Security and Defence, 24 March 2022; at https://www.eeas.europa.eu/eeas/strategic-compass-security-and-defence-0_en.

[22] Connecting Europe and Asia—Building blocks for an EU Strategy, 19 September 2019; at https://www.eeas.europa.eu/sites/default/files/joint_communication_-_connecting_europe_and_asia_-_building_blocks_for_an_eu_strategy_2018-09-19.pdf.

[23] The Global Gateway, 1 December 2021; at https://ec.europa.eu/info/sites/default/files/joint_communication_global_gateway.pdf.

[24] EU Strategy for cooperation in the Indo-Pacific-Council conclusions, 16 April 2021; at https://data.consilium.europa.eu/doc/document/ST-7914-2021-INIT/en/pdf; The EU strategy for cooperation in the Indo-Pacific, Joint Communication, 16 September 2021; at https://www.eeas.europa.eu/sites/default/files/jointcommunication_2021_24_1_en.pdf.

[25] See Michael Reiterer, chapter "The Primacy of EU Law Over National Law: Rule of Law Contested—Reflections on the Case of the Polish Constitutional Court", in this volume.

[26] Joint Statement of the Russian Federation and the People's Republic of China on the International Relations Entering a New Era and the Global Sustainable Development, 4 February 2022; at http://en.kremlin.ru/supplement/5770.

[27] Informal meeting of the Heads of State or Government. Versailles Declaration. 10 and 11 March 2022; at https://www.consilium.europa.eu/media/54773/20220311-versailles-declaration-en.pdf.

process of the Conference on the Future of Europe[28] could get a new meaning and task—beyond talk shops at the periphery of European citizens.

Europe has got used to decades of stability, prosperity and peace—blending out signs of alarm whether the increasing income gap among nations, climate change or clear threats formulated by Putin at the 2007 München Security Conference,[29] partly implemented in 2014 with the annexation of the Crimean Peninsula. The loss of trust in Putin will translate into a loss of trust in Russia; the sanctions and the withdrawal of foreign companies will have an impact for years on Russia's economy and standing in the world. The pariah status endangers its voice being heard, in international organisations, sports and culture. Trading the conference rooms with the battle field, breaching agreements and the law, diverting attention and funds from the necessary fight against climate change and environmental degradation endangers future generations, first and foremost the Russian. However, in the long run, the biggest country on the Eurasian landmass will have to return to the international community. Also in the past arrangements have always been found with villain forces, especially once the main perpetrator was gone.

Nevertheless, the speed of the unravelling of the obviously shaky house of the rule of law described earlier and built over decades, the dominance of economic and energy interests over professed values, the return of the outlawed use of force should be more than a wake-up call. The development from soft to smart to hard power, financing even weapons in support of the Ukraine, is a particular challenge for the EU, as it is counter intuitive with its underlying principles, requiring a re-think and re-conceptualization of the international order.

I argue in another publication[30] that the LIO needs to become an ***Inclusive*** Liberal Order, preserving its values but underling inclusiveness and cooperation, freeing thereby the notion from the neo-liberal connotation which is perceived negative, especially by those who were not part of its construction and did not get the full benefits from it.

While focusing on the Sino-American competition, regarding China as the main security threat, wondering whether a new cold war was about to start, Russia started a hot war which China could use for its advantage: supporting tacitly or openly Russia will give China a sway over Russia, not least with an economy which has grown ten times larger than the Russian one and which is more diversified including mastering up-stream technologies. Observing the unified reaction by the EU and the US and their allies and partners, China which is dependent on their markets for economic growth, will factor in this analysis in deciding how to proceed with Taiwan.

---

[28] https://futureu.europa.eu/pages/about.

[29] Speech President Putin, 10 February 2007; at https://www.ardmediathek.de/video/dokumentationen/10-02-2007-putin-kritisiert-usa-politik/phoenix/Y3JpZDovL3Bob2VuaXguZGUvMjUyNDU1Mw.

[30] Michael Reiterer (2023). Connecting Europe and Asia: From Connectivity to Global Gateway, from Asia to the Indo-Pacific—Building an Inclusive Liberal International Order, in Kim Shihong, Michael Reiterer (eds.) Connecting Europe and Asia: Security, Economy and Mobility. HUNIE publisher, Hankuk University for Foreign Studies (HUFS), Seoul; 2023 (forthcoming).

In another Epilogue in three years' time, it would timely to evaluate whether the long over-due institutional reforms of the UN and especially its Security Council have been triggered by this crisis. Whether multilateralism has survived or whether alliance systems mostly in the form of hub and spoke, cooperation models of the willing have taken over and the more powerful arrange themselves in a Westphalian world worshipping Leviathan.

The optimist would argue that after all the major catastrophes, World War I and II, efforts were made to strengthen international cooperation, through the League of Nations, the United Nations. The advantage this time could be, that there is no need to start from scratch but to reform the existing institutions.

Preserving the status quo obviously is no option; it would endanger the chance to preserve the valuable. More attention will be required to provide effective mechanisms to collectively implement what has been agreed, to correct deviations and breaches—otherwise we are back to the law of the jungle, to politics of power leading to power politics.

The time window for reform may be small: it needs the US back as President Biden put it, and China hesitating to full-heartedly embrace Russia as bigger brother in recognition of its economic interdependence with Europe and the US. The strive for more resilient lines of production and value chains can lead to adaptations (reshoring) and more autonomy. While this can be positive, the process needs to be steered to avoid autarky turning into protectionism and the ensuing loss of efficiency. In political terms, this could translate into erecting spheres of influence, exclusive and excluding alliances, further binary thinking with the known negative consequences.

In concluding, I refer back to the closing paragraph of three years ago—we are in for a task which needs co-walkers, an immediate start and energy for the marathon, not easy for the untrained!

The Primacy of EU Law Over National Law: Rule of Law Contested—Reflections on the Case of the Polish Constitutional Court

Michael Reiterer

1 Introduction: The Law-Based Integration Model of the European Union

In order to understand the Polish case, one has first to zoom out of the case and zoom into the very nature of European integration: Unlike other regional integration mechanisms, like ASEAN, the EU has been built from the outset on the rule of law—the European Court of Justice (EUCJ) therefore is an essential part of the EU´s institutional structure.

Policies of the EU are anchored in law, not just in words but also in deeds—the EUCJ applies law, decides on sanctions if necessary. In addition, the Court interprets law and thereby either fills lacunas or, and this aspect is increasing, decides de facto political issues referred to it by politicians who prefer delegating decisions to an authoritative neutral institution over taking political decisions themselves. The latter aspect is, however, rightly criticised as it opens the door too widely for political decision making by an institution which was not set up for this purpose and whose organs (judges) are not democratically empowered to do so beyond the practice developing principles through *juris prudence*. Thus, politicians should not evade their political responsibility and accountability vis-à-vis the sovereign, their electorate.

In the Anglo-Saxon tradition—the EU law has to merge continental and Anglo-Saxon traditions of law, which has not changed after BREXIT—the Court is instrumental in developing EU law in establishing principles through important decisions like the **supremacy of EU law** over the law of member states (Costa vs. ENEL), the principle of **proportionality** (Fèdèration Charbonnière de Belgique Internationale Handelsgesellschaft, Fedesa) or **mutual recognition** (Cassis de Dijon) to name just a few.

M. Reiterer (✉)
Centre for Security, Diplomacy and Strategy, Brussels School of Governance, Vrije Universiteit Brussel, Brussels, Belgium
e-mail: Michael.Reiterer@vub.be

M. Deguchi and K. Yakushiji (eds.), *Europe and Asia as a Legal Area for Fundamental Rights*, https://doi.org/10.1007/978-981-19-7542-4_6

While the jurisprudence of the Court may challenge the policies of member states, it can also be instrumental in inciting member states to take action to remedy a situation or fill a lacuna.

Furthermore, the Court also delimits the competences of the EU institutions.

Important in assuring the rule of law, the Court makes not only sure that legal acts are **based on law**, but also on the **correct treaty provision** as the legal base has legal consequences in substance and procedure.

All legal acts of the Union, regulations, directives and decisions may be challenged in court by EU institutions, member states or citizens. National courts may refer questions of EU law to the European Court for a legal opinion, then to be used in a national decision. This serves the overall goal of achieving security and predictability within the EU, in particular, but not only, in the Single Market.

The **law-based approach to European integration** was essential from the outset: law always protects the weaker. At the cradle of the EU there were six states: three large ones (France, Germany, Italy) and three small ones (Belgium, The Netherlands, Luxembourg). For the latter three, in addition to the common political goal to establish peace on the war-torn European continent, rule of law was an important equaliser.

This feature of European integration has gained in importance through the **transfer of competences from the national level to the EU**, including **directly applicable EU law**. This strengthened in turn the EUIJ. These transfers were the result of consecutive changes in the EU treaties and are therefore part of the primary law of the EU. Treaty changes need not only consensus of member states but also ratification according to their national legal orders; thereby they are democratically legitimised.

Therefore, EU law, its foundations and primacy are widely respected. However, the contestations in Poland and Hungary demonstrate the importance to defend and uphold this essential characteristic of European integration.

This strong position of the European Courts (European Court of Justice, General Court) and their inclination to adjudicate integration-friendly with a centralistic spin—a tendency inherent in apex courts—has often led to discussion and irritation, especially concerning the further development of EU law to promote integration. The opinions range from unintended development as part of legal proceedings, intended activism by the Court to facilitate integration or producing results wished for by member states.

In legal terms, this led to the discussion whether the Court respects limits inherent in EU law or acts, *ultra vires*, beyond its competence but creating nevertheless law. Linked to this issue is whether EU law supersedes national law, the primacy issue, as part of the supra-national integration process of the European Union.

2 The Sovereignty Issue

The depth of integration within the European Union makes EU/European law relevant for citizens, enterprises and states themselves. This raises on the one hand the issue of sovereignty and of democratic legitimisation of EU law making on the other. The COVID-19 crises added another dimension as it broke temporarily basic principles of the EU, like free movement of persons and goods, and lead to the discussion of securing production and value chains. "Sovereignty" came back with force in the political discussion, also in the form of de-globalisation, reshoring, or the creation of national champions through industrial policy. The latter could also get a positive spin in the long-run: it could further the insight, that only a united and strong Europe will compete successfully in the global market place.

"**Strategic autonomy**" also serves as a cover to take up this problem. In my view, "**strategic responsibility**" would be a better term, fitting in a cooperative concept, indicating the need not only for burden sharing but actually burden shouldering. There is an urgent need to narrow gaps in societies and within the EU. If not, contestation will gain traction as the system is perceived as not delivering on promises or expectations. Doubting, questioning the utility of the EU system facilitates politically putting the primacy of EU rules and regulations, as well as law, into doubt.

On the other hand, the growing importance of policy areas like fighting climate change, digitalisation, cybersecurity, global connectivity makes it abundantly clear, that these policy areas need international cooperation beyond the nation state and sovereignty.

The impression of losing control opens the door for nationalism, populism and ultimately isolationism—putting at risk not only European integration but also the international system. The latter is often referred to as the 'Liberal International Order', which is built around multilateralism epitomised by the system of the United Nations and the Bretton Woods system.

3 Primacy of EU Law Contested

The contestation of the primacy of the EU in general and EU law in particular has shown two faces: First, questioning a particular policy, like the Public Sector Purchasing Programme of the European Central Bank, or, second, fundamental principles, like the rule of law, as it is the case of the ruling of the Polish Constitutional Court. These two examples also demonstrate, that even founding members of the EU, like Germany, can harbor doubts, not only more recent member states, like Poland and Hungary.

As the European Commission put it in its 2020 Rule of Law Report, Country Chapter on the rule of law situation in Poland, "Poland's justice reforms since 2015 have been a major source of controversy, both domestically and at EU-level, and have raised serious concerns, several of which persist." Poland is on a year-long escalation course with the EU on issues ranging from the independence of courts, media pluralism and freedom, anti-corruption measures, out-manoeuvring checks and balances in the legislative process,[1] LGBT rights, to the closing the Turów mine extended unilaterally in violation of environmental regulations.[2]

In order to **maintain an independent judiciary**, the EU requests the Polish government to dismantle a disciplinary chamber for judges found to endanger the independence of the judiciary and therefore ruled illegal by the EUIJ. As becomes clear from the statement by the Polish Judge *Bartlomiej Sochanski*, "***The EU Treaty is subordinate to the constitution in the Polish legal system … and, like any part of the Polish legal system, it must comply with the constitution***",[3] the Polish Court holds, that it has a right not only to check the constitutionality of EU law but also the rulings of the Court of Justice of the European Union.[4] This position[5] contests the primacy of EU law, a cornerstone of the EU system, which the European Commission, as the guardian of the treaties as well as member states, cannot accept. The Court confirmed in its judgment of 21 December 2021 (C-357/19 and others, Euro Box Promotion) the EU's obligation of judicial independence of constitutional courts.[6]

In order to suspend the powers of the Supreme Court's Disciplinary Chamber, considered a breach of EU-law, the EUCJ followed in full a request by the EC of March 2021 granting interim measures[7] in July 2021 requesting the suspension of the reorganisation of the judiciary, and, importantly to allow the direct application of and reference to EU law. In reaction to the non-application of these measures by the Polish authorities, the EC followed up with the EUIJ "*to impose financial penalties on Poland to ensure compliance with the Court's interim measures order requested under Article 279 TFEU (of 14 July 2021). On 27 October 2021, the Court of Justice* ***imposed €1 million as a daily penalty payment*** *on Poland for as long as the interim*

---

[1] European Commission Staff Working Document (2020). 2020 Rule of Law Report, Country Chapter on the rule of law situation in Poland. 30 September 2020; EUR-Lex, at https://eur-lex.europa.eu/legal-content/EN/TXT/?uri=CELEX:52020SC0320.

[2] Wojciech Kosc (2021). "Poland digs in over mine spat with EU". Politico, 27 December 2021; at https://www.politico.eu/article/poland-digs-in-over-mine-spat-with-eu/.

[3] Anna Wlodarczak-semczuk (2021). "Polish court rules some EU law is unconstitutional, deepening dispute". Reuters, 7 October 2021; at https://www.reuters.com/world/europe/polish-constitutional-tribunal-some-articles-eu-treaties-unconstitutional-2021-10-07/.

[4] For details on the Polish case see Marta Lasek—Markey (2021). "Poland's Constitutional Tribunal on the status of EU law: The Polish government got all the answers it needed from a court it controls". European Law Blog, 21 October 2021; at https://europeanlawblog.eu/2021/10/21/polands-constitutional-tribunal-on-the-status-of-eu-law-the-polish-government-got-all-the-answers-it-needed-from-a-court-it-controls/.

[5] Constitutional Court of Poland (2021). "Article 6(1), first sentence, of the Convention for the Protection of Human Rights and Fundamental Freedoms, insofar as the term 'tribunal' used therein comprises the Constitutional Tribunal". K6/21 at https://trybunal.gov.pl/en/hearings/judgments/art/11709-art-6-ust-1-zd-1-konwencji-o-ochronie-praw-czlowieka-i-podstawowych-wolnosci-w-zakresie-w-jakim-pojeciem-sad-obejmuje-trybunal-konstytucyjny (accessed 30 December 2021).

[6] Verfassungsblog on Matters Constitutional (2022). "From Romania with Love". 14 February 2022; at https://verfassungsblog.de/from-romania-with-love/.

[7] European Court of Justice (2021). Interim Relief, Order by the Vice-president of the Court, 6 October 2021; at https://eur-lex.europa.eu/legal-content/EN/TXT/PDF/?uri=CELEX:62021CO0204(01)&from=EN.

measures order of 14 July 2021 has not been fully complied with."[8] This lead in December 2021 to the launch of the formal infringement procedure (see p. 10). The European Commission threatened to withhold unpaid penalties from payments due to Poland,[9] a decision finally taken in February 2022.

Similarly, Hungary, or more precisely PM Orban[10] and his Fidesz party are also at odds with the EU on human rights, LGBTI (Children Protection Act[11]) and democracy in general. However, PM Orban was restrained by the Hungarian Constitutional Court on the primacy of EU law. The Court ruled that the legal challenge by the Hungarian government "*cannot be the subject of a review*" of the European court's judgment, nor can it lead to an "*examination of the primacy of EU law.*"[12]

4 What Is at Stake?

The primacy of EU law is one of the pillars of the EU legal system as it is essential to provide EU citizens with the same rights and obligations through the equal application of EU law. This principle is also necessary to allow the EU to carry out the many EU policies in an uniform and equal manner throughout the Union. If national laws were to prevail, the uniformity, predictability and reliability of the EU system would be broken. Therefore, in case of conflict between EU law and the national law of a member state, the EU law takes precedence over national law.

In order to assure uniformity, the date of accession of a member state to the EU is not relevant. With the accession to the EU a candidate state accepts the status quo of EU law at the moment of accession. There is no picking and choosing in arguing that a certain law predates accession.[13]

Critics of the principle of the primacy of EU law base their argument on the fact that this principle is not enshrined in the EU treaties, but has been developed through case law (jurisprudence) of the European Court of Justice. Thus, the Court was

---

[8] European Commission (2021) "Rule of Law: Commission launches infringement procedure against Poland for violations of EU law by its Constitutional Tribunal". Press release, 22 December 2021; at https://ec.europa.eu/commission/presscorner/detail/en/IP_21_7070 (emphasis added).

[9] *The Irish Times* (2022). "Brussels ready to recoup unpaid fines from Poland as rule of law rift widens". 14 January 2022; at https://www.irishtimes.com/news/world/europe/brussels-ready-to-recoup-unpaid-fines-from-poland-as-rule-of-law-rift-widens-1.4776348.

[10] *New York Times* (2021). "How the E.U. allowed Hungary to become an illiberal model". 3 January 2022; at https://www.nytimes.com/2022/01/03/world/europe/hungary-european-union.html?referringSource=articleShare.

[11] Euronews (2021). "EU begins legal action against Hungary over anti-LGBT law". 15 July 2021; at https://www.euronews.com/2021/07/15/eu-begins-legal-action-against-hungary-over-anti-lgbt-law.

[12] Deutsche Welle (2021). "Hungarian top court declines to rule on EU law in asylum case". 10 December 2021; at https://www.dw.com/en/hungarian-top-court-declines-to-rule-on-eu-law-in-asylum-case/a-60077221.

[13] See EUR-lex. Glossary of Summaries. Primacy of EU law. Accessed 27 December 2021 at https://eur-lex.europa.eu/summary/glossary/primacy_of_eu_law.html.

empowering itself. However, developing binding principles through jurisprudence is a legitimate source of law in general, not limited to the Court of Justice.

Already in 1964, the Court had declared[14] that the laws adopted by European institutions must be integrated into the legal systems of EU countries, which are obliged to comply with them. EU law therefore has primacy over national laws. Subsequent cases confirmed this principle.[15]

5 The Jurisdiction of the EUIJ Is Not Unlimited

Contrary to some negative propaganda, the EUIJ has, not unlimited jurisdiction in all instances of European integration. It is limited to areas member states have transferred sovereignty to the EU like the Single Market, transport, environment.

Justice and Home affairs, social policy and taxation as well as the Common Foreign and Security Policy were traditionally not covered. However, Justice and Home Affairs gradually became subject to judicial control, not least because of the Schengen system and the Charter of Fundamental Rights which became binding on EU institutions in 2000. On the other hand, the EUIJ has resisted attempts to Europeanise taxation through legal proceedings.

The EU joining the European Convention on Human Rights (ECHR) of the Council of Europe has been decided in 2009 (Treaty of Lisbon). However, a first agreement reached was rejected by the EU Court of Justice in 2014 as not compatible with EU law. In 2020 negotiations have resumed with a new mandate. The EU's accession to the ECHR will make it possible for individuals to take complaints against the EU to an independent international court—the European Court of Human Rights in Strasbourg. This poses another facet of the problem of supremacy of EU law.

The German Constitutional Court has developed three **carve-outs** from the primacy of the EU law which are widely followed by other apex-courts of member states.[16] They have been below the level of contesting the primacy of EU law, which makes the Public Sector Purchase program (PSPP) judgement—widely regarded as violating EU-law—more perilous for the unity of EU law.

The three carve-outs are:

i. **'Solange' reservation**: the German constitutional court can review EU legal acts as long (*solange*) the protection of fundamental laws by the European Court is not adequate. This reservation is becoming obsolete as the Charter of Fundamental

[14] Costa v ENEL (Case 6/64).

[15] Internationale Handelsgesellschaft mbH v Einfuhr- und Vorratsstelle fur Getreide und Futtermittel (Case 11/70); Amministrazione delle Finanze dello Stato v Simmenthal SpA (Case 106/77); Marleasing SA v La Comercial Internacional de Alimentacion SA (Case C-106/89).

[16] Niels Petersen, Konstatin Chatziathanasiou (2021). "Primacy's twilight?" European Parliament Think tank. 27 April 2021; at https://www.europarl.europa.eu/thinktank/en/document/IPOL_STU(2021)692276.

Rights of the European Union[17] has become binding on EU institutions and the EU is in the process of acceding to the European Convention of Human Rights[18] under the auspices of the Council of Europe;

ii. In a similar manner, the **constitutional identity review**—EU legal acts violating core guarantees of the German constitution—loses relevance through the tighter legal framework on the European level;

iii. the ***ultra vires*** test: the German court wants to determine whether legal acts are issued by the European institution mandated to do so.

The last one is the critical one, dealing with the '*Kompetenz-Kompetenz*'[19] to which the German court applies the proportionality test to define competences. Applying standards of 'manifestly inappropriate, manifest error, misuse of power' or 'exceeding the power of discretion' cover a wide field. Concerning the latter, the institution issuing a legal act should have made an impact assessment and have taken all relevant facts into account. A proportionality test must reveal that the mentioned flaws lead to a result of structural importance.

The salient question, however, remains to determine whether the EUIJ acts *ultra vires*, a dilemma not unfamiliar with apex courts in general, but of special significance in the case of the EU on its way to "ever closer" integration.

6 The Issue of Primary EU-Law

It is noteworthy to consider Declaration 17 annexed to the Treaty of Lisbon. This Declaration confirms the primacy of EU law as developed by jurisprudence and adds a declaration by the legal service to this end. The significance of this Declaration lays also in the fact that the Treaty of Lisbon—in contrast to the draft European Constitution[20] which was not adopted after two negative referenda in France and The Netherlands—does not explicitly enshrine the primacy in the EU's prime law, the treaties. However, and this clarifies Declaration 17, this omission was not meant to negate the primacy of EU law but was part of the drive at the time by some member

[17] Charter of Fundamental Rights of the European Union (2012); at https://eur-lex.europa.eu/legal-content/EN/TXT/PDF/?uri=CELEX:12012P/TXT&from=EN.

[18] Council of Europe (1950). Convention for the Protection of Human Rights and Fundamental Freedoms.; at https://www.echr.coe.int/documents/convention_eng.pdf.

[19] European Parliament (1997). The Division of Competences in the European Union. H. Adjudicating the Dilemma of Competences—Judicial Kompetenz-Kompetenz; at https://www.europarl.europa.eu/workingpapers/poli/w26/adju_en.htm.

[20] "Article 10: Union law

1. The Constitution, and law adopted by the Union's Institutions in exercising competences conferred on it, shall have primacy over the law of the Member States.

2. Member States shall take all appropriate measures, general or particular, to ensure fulfilment of the obligations flowing from the Constitution or resulting from the Union Institutions' acts." Treaty Establishing a Constitution for Europe (18 July 2003); at https://eur-lex.europa.eu/legal-content/EN/TXT/PDF/?uri=CELEX:52003XX0718(01)&from=EN.

states (UK, Poland) to avoid any reference to supranationalism and statehood to which we also owe the disappearance of the notion of 'constitution', 'EU-law' or titles like 'European foreign minister'.

> It results from the case-law of the Court of Justice that primacy of EC law is a cornerstone principle of Community law. According to the Court, this principle is inherent to the specific nature of the European Community. At the time of the first judgment of this established case law (Costa/ENEL, 15 July 1964, Case 6/641 [1] there was no mention of primacy in the treaty. It is still the case today. The fact that the principle of primacy will not be included in the future treaty shall not in any way change the existence of the principle and the existing case-law of the Court of Justice.
>
> > [1] It follows (…) that the law stemming from the treaty, an independent source of law, could not, because of its special and original nature, be overridden by domestic legal provisions, however framed, without being deprived of its character as Community law and without the legal basis of the Community itself being called into question.

The primacy of EU law is of course not without any foundation in the Treaties, the primary law of the EU, itself: Article 344 of the Treaty on the Functioning of the EU (TFEU) stipulates that Member States are obliged to submit disputes concerning the application and interpretation of EU law only to the institution foreseen in the Treaty i.e., the Court of Justice. This is supported by Article 267 TFEU which regulates the referral of questions of the interpretation of EU law to the Court of Justice which Member States are obliged to do, and consequently, apply the interpretation given.

Building on this history and the treaty provisions, the European Commission was clear in its reaction to the decision of the Polish Court:

The Polish President Duda vetoing in December 2021 a law criticised by the US for targeting an US broadcaster TVN owned by Discovery[21] is a clear indication that pressure works. The background to this move is geopolitical: Poland needs US support in the growing conflict with Russia as well as Byelorussia's migration blackmail. This raises, however, an important political question in relation to the EU: Does Poland take the support of the EU for granted because of EU-membership and therefore picks and choses what to respect?

Similarly, PM Orban is in need of the €7 billion COVID-19 recovery funds earmarked for Hungary.

---

[21] Official website of the President of Poland (2021). The President vetoed the Broadcasting Act. 27 December 2021; at https://www.prezydent.pl/aktualnosci/wydarzenia/prezydent-zawetowal-ustawy-o-radiofonii-i-telewizji,47225?utm_source=POLITICO.EU&utm_campaign=c859bd31a7-EMAIL_CAMPAIGN_2021_12_28_05_59&utm_medium=email&utm_term=0_10959edeb5-c859bd31a7-190655620 (accessed 28 December 2021).

7 The Heart of the EU—Its Values and Principles

Article 2 of the Treaty of the European Union[22] enshrines the values on which the integration process is built and wants to maintain:

> The Union is founded on the values of respect for **human dignity, freedom, democracy, equality, the rule of law and respect for human rights**, including the rights of persons belonging to **minorities**. These values are common to the Member States in a society in which **pluralism, non-discrimination, tolerance, justice, solidarity and equality between women and men prevail**.

The political defence of the values of Article 2 is **Article 7**[23]:

> 1. On a reasoned proposal by one third of the Member States, by the European Parliament or by the European Commission, the Council, acting by a majority of four fifths of its members after obtaining the consent of the European Parliament, may determine that there **is a clear risk of a serious breach by a Member State of the values referred to in Article 2**. Before making such a determination, the Council shall hear the Member State in question and may address recommendations to it, acting in accordance with the same procedure.
>
> The Council shall regularly verify that the grounds on which such a determination was made continue to apply.
>
> *2. The European Council, acting by unanimity on a proposal by one third of the Member States or by the Commission and after obtaining the consent of the European Parliament, may* ***determine the existence of a serious and persistent breach by a Member State of the values referred to in Article 2****, after inviting the Member State in question to submit its observations.*
>
> *3. Where a determination under paragraph 2 has been made, the Council, acting by a qualified majority, may decide to* ***suspend certain of the rights deriving from the application of the Treaties*** *to the Member State in question, including the* ***voting rights*** *of the representative of the government of that Member State in the Council. In doing so, the Council shall take into account the possible consequences of such a suspension on the rights and obligations of natural and legal persons. The obligations of the Member State in question under the Treaties shall in any case continue to be binding on that State...*

Concerning Article 7 it may be useful to recall the political environment which induced this article: In 2000, thus within the period of elaboration of a European Constitution[24] by the European Convention, the ultra-right Austrian Freedom Party became part of a coalition government with the conservative People's Party. At the time, there was no basis in the EU treaties to act; therefore, the then 14 member states politically boycotted representatives of the Austrian government. This boycott took place technically outside the EU legal order through a coordinated behaviour of government representatives of the fourteen member states.

---

[22] Consolidated version of the Treaty on European Union. Official Journal of the European Union, C 326/13, 26 October 2012; at https://eur-lex.europa.eu/resource.html?uri=cellar:2bf140bf-a3f8-4ab2-b506-fd71826e6da6.0023.02/DOC_1&format=PDF emphasis added.

[23] Ibid., emphasis added.

[24] The draft was signed in Rome on 29 October 2004 by representatives of all 25 member states; 7 held referendums, France and The Netherlands rejected the project which led after a reflection process to the Treaty of Lisbon.

Article 7, introduced by the Lisbon Treaty, provides now a basis for political actions; however, with the mentioned burdensome procedure. As it is a political instrument, it can be used to criticise and even sanction political acts below the level of the breach of a legal obligation e.g., the "*risk of a serious breach*" suffices for its application.

In addition to Article 7, the EU can draw on treaty provisions and has enacted supplementary mechanisms to protect the rule of law within the EU either politically or legally.[25]

Legal steps are:

1. a legally binding **declaration** that a Member State has violated a given rule of EU law (Articles 258–260 TFEU);
2. a legally binding **interpretation** of EU law confirming that a given Member State's laws, regulations or practices violate the rule of law (Article 267 TFEU);
3. a **financial penalty** imposed upon a Member State (Article 260(2) TFEU) for non-respect of a judgment rendered at the end of an infringement procedure; as well as
4. the **suspension** of a Member State's voting rights in the EU (Article 7 TEU).

Given the persistent challenge of the rule of law by Poland and Hungary and in order to press them to fulfil all their obligations under the Treaties, the EU has set-up in 2019 a conditionality mechanism,[26] which seeks to protect the EU-budget from violations by member states. Most importantly, this mechanism allows to with-hold substantial CoVID-19 Recovery Fund payments. Contested in court by the two member states, as it is their legal right, the Advocate General of the Court found that the conditionality regulation is compatible with existing sanctions mechanisms under Article 7 of the EU treaty, and that there is a "*sufficiently direct link*" between rule of law breaches and the implementation of the EU budget.[27]

The Court of Justice followed in his February 2022 ruling this line of argument and "dismissed the actions brought by Hungary and Poland in their entirety"[28] e.g., confirmed that the conditionality mechanism falls within the competence of the EU

---

[25] Rafal Manko (2019). Protecting the rule of law in the EU. EPRS | European Parliamentary Research Service, November 2019; at https://www.europarl.europa.eu/RegData/etudes/BRIE/2019/642280/EPRS_BRI(2019)642280_EN.pdf.

[26] Regulation (EU, Euratom) 2020/2092 of the European Parliament and of the Council of 16 December 2020 on a general regime of conditionality for the protection of the Union budget. Official Journal of the European Union L 433 I/1; at https://eur-lex.europa.eu/legal-content/EN/TXT/PDF/?uri=CELEX:32020R2092&from=EN.

[27] European Court of Justice (2021). InfoCuria, case law, Opinion of Advocate General Campos Sanchez-Bordona, Case C-156/21, Hungary v European Parliament and Council of the European Union, 2 December 2021; at https://curia.europa.eu/jcms/upload/docs/application/pdf/2022-02/cp220028en.pdf https://curia.europa.eu/juris/document/document.jsf?text=&docid=250424&pageIndex=0&doclang=EN&mode=req&dir=&occ=first&part=1&cid=4861192.

[28] Court of Justice of the European Union (2022). PRESS RELEASE No 28/22 Luxembourg, 16 February 2022; at https://curia.europa.eu/jcms/upload/docs/application/pdf/2022-02/cp220028en.pdf.

in establishing financial rules; Article 7 procedures and the conditionality mechanism pursue different aims; Member states can establish with sufficient precision the essential content and the requirements of essential principles like the rule of law.

Nevertheless, the **Article 7 procedures**, set up to face the "*clear risk of a serious breach by a Member State of the values referred to in Article 2*" has remained a weak remedy because of the unanimity and majority requirements in its application.[29] Therefore, the European Parliament pushed the European Commission to make use of the conditionality instrument in relation to Poland and Hungary, "where there is a risk of funds flowing into the wrong channels".[30] The EC was first reluctant to make use of this strong measure[31] and preferred continuing to find a political solution.

Seeking the opinion of the EUIJ first, before applying conditionality legally, was part of the compromise the EC reached with the member states concerned to get their support for the mechanism, much to the dislike of the European Parliament.

Therefore, on 22 December 2021, the European Commission launched an infringement procedure against Poland "because of serious concerns with respect to the Polish Constitutional Tribunal and its recent case law. The Constitutional Tribunal, in its rulings of 14 July 2021 and 7 October 2021, considered the provisions of the EU Treaties incompatible with the Polish Constitution, expressly challenging the primacy of EU law. Poland has two months to reply to the letter of formal notice.

> The Commission upholds and reaffirms the founding principles of the Union's legal order, namely that:
>
> - EU law has primacy over national law, including constitutional provisions;
> - all rulings by the European Court of Justice are binding on all Member States' authorities, including national courts.
>
> We will analyse the ruling of Polish Constitutional Tribunal in detail and we will decide on the next steps. The Commission will not hesitate to make use of its powers under the Treaties to safeguard the uniform application and integrity of Union law.
>
> The European Union is a community of values and of law, which must be upheld in all Member States. The rights of Europeans under the Treaties must be protected, no matter where they live in the European Union.
>
> The European Commission has the task of safeguarding the proper functioning of the Union's legal order and it will continue to ensure that.[32]

---

[29] Article 7 "2. The European Council, acting by unanimity on a proposal by one third of the Member States or by the Commission and after obtaining the consent of the European Parliament, may determine the existence of a serious and persistent breach by a Member State of the values referred to in Article 2, after inviting the Member State in question to submit its observations."

[30] European Parliament, Parliamentary questions on application of the new regime of conditionality for the protection of the Union budget 8 October 2021; at https://www.europarl.europa.eu/doceo/document/P-9-2021-004585_EN.html#def1.

[31] Legal Service of EP, Analysis of EC response, 27 August 2021; at https://www.politico.eu/wp-content/uploads/2021/10/21/Legal-Service-Opinion.pdf.

[32] European Commission, Statement 7 October 2021. "European Commission reaffirms the primacy of EU law"; at https://ec.europa.eu/commission/presscorner/detail/en/statement_21_5142.

The Commission considers that these rulings of the Constitutional Tribunal are in **breach of the general principles of autonomy, primacy, effectiveness and uniform application of Union law and the binding effect of rulings of the Court of Justice of the European Union.**"[33]

8 Conclusions

While the EU is built on law, it is a political project with peace as the ultimate and continuous ideal in realising the **goals defined in Article 2**.[34] Contesting this key 'value article' Article 1 ("'the Union', on which the Member States confer competences to attain objectives they have in common … a process of creating an ever-closer union among the peoples of Europe) and Article 19 setting up the European Court of Justice,[35] goes right to the heart of the European Union and therefore requires a robust legal but even more importantly, political answer.

Essential is the political commitment. Rule of law serves realising the goals in a transparent, equal manner. Membership in the EU grants rights but also establishes obligations—a dichotomy sometimes forgotten or questioned. Pick and choose is the end of a community whether in terms of values or finance.

This attitude has ultimately led to the break-down of the negotiations between the EU and Switzerland to maintain a level playing field through the application of the same state of EU law relevant for the Single Market in which Switzerland wants to participate. The participation of a non-member state in the Single Market can obviously not change the EU legal system, which is built on the primacy of the EU and its implementation through the EUIJ.

The primacy of EU law is THE instrument to achieve community goals, to empower and protect EU-citizens and maintain trust in the legal system. As the President of the European Commission, Ursula von der Leyen, put it, "When they joined, the Polish people put their trust in the EU. They expected the EU to defend their rights. And rightly so. The EU-Commission protects the rights of EU citizens, wherever they live in our Union."[36] Furthermore, one of the major achievements of the EU is to replace the battle fields with conference rooms—may the best argument be the best weapon.

---

[33] European Commission (2021) Press release, 22 December 2021.

[34] "*The Union is founded on the values of respect for* ***human dignity, freedom, democracy, equality, the rule of law and respect for human rights****, including the rights of persons belonging to* ***minorities****. These values are common to the Member States in a society in which* ***pluralism, non-discrimination, tolerance, justice, solidarity and equality between women and men prevail***" (emphasis added).

[35] Article 19.1 TEU: "The Court of Justice of the European Union shall include the Court of Justice, the General Court and specialised courts. It shall ensure that in the interpretation and application of the Treaties the law is observed. Member States shall provide remedies sufficient to ensure effective legal protection in the fields covered by Union law."

[36] Ursula von der Leyen (2021). https://twitter.com/vonderleyen/status/1450385524867444741.

An institutional, legal proposal to solve the problem is to introduce as part of the reform of the treaties—thus not anytime soon—a separate chamber at the Court of Justice, composed equally of judges from the Court and the apex courts of member states, with the sole task of interpreting EU competences. This could become a means to render such decisions more objective, as the Court of Justice is perceived by some as too European or biased in favour of (ever closer) European integration.[37]

Legal instruments and remedies are necessary to maintain the system, but cannot replace the political will to implement laws and regulations, to carry the integration project forward. EU membership has been entered freely by all members and they have to right to leave (BREXIT), undesirable as this is and negative in consequences primarily for the United Kingdom but also the EU.

Cashing in only financial advantages without delivering on values is breaking the commitment entered into when joining the EU. The usage of the same terms but assigning them different meanings or coining contradictory terms like 'illiberal' democracy or applying fundamental rights selectively, cannot camouflage divergent opinions. If they cannot be settled in the political process there are abundant legal possibilities and guarantees to ask for clarification whether measures are covered by the existing legal framework. But at the end, there is the obligation to accept a legal verdict based on the supremacy of EU law.

Non-respect cannot become a bargaining chip or a token for blackmail. As the last and absolutely undesirable solution, a member state continuously contesting and undermining essential principles on which the EU is built, such as the rule of law and its primacy, may be reminded that "*Any Member State may decide to withdraw from the Union in accordance with its own constitutional requirements*" (Article 50 EUTF). Interaction with citizens and discourse not exclusion can prevent such a negative development, as BREXIT has proven.

This, however, seems to be one bridge too far for Poland, one of the countries profiting most from EU funding and where support for the EU in the population is high,[38] despite the negative propaganda by the government. Finally, 3 February 2022, the Polish President *Andrzej Duda* has taken a first step to settle the "Battle of the Courts" in submitting legislation to dismantle the controversial disciplinary chamber for judges. (Judges of this chamber could either retire or be moved to other Supreme Court chambers. Disciplinary cases would be heard by a new panel composed of 11 Supreme Court judges chosen through a draw.)[39] However, as the Chamber will be replaced by another body appointed by the President, this might not qualify as

[37] Petersen, Chatziathanasiou (2021).

[38] Future of Europe 2021-Special Eurobarometer 96.1 (2022) "62% Membership in the EU is a good thing. Bad thing: 10%"; at https://europa.eu/eurobarometer/surveys/detail/2554

[39] Aljazeera (2022). "Poland's president proposes bill to end rule of law row with EU". 3 February 2022; at https://www.aljazeera.com/news/2022/2/3/polands-president-proposes-bill-to-end-rule-of-law-row-with-eu. See also Judgment in Case C-430/21, Press release No 31/22, Luxembourg, 22 February 2022, on primacy of EU law and prohibition of disciplinary measures against judges; at https://curia.europa.eu/jcms/upload/docs/application/pdf/2022-02/cp220031en.pdf.

one of three "milestones" requested by the President of the European Commission[40] e.g., abolishing the disciplinary chamber, rewriting its rules and allowing judges sanctioned or suspended by the chamber to have their cases reviewed.

Also on 3 February 2022, the European Court of Human Rights had ruled that "that the Civil Chamber of the Supreme Court, which had decided on a case concerning it, had not been a "tribunal established by law" and had lacked impartiality and independence."[41] Therefore, there is a violation of Article 6 § 1 (right to a fair hearing) of the European Convention on Human Rights.[42]

Furthermore, a million euro a day penalty for not suspending the court organisation; withholding the approval of Poland's Resilience and Recovery Facility e.g., the Covid-19 recovery fund spending plan of €36bn; offsetting of payments for monthly penalties of €15 million from Poland's allocated EU funds as a result of Warsaw's continued refusal to pay a €500,000 daily fine for keeping open the Turow power plant[43]; all these may be more convincing arguments than rule of law and the primacy of EU law! In terms of geopolitics, the flagrant breach of international law by Russia in invading the Ukraine might also weigh in! The need to receive EU funding in support of more than 3 million Ukrainian refugees in Poland is another strong argument.

2022 was a crucial year to manage a strained political situation in Poland.[44] Hungarians voted with a surprisingly clear margin to keep PM Orban in power. This triggered President von der Leyen to announce in a debate about the rule of law at the European Parliament that the Commission has launched the next step of the rule of law conditionality mechanism.[45] After the re-election of PM Orban

---

[40] Ursula von der Leyen (2022). Speech by President von der Leyen at the European Parliament Plenary on the rule of law and the potential approval of the Polish national recovery plan, 7 June 2022; at https://ec.europa.eu/commission/presscorner/detail/en/SPEECH_22_3528.

[41] The case is one of 94 currently pending applications against Poland, mostly lodged in 2018–2022, concerning various aspects of the reorganisation of the Polish judicial system initiated in 2017.

[42] European Court of Human Rights (2022). Judgment Advance Pharma SP. z o.o v. Poland "Systemic dysfunction in judicial appointments procedure in Poland". Press Release, ECHR 039 (2021) 03.02.2022; at https://hudoc.echr.coe.int/app/conversion/pdf/?library=ECHR&id=003-7249361-9866930&filename=Judgment%20Advance%20Pharma%20SP.%20z%20o.o%20v.%20Poland%20-%20Systemic%20dysfunction%20in%20judicial%20appointments%20procedure%20in%20Poland.pdf.

[43] Reuters (2022). "EU notifies Poland it will withhold its EU cash to cover unpaid fines". 8 February 2022; at https://www.reuters.com/world/europe/eu-notifies-poland-it-will-withhold-its-eu-cash-cover-unpaid-fines-2022-02-08/ (case C-121/21 Czechia v Poland on Turów).

[44] Lily Bayer (2021). "Next year will be critical for the rule of law—Europe's troublemakers face tough electoral challenges". Politico, 27 December 2021; at https://www.politico.eu/article/eu-europe-rule-law-elections-hungary-viktor-orban-fidesz-poland-pis-donald-tusk-slovenia-janez-jansa/.

[45] European Parliament, Press release 5 April 2022. Question time with Commission President Ursula von der Leyen, at https://www.europarl.europa.eu/news/de/press-room/20220401IPR26529/question-time-with-commission-president-ursula-von-der-leyen.

the formal letter of notification was sent.[46] However, PM Orban remained defiant, linking agreement to the sixth sanction package against Russia which includes an oil-embargo to compensatory payments. However, no payments from the EU are possible as long as the rule-of-law mechanism is in force. Prolonging the state of emergency which was at the time imposed because of COVID-19 due to the war in neighbouring Ukraine, is another measure rule-of-law defying measure by Orban, destroying, not rebuilding trust.[47]

It would have been timely for the EU to act before the right-wing populist 'illiberal democracy' takes hold and transforms Hungary into an authoritarian regime where 'democracy' serves for branding but not as the guiding principle for politics. The war in the Ukraine and the modalities of the election with heavy involvement of the government on behalf of a party, a biased media opaque campaign funding influenced the elections in Hungary as criticised by the OSCE observer mission,[48] rather unusual in the case of an EU member state.

When I was a university student in the 1970s, a professor of constitutional law warned us: when a country has 'democratic' in its name, mistrust the wrapping. We are not there yet, but we don't want to get there and therefore the primacy of EU law is not an issue for specialists and seminars but an important legal and political issue for all members of the European Union and its citizens.

[46] Politico (2022). "In major first, EU triggers power to cut Hungary's funds over rule-of-law breaches". 27 April 2022; at https://www.politico.eu/article/eu-european-commission-rule-law-mechanism-hungary-funds/.

[47] Hungary Today (24 May 2022). "Government declares state of emergency due to war"; at https://hungarytoday.hu/pm-orban-government-declares-state-of-emergency/.

[48] OSCE International Election Observer Mission. Hungary—Parliamentary Elections and Referendum, 3 April 2022. Preliminary Conclusions; at https://www.osce.org/files/f/documents/4/6/515111_1.pdf.

Human Rights Limitation in the Rule of Law from Vietnam's Practice

Nguyen Linh Giang

Human rights are always full of conflicts. It could be the conflict among the rights of oneself; conflict between the rights of one person to another; rights of an individual to a collective's rights; and rights of the State to the rights of its people. If these conflicts are not settled or resolved harmoniously, society will not be able to exist and progress. To resolve these conflicts, we need human rights limitation.

Naturally, human rights will always accompany with limitations. But how to efficiently and effectively limit these rights? Which rights are to be limited? Where do we draw the line between freedom to act and limitation of rights? These are all important matters, since if there is no guiding principle, human rights could be arbitrarily limited. Therefore, along with the recognition of basic human rights, the Constitution needs to stipulate principles and mechanisms to legitimately and effectively limit these rights.

1 The Legitimacy of Limiting Human Rights

The French revolution had set a principle: Men are born and remain free and equal in rights.[1] However, this idea of freedom cannot be exercise freely and without any limits in practice. The nature of man is always looking for self-interest, therefore, when it comes to enjoying one's rights, naturally everyone will want to expend it to the maximum and to satisfy their desire at the highest possible level. If such desire exceeds the acceptable limit, it will intrude others people's rights or public interest.

[1] Article 1 Declaration of the Rights of Man and of the Citizen 1789.

N. L. Giang (✉)
Institute of State and Law, Vietnam Academy of Social Sciences, Hanoi, Vietnam
e-mail: linhgiang@isl.gov.vn

M. Deguchi and K. Yakushiji (eds.), *Europe and Asia as a Legal Area for Fundamental Rights*, https://doi.org/10.1007/978-981-19-7542-4_7

What will society become if everyone keeps maximizing their rights without minding the limits?

It is necessary to prevent an individual from abusing their rights through restrictive terms. Abuse of rights can be defined as when one exercises their rights contrary to the initial objectives, scope of right protection and the spirit of the right. It should be perceived as an illegal, prohibited behavior as it can affect the rights and freedom of others. To prevent a person from exercising their rights that could possibly influence, threaten the rights and freedom of others, the State must be responsible to maintain order, to protect the rights of its member.

Hence, limiting human rights can be viewed as a tool to better protect rights. This constitutional principle is an important basis to ensure the constitutionality of limiting rights. The Constitution can inherit from international law on human rights, or countries can study each other to construct a chapter on human rights that reflects the progress of humanity. However, these regulations will lose its value if they are to be "narrowed" arbitrarily by statutes, by laws. Therefore, it should be more important to prevent such arbitrary restrictions than to recognize these rights.

Limiting the right is to set a boundary for one's action to not affect social interests or individual interests, rights. It is not a violation of rights to limit human rights but rather a justifiable action to create a space for each individual to freely act and enjoy their own rights within it. The possible risks for this are when we limit too strictly or too loosely on one's rights. Both of these risks need to have preventive measures.

The State, with its mission to ensure public order and safety and the social interest, also have to respect, protect the rights and freedom of man and citizen. A society that lacks freedom cannot expect to have a healthy and stable politic, economic, social and cultural development. If a State does not establish the rule of law, the rights of its citizen will not be guaranteed. Hence, on one hand, the State need to create a space for each individual to exercise their rights and freedom and protect it when they are being violated[2]; on the other hand, the State also need to limit this space to a certain scope. The State, has the obligation to respect and enable the rights of its citizen as well as the obligation to protect these rights against the violation from other subjects and the State itself.

Thus, the nature of the limitation of human rights is to balance between the legitimate rights of each individual versus the community interests. Limiting human rights is necessary. The clauses to limit these rights need to be carefully and thoroughly explained in accordance with widely accepted rules to protect the basic human rights and should not be interpreted beyond its normal concepts.

---

[2] See also: Nguyen Van Hien, Truong Hong Quang, The principles to limit human and citizen rights under the Constitution of 2013, Justice Publisher, Hanoi, 2018, pp. 24–25.

2 The Principles on the Limitation of Human Rights

Human rights are not absolute, thus, in situations necessary for the public interest or to protect social order, state security, morals, public health, or the legitimate rights and interest of others, such rights can be limited. This has been widely accepted worldwide and can be seen reflected in the law of many countries. Limitations of human rights could come from the right itself, for example, an individual's freedom of speech can be limited in case of slander, expose of state secrets, other people's private secrets... But human rights can also be temporarily suspended due to special circumstances, such as freedom of movement can be limited in the war, natural disasters and epidemics or in restricted areas for national security or defense reasons... This limitation can be short-term or long-term, apply in a part or in the whole country.

The limitation of human rights was recognized in the Universal Declaration of Human Rights in 1948 (UDHR) and some international conventions on human rights. The nature of limiting human rights is to allow states to impose certain conditions on the implementation/enjoyment of certain human rights.[3]

2.1 *Principles on the Limitation of Human Rights Under International Human Rights Conventions*

The recognition of the principle on human rights limitation in international human rights conventions is the permission for member states of the convention to set limitations on human rights. However, this limitation must not be imposed arbitrarily and have to follow some important rules.

The International Covenant on Civil and Political Rights (ICCPR) and the International Covenant on Economic, Social and Cultural Rights (ICESCR) recognized the obligations of member states in protecting human rights in various areas. However, both Covenants have their own restrictions on human rights.

According to Article 4 of ICESCR, the limitation of human rights must follow these important principles:

2.1.1 It Must Be Regulated by Law

This principle address that limitations of human rights must be regulated by law. However, defining what is considered to be "law" still remains a controversial question.[4] Some countries set these limitations through legal documents, some through

[3] See also, Q&A on human rights, Research Centre for Human and Citizen's Rights, Faculty of Law, Vietnam National University, Hong Duc publisher, 2011, p. 72.

[4] Alkema believed that "law" are rule set by the legislature, See also E. Alkema, Studies on European Human Rights (Deventer, 1978), p. 42; Contrary to this, Van Dijk and Van Hoof argued that this definition must be viewed broadly to include "all competence agencies with the right to build law",

by-laws or court orders... The European Court of Human Rights lets member countries answer this question on their own since they are in the most favorable position to understand the nature of their legal system.[5] The case-law of the European Court of Human Rights showed that law must be viewed broadly, not just include rules made by the legislature, but also from the court, which are the case laws in the Common-law countries,[6] international obligations that bind the member states,[7] other secondary sources like royal edict, emergency resolutions, and other internal regulations base on the law.[8]

The requirements for the Law is to be consistent with other international conventions, must be available, public, clear and indiscriminate toward other people. The explanation and application for this can be found in the practice of the European Court of Human Rights. According to the Court, the principle to limit human rights must be evaluated based on three criteria: (1) The limitation must be prescribed by law; (2) It must be easily accessible; and (3) It must be transparent and predictable.

- The limitation must be prescribed by law

The law granted the right to intervene to the State and so it must have some regulations to limit such power of the State.[9] This is an important basis for monitoring and therefore assessing the intervention of the State in a specific situation to be beyond its authority or not.

- It must be easily accessible

The accessibility of the law means the law itself must be publicly publish under various forms, media for the people to access when needed. Also, the accessibility of the law depends on how easy or the people to perceive it and the language written in the law, as well as how to effectively apply it in practice.

- It must be transparent enough for the people to predict the legal consequences of their behavior

The transparency and predictability of the law are a necessary condition for individual to shape their behavior in practice. The transparency is evaluated base on the

---

including case law from courts in the Common law countries, See also Van Dijk and Van Hoof, Theory and Practice of European Convention on Human Rights (2nd ed) (Deventer, Boston: Klumer, 1990), p. 372.

[5] *Kruslin, ibid*, paragraph 29; *Malone v. The U.K.*, ECtHR App No. 8691/79 (1984), paragraph 79; *Barthold v. Germany*, ECtHR App No. 8734/79 (1985), paragraph 48; *Campbell v. The U.K.*, ECtHR App No. 13590/88.

[6] *Malone v. UK, ECtHR App No.8691/79 (1984)*, paragraph; *Sunday Times, ibid*, paragraph 47; *Tolstoy Miloslavsky v. The U.K.*, ECtHR App No. 18139/91 (1995), paragraph; *Kruslin, ibid*, pp. 28–29; *Barthold, ibid*; *Markt Intern v. Germany*, ECtHR App No.10572/83 (1989).

[7] *Groppera and Others v. Switzerland*, ECtHR App No.10890/84 (1990).

[8] *Vagrancy v. Belgium*, ECtHR App No. 2832 2835 2899/66 (1971), paragraph 93; *X v. Switzerland*, App No. 7736/76 (1970), paragraph 206, 207; *X v. The U.K.*, App No. 7308/75 (1979), paragraph 32, 34–35.

[9] *Silver, ibid, paragraph 83*; *Herczegfalvy* (1992), paragraph 89.

content of the text, the area it regulates, as well as the number and eligibility of the regulated subject.[10] However, many regulations are general, hence, the interpretation and application of them is much depend on practice.[11]

Thus, it can be seen that the assessment on the limitations on human rights has relatively wide amplitude, and depends on the application of each country. Nonetheless, it is a non-abstract, easy to assess criterion and only depends on each country definition of "law" or "legal document".

2.1.2 The Limitations Set Forth Must not Go Against the Nature of Related Rights

This principle aims to ensure the limitations set by the State will not change or damage the nature of the rights. Obviously, to assess whether a limitation can or cannot affect or go against the nature of a right is not easy and must be done in specific situation. It must not lose the nature of the right and must be viewed within the context of the right.

The Limburg principles on the implementation of the ICESCR 1986[12] has some explanation on the context, which demands that the limitations set forth must not be interpret or apply to cause harm to the nature of related rights. Example: Absolute rights must not be limited. If they are to be limited, the very nature of those rights will be altered.

2.1.3 Human Rights Limitation is Necessary in a Democratic Society and Its Primary Aim is to Promote Public Interest

This principle has two implications regarding "democratic society" and "public interest". These are two concepts that are viewed quite broadly and can be assessed differently, depending on the circumstances of different countries.

+ *Democratic society:* For a long period of time there had been differences between eastern and western take on the definition of democratic society. There are also little mentions in the United Nation's document on this concept of democratic society, mostly in Article 21, 22 of ICCPR. However, regardless of the notion, in a democratic society, basic human rights and freedom of its citizen must be respected and ensure transparency in the decision-making process of the States.

[10] *Malone, ibid,* paragraph 68; *Sunday Times, ibid,* paragraph 49; *Wingrove v. The U.K.*, ECtHR App No. 17419/90 (1996), paragraph 40–44.

[11] *Silver, ibid*, paragraph 88; *Tolstoy Miloslavsky, ibid*; *Goodwin v. The U.K.*, ECtHR App No. 17488/90 (1996), paragraph 32–34.

[12] The Limburg principles was elaborated by a group of experts in international law, convened by the International Commission of Jurists, the Faculty of Law of the University of Limburg (Netherlands) and the Urban Morgan Institute for Human Rights (University of Cincinnati, Ohio, USA), met at Maastricht form 2 to 6 June 1986 to consider the nature and scope of the obligations of States parties to the ICESCR.

+ *Public interest* or *general welfare:* Following Article 4 of ICESCR, member states can only apply such limitations when the conditions are met, and cannot limit human rights on the basis of lack of resources but to take steps to maximizing available resources to gradually realize ICESCR regulations. According to Article 4 of ICESCR, the limitation of economic, social and cultural rights is for the sole purpose of "promoting the general welfare".

An example for this is the curfew and limitation of the freedom of movement in case of terrorism or armed conflict. When facing natural disasters, terrorism attacks or armed conflicts that could affect the whole society, to ensure public interest and protect the safety of individuals; freedom of movement could be limited. Nonetheless, terrorism attacks or armed conflicts cannot justify the act to limit people's rights to food and health. Also, member States have the obligation to prove which situations could be considered as public interest or general welfare.

Although limiting human rights is prescribed in ICESCR, but these principles can be applied to all human rights. Therefore, limitations of human rights are not only applicable for economic, social and cultural rights but also for civil and political rights. Rights that can be limited in ICCPR include those that are not absolute, such as: Privacy and Family (Article 17, 23 ICCPR); freedom of religion and belief (Article 18 and 4.2 ICCPR); freedom of speech (Article 19, 20 ICCPR and Article 4.4a); freedom of assembly and association…

2.2 The Principles on Limitation of Human Rights in the Law of Many Countries in the World

Overall, there are certain common principles to limiting human rights as follow:

(1) The principle of respect for the dignity of individual

Respecting human dignity is the first and foremost principle of the Universal Declaration of Human Rights. In free societies operated by the rule of law, the functions of state agencies are to establish and maintain the conditions to protect human dignity. For example, torture or humiliate people with violence and inhumane acts must not be allowed, even when that person is currently in detention or in custody.

(2) The principle of legality

This principle stated that everyone is free until there are limitation set forth by the law. This limitation must be clearly indicated in the law and have appropriate measures to prevent the possibility of abusing these limitations or arbitrarily setting up limitations.

(3) The principle of the rule of law

This principle was established for democratic purposes, to limit State power and protect basic human rights. The limitation will be set when it is needed in a democratic society for the purpose of promoting general welfare or protect public order, national security, moral, public health or the rights and interest of others.[13]

(4) The principle of equality and non—discrimination

This principle is an important element in the theory of limiting human rights. Limitations for rights must be a universal limitation, which will apply to all rights, not just a particular one. The limitation must ensure that there is no discrimination on the ground of race, color, sex, language, religion or social origin.[14]

(5) Principle of proportionality

The principle of proportionality represents the appropriateness between the tools; means and measures taken to achieve a legitimate purpose must be reasonable, necessary, appropriate and proportionate. The optimal and proportional solution is one that has the less limitation to rights but bring about greater benefit than the damage caused by the restriction. This represents the relationship between limitation and its purpose. Limiting rights must aim for legitimate/justifiable purposes; the limitations must be reasonable, necessary and appropriate.

3 The Practice of Limiting Human Rights in Vietnam

For the first time in Vietnamese constitutional history, the limitation of human rights has been recorded in a Constitution. Clause 2 Article 14 of the 2013 Constitution stipulates: *"Human rights and citizens' rights shall only be restricted when prescribed by law in imperative circumstances for the reasons of national defense, national security, public order and security, social morality and public health"*. According to this Article, the principles of limiting human rights under the Vietnamese Constitution require:

—Limitations on human rights must be made as prescribed by law.

—Limitations on human rights can only occur in imperative circumstances for the reasons of "national defense", "national security", "public order and security", "social morality" and "public health".

3.1 Limiting Human Rights as Prescribed by Law

According to this principle from Vietnam's point of view, limiting human rights must be implemented by laws, which passed by the National Assembly—a legislative body. In Vietnam, legal texts include the Constitution, codes and other legal documents promulgated by executive agencies. The drafters for the Constitution of 2013 feared

[13] Article 4 ICESCR.

[14] Article 4 Sect. 1 ICCPR.

that if the Constitution allowed limitations on human rights to be regulated by legal texts in general, human rights could be arbitrarily violated by executive agencies, since they are responsible for the enacting of legal documents to limit human rights. These actions, if they occur, will "neutralize" the Constitution or laws enacted by the National Assembly. Therefore, only the documents of the National Assembly labeled "law" is allowed to limit human rights. This provision of the Constitution shows the requirements for the State to limit human rights is stricter than that of internationals conventions, thus provides more protection for human rights.

However, in practice, Vietnam still have some limitations prescribed by sub-law documents. For example, freedom to conduct business has been prescribed in the Constitution of 2013. The Law on Enterprise of 2020 and the Investment Law of 2020 were enacted with the approach to freedom to conduct business in the direction of simplifying licensing conditions and procedures, lifting restrictions, expanding rights for business. However, the freedom to conduct business still faces a number of barriers because of the business conditions prescribed in sub-law documents. Currently, Vietnam has 5719 business conditions involving 227 conditional business lines, a relatively.[15] According to our assessment, some conditions set out for some business lines do not affect the public interest, public morality or national security. The regulation on the difference in retirement age between male and female under Vietnam's current labor law is also considered to be causing gender inequality, going against the spirit of the Constitution.

These regulations, although being criticized as an arbitrary limitation to human rights, yet it still exists and being applied in practice. Thus, limiting human rights as prescribed by law in Vietnam is a justifiable requirement, but quite difficult to implement in practice.

3.2 Principles of "National Defense", "National Security", "Public Order, Safety", "Public Morality", "Public Health"

—Limiting human rights for national defense, national security reasons: National defense and national security are two important and vital objectives in every States in the world. By using national defense and national security, States have been setting up "barriers" to limit human rights. The struggle with terrorism in recent years is an exemplary display to this fact. A series of personal freedoms have been "sacrifice" for the reason of national security and terrorist attack. This raises the question of, were the State abusing this term? How to have a correct view on this term? How to apply it properly? Such questions are not easy to solve.

According to Vietnam's Law on National security of 2004, "national security" is defined as: The stability and sustainable development of the socialist regime and the

[15] VCCI (2017), *Report on the review of business conditions and freedom to conduct business in Vietnam.*

State of the Socialist Republic of Vietnam, the inalienability of the independence, sovereignty, unity and territorial integrity of the fatherland. It can be seen that the definitions of national security, national defense in Vietnam have much in common with many countries in the world. However, to apply this principle in practice is no easy task, especially from the State point of view—who is directly responsible for the protection of national security.

—*Limiting human rights for public order, public safety reasons:* Limiting human rights for public order and public safety reasons is commonly stipulated in the Constitution of many countries around the world. However, the use of these terms varies in different countries. The equivalent terms commonly which use in this area are "public security", "public order" …

Currently, there is no legal definition of "public order and safety" in Vietnamese legal documents. The Law on The People's Public Security Forces of 2014 prescribed: Maintenance of public order and safety means preventing, detecting, stopping and fighting against crimes and illegal acts related to public order and safety. The definition of public order and safety in Vietnam currently is being understood in a narrower view than the common definition in the world. Public order and safety is viewed more broadly to matters such as the protection of human rights, social harmony, fighting against the abuse of rights from the State, protection of personal freedom… Meanwhile, in Vietnam, since there is no mechanic to interpret the law and the case law system is underdeveloped, public security is still related to combat and prevention of crime.

—*Limiting human rights for social morals reasons*: Because individuals cannot live in isolation, they have to respect others' rights and freedom and respect the social morality that is universally accepted. The definition of social morality may differ in the perspective of each person, each State, each region, and each historical period. The establishment of limitations of human rights for moral reasons must have strict constraints because of the dangers of abusing these polysemous terms.[16]

Nowadays, Vietnam does not have any legal definition on "social morality". According to the traditional concept, morality is the criteria to distinguish the wrong from the right, good from bad actions. Social morality is ideas and beliefs on the requirements for good behaviors. At the same time, social morality is a good life and good behaviors.

However, the moral standards in different societies, different periods also vary in the level and the way of expression. Therefore, along with the time and space, moral standards also change to different, sometimes even contradictory concept. For example, in the past in Vietnam and in the world, majorities of people think that it is unacceptable for two same-sex persons to love each other and live together. It's a violation of the habits and customs, the social morality. Nonetheless, the social concept on this issue has changed more and more. This concept has also led to the

---

[16] Erica Irene A. Daes, The individual's duties to the community and the limitations on human rights and freedoms under Article 29 of the Universal Declaration of human rights. A contribution to the freedom of the individual under law, United Nations, New York, 1983, p. 175.

important change in the law of many countries. Particularly, many countries in the world have approved the legal texts on the same-sex marriage.

Nevertheless, social morality is quite an abstract concept difficult to define, difficult to quantify and very difficult to evaluate what is the standard and what is a violation of social morality? This is a barrier in explaining and applying the Constitution related to this issue.

—*Limiting human rights for public health reasons*: Public health is also an important factor to consider in the process of protecting human rights and besides, it's a sensible reason for the countries to limit human rights. For example, in case of epidemics, many human rights may be limited such as: right of movement, right to freedom of assembly…these limitations aim at controlling disease and preventing the epidemic from spreading. Therefore, public health is an important reason to limit human rights. The matter is just how limited? And how the limitation regulations should be developed to avoid abuse and influence on people's personal freedom.

Although Vietnam has passed the Law on people's health protection in 1989, there is no definition on "public health". In general, according to the general way of understanding in Vietnam, "public health" is understood as an organizational system among people who interact and impact each other in social environment. Public health revolves around the issues of disease prevention, epidemic control, health care and environment.

In terms of limiting human rights for public health reasons, it seems that Vietnam also has a common understanding with the world. Limiting the freedom to conduct a business as well as advertisements related to alcohol, tobacco, milk, and functional foods in the past is proves this remark.

It can be seen that the current regulation and the understanding of Vietnam are quite similar to those of international laws on human rights as well as the Consititution and the laws of many countries in the world. Nevertheless, in order to realize the principles on limitation of human rights in reality, it's necessary to have a state supervisory mechanism in the implementation of the principle of limiting human rights. In many countries in the world, supervising the implementation of Constitutional provisions on human rights is often delegated to Constitutional judiciary such as Constitutional Court or Constitutional Council. Clause 2 Article 119 of the current Constitution of Vietnam provides: "the mechanism of the Constitutional protection by law". However, until now there has been no law that concretizes this provision of the Contitution on mechanism of the Consitution protection. Protection of Constitution is basically applying according to the regulations issued before the current Constitution takes effect.

4 Conclusion

The common opinion in the world is that human rights need to be limited. However, limitation of human rights is a sensitive field and sometimes too hard to evaluate the rationality and the appropriateness of State decisions. Therefore, one important human right obligation is that the State has to find out the way to limit human rights in the acceptable scope in different contexts.

From the practice of limiting human rights in Vietnam, some lessons learnt can be drawn such as: (1) Limitation of human rights should be stipulated in the Constitution and the relevant laws. (2) Limitation of human rights should only be set in the necessary circumstance for the common interest or social welfare, for the "defense" reason, "national security", "social order and safety", "social morality ", "public health" and aimed at protecting the legitimate interests of others. (3) Limitation of human rights must abide by the rule of law, the legitimation, the rationality, the necessity and the appropriateness; respect the human dignity; equality and no discrimination. (4) Limitation of human rights associates with controlling State power by the mechanism of the Constitution protection.

Protection of Personal Data as Property in the Chinese Constitutional Order

Libin Xie

1 Question to Consider

Everyone is aware that the unauthorised use of personal data entails risks. There is therefore a broad consensus that personal data must be protected from misuse. Chinese lawmakers have already reacted to this in part. For example, § 253 of the Chinese Criminal Code 2015 was amended to make the illegal sale or provision of personal data to third parties, theft or other acquisition of personal data a punishable offence. In addition to protection against misuse, another aspect of the problem should also be taken into account: The issue of personal data includes an ownership dimension that has so far tended to take a back seat and is only neglected by academics. It is therefore of great importance to clarify scientifically whether personal data (could) constitute property.

Against this background, the present study attempts to clarify whether personal data fall within the scope of protection of property within the meaning of Art. 13 of the Chinese Constitution (hereinafter referred to as "CV") and, if so, how constitutional protection can be implemented simply by law. After a conceptual clarification, it must first be clarified to what extent personal data possess assets. Subsequently, the allocation of the property value under different constitutional aspects is discussed before an interim result is presented. In the last part, it has to be examined how the constitutionally justified protection of personal data is to be implemented by simple law. The study takes German-language works on similar problems into account. The arguments that fit the Chinese circumstances are adopted selectively.

L. Xie (✉)
Chinesisch-Deutsches Institut Für Rechtswissenschaft, China University of Political Science and Law, Beijing, China
e-mail: libinxie@hotmail.de

M. Deguchi and K. Yakushiji (eds.), *Europe and Asia as a Legal Area for Fundamental Rights*, https://doi.org/10.1007/978-981-19-7542-4_8

2 Personal Data: Definition and Commercial Value

Personal data can be understood as various things. There is still no agreement on this in sight.[1] In several legal acts, such as the Law on Internet Safety and the decision of the Standing Committee of the National People's Congress to improve the protection of Internet information, different definitions are used.[2] For the purpose of this study, it first includes information about an identified or identifiable person such as names, age, sex, ethnic origin, religious beliefs, health, sexual orientation. In addition, information that records a person's behaviour is also to be understood as personal data. Personal data must be distinguished from industry data by the fact that industry data such as technical data of a car or an engine on an aircraft have no or no significant personal reference at all, while personal data is always based on specific individuals.

Personal data is collected on a massive scale in the course of the ubiquitous digitalisation of the world we live in. In the information age, people of almost every age and in every situation can no longer be left alone and live unnoticed. Everyday behaviour is recorded around the clock using the Internet, smartphones, navigation systems, fitness wristbands, Google Glass and other smart things, with the result that everyone automatically becomes a data producer. People are increasingly becoming intensively observed objects.

The continuously disclosed personal data, the quantities of which are difficult for laymen to fill, have long since become an increasingly important economic factor. Companies are continuously developing innovative business models that deal with data collection, storage, collection, networking, processing, exploitation and even marketing. For example, a widespread business model uses personal data to market goods and services. First of all, the consumer behaviour of a person is recorded in detail and completely by linking the collected personal data, including at first glance rather irrelevant personal data, and assigned to this person. The networking and aggregation of the data makes it possible to get to know the person concerned down to the last detail. In the end, profiles of consumers are created. Search engines and online sellers use such profiles for targeted, individual and tailor-made advertising for goods and services. Technically, the process is silent and completely hidden, for example because a plugin introduced on a website ensures that a user's data is automatically transferred to the provider of the plugin.[3] On the basis of such data, the provider immediately learns who is currently accessing the website and which goods and services could be of interest to the person at what prices. On the basis of such information, new, tailor-made goods and services are offered at prices acceptable to

[1] See Guo Minglong, Lun Ge Ren Xin Xi Zhi Shang Pin Hua, in: Fa Xue Lun Tan 2012 Nr. 6, p. 108 et seq; Xie Yuanyang, XInxilu Shijiao xia Geren Xinxi de Jiazhi, in: *Tsinghua University Law Journal* 2015 No. 3, S. 97 et seq; Yang Weiqin, Jjiazhi Weidu zhong de Geren Xinxi Quanshu Moshi Kaocha, in: Faxue Pinglun 2016 No. 4, p. 66 f.

[2] See Yu Zhigang, "Gongmin Geren Xinxi" de Quanli Shuxing zu Xingfa Baohu Silu, in: Zhejiang Shehui Kexue 2017 No. 10, p. 5 et seq.

[3] LG Düsseldorf MMR 2016, 328, 329 m. Anm. Föhlisch/Pilous.

the provider. Companies can offer consumers the same goods and services at different prices, depending on how financially strong the potential buyers are and how urgent the need is. As a result, companies can make lucrative profits. Such practices are by their very nature not uncontroversial. In practice, there have already been legal disputes in China. In 2014, a court had to deal with the question of whether Baidu, the leading search engine in China, could use cookies to record Internet behaviour of Internet users and exploit it for commercial purposes, which raised more questions than it answered.[4] Personal data can also be used for other business models. For example, companies can analyze personal data such as the income situation of many citizens to assess future consumption needs. The development of artificial intelligence is unthinkable without large amounts of personal data. Overall, the possibilities for commercial exploitation of personal data are unlimited.

What is certain is that profits are generated by the exploitation of personal data in a wide variety of business models. Seen in this light, personal data is an asset. To whom the asset of personal data is to be allocated, is clarified below.[5]

3 The Constitutional Classification of the Commercial Value of Personal Data

The question of who is entitled to the asset of personal data is to be answered taking into account a number of constitutional aspects.

3.1 Justice Commandment of the Article on Socialism

China is a socialist country (Art. 1 para. 1 CV). Therefore, social balance must not be disregarded when shaping the legal system. As long as there is no equal balance of power between two parties, the state should limit the strong with different forms and support the weak if the social balance of power is difficult to reconcile with the general concept of justice. For the question of interest here, a fair balance must be established between the company using the personal data and the original owner.[6]

In reality, there is no equal relationship between citizens as data producers and companies as data users. Due to economic strength, technical and economic superiority and a clear information advantage, companies are in a position to collect and use personal data unilaterally. This situation can be counteracted by assigning personal data to their owners under property law. The recognition of personal data as property

---

[4] Civil decision 5028 from Nanjing Intermediate People's Court 2014.

[5] Wandtke, Ökonomischer Wert von persönlichen Daten, MMR 2017, 5.

[6] Libin Xie, Chinesisches und deutsches Wirtschaftsverfassungsrecht, Köln 2007, p. 17; zum ähnlichen Sinngehalt des deutschen Sozialstaatsprinzips siehe etwa Zippelius/Würtenberger, Deutsches Staatsrecht, 32nd ed., p. 132.

will significantly strengthen the position of consumers. This will force companies to negotiate with individuals and make them interesting offers to acquire the right to use personal data of individuals. Individuals will be able to negotiate with companies themselves on the disclosure of their personal data according to their own priorities. This could create a socially balanced relationship between the citizen as data owner and the company.

3.2 The Principle of Equal Treatment

According to the equality clause of Art. 33 para. 2 CV, substantially equal and substantially unequal shall be treated as equal and unequal respectively.[7] From this perspective, personal data should be treated like trade secrets. There are no major differences between the two which require or justify different treatment. Since trade secrets are protected as property, this protection of personal data should not be withheld. On the other hand, the objection can be raised that trade secrets can be traced back to the personal contribution invested in them. Since the advantages acquired through personal contribution are more likely to be recognised as property, trade secrets should be protected as property for this reason. On the other hand, personal data are not linked to the personal contribution of the persons concerned, but rather to the investments made by companies. This objection cannot stand up to a thorough analysis. Not all business secrets can be traced back to personal contribution. For example, the list of regular customers is not the result of an own contribution. Therefore, personal data such as trade secrets should be protected as property.[8]

In order to prevent or minimise violations of personal rights in the form of misuse of personal data, personal data should be recognised as constitutional property.

3.3 Institutionalized Prevention of Misuse of Personal Data

In order to prevent or minimise violations of personal rights in the form of misuse of personal data, personal data should be recognised as constitutional property.

In the business world, activities are based on cost–benefit calculations. If a (potential) infringer has to reckon with the corresponding economic disadvantages, he will of his own accord refrain from business models that generate profits through the misuse of personal data. In current practice, the misuse of personal data is merely a violation of personal rights. As a rule, the person whose personal data are misused cannot claim any damages, as no material damage is generally recognised. From an economic perspective, the established protection mechanism for personal rights

[7] More on this Libin Xie, Chinesisches und deutsches Wirtschaftsverfassungsrecht, Cologne 2007, p. 77 et seq.

[8] Liu Deliang, Ge Ren Xin Xi de Cai Chan Quan Bao Hu, in: Fa Xue Yan Jiu, 2007 No. 3, 88.

therefore does not act as a sufficient deterrent to prevent the misuse of personal data. In order to combat legal infringements efficiently, the costs of legal infringements should be increased. An effective means of increasing the costs of infringements is to recognise personal data as property and to charge the infringer with property rights accountability.

3.4 Favourable Framework Conditions for Sustainable Data Management

Promoting economic growth is a legitimate objective. When the economy is doing well, many constitutional goals can be achieved better and faster. Guaranteeing fundamental social rights is a good example. The Chinese constitution provides for a number of basic social rights, the realisation of which depends on financial resources. Citizens can only enjoy basic social rights within the bounds of what is financially possible. In this spirit, Art. 14 (4) CV provides: "The state shall establish a balanced social security system consistent with the level of economic development". In view of the importance of economic growth for the realisation of the constitutional goals, it is constitutionally necessary to create favourable framework conditions for the national economy.

In the digital age, the information economy is becoming more and more important for the entire economy as an industry for which, among other things, the exploitation of personal data is indispensable. In order to promote the growth of this branch of the economy, data of all kinds, including personal data, should be able to flow as unhindered and orderly as possible so that added value is possible at all.[9] Where personal data are protected exclusively or principally by personal rights, the collection, processing, disclosure and use of personal data as potential violations of personal rights are generally suspected. In order to protect personal rights, personal data should be collected, processed, passed on and used as rarely as possible. This conflicts with the needs of the information economy. If personal data is protected as the property of the data subjects, companies can acquire the authority to collect their personal data and make use of it by agreement with the individuals. In this way, the information economy can develop rapidly, which ultimately benefits the welfare of the community. This is also in the interest of citizens as holders of their personal data, as they will benefit from the facilitation provided by innovative business models.

[9] Hu Ling, Shangze Moshi Shijiao Xiade "Xinxi/Shuju" Chanquan, in: Shanghai Daxue Xuebao (Shehui Kexueban) 2017 No. 6, 6.

3.5 *Personal Data as an Intangible Asset*

While the previous study indicates the recognition of personal data as property in principle, two reasons for not doing so will be examined below.

While the previous investigation basically points to the recognition of personal data as property, two reasons for not doing so will be examined below. One could argue that personal data as intellectual property cannot be protected by Art. 13 CV. The Chinese constitution is characterised by a concrete, imagined understanding of property. This is expressed in several places in the constitution. Art. 9 para. 1 CV provides, among other things, that "mineral resources, waters, forests, mountains, grass steppes, wasteland, beaches and other natural resources belong to the state". Before the 2004 constitutional amendment, the state expressly protects "the right of citizens to ownership of their legally acquired income, savings, houses and other legal assets" under Art. 13 (1) CV. An overall view of the Chinese constitution makes it clear that the Chinese constitution is based on material goods when it comes to property protection.

This reasoning must be contradicted. In order to grasp the constitutionally guaranteed property correctly, one must free oneself from a traditional, conscious or unconscious, concrete, thought understanding of property. It cannot be denied that the understanding of property, which is shaped by material goods, is reflected in several passages of the Chinese constitution. However, constitutional property is not an unchangeable entity, but must be constructed dynamically. As a fundamental right, the guarantee of property serves to guarantee citizens the material prerequisite for their freedom. For this reason, the scope of protection of property must be broad. Accordingly, intellectual property rights must also be recognised as property. This is also confirmed by the amendment of Art. 13 CV in 2004, which departed from the previous list of objects and opted for a general formulation of "private property".

In summary, it is clear that the protection of personal data as property would not fail because personal data constitute an intellectual property.

3.6 *Potential Impairment of Interpersonal Communication*

Another argument against the recognition of personal data as property is that this is incompatible with the constitutionally guaranteed freedoms of communication such as freedom of speech and freedom of the press (Art. 35 CV). The following could be stated as reasons. In order to exercise basic rights of communication sensibly, it is necessary for citizens to obtain comprehensive information. Only on the basis of the information acquired can the citizen communicate facts to other fellow citizens at all, form an opinion and participate meaningfully in the exchange of ideas with others. If personal data are generally excluded from public information traffic, meaningful interpersonal communication would be excluded. This would be the case if personal data were protected as property. For example, private individuals as owners of their personal data could restrict or prohibit the use of such information by their fellow citizens, with the result that normal interpersonal communication would no longer take place.[10]

On closer inspection, this objection is unfounded. The recognition of personal data as property does not lead to an unreasonable restriction of the freedom of communication. Even basic communication rights are by no means unlimited in themselves. For example, an absolute, unlimited freedom of speech is foreign to the Chinese constitution. While according to Art. 35 CV citizens may both claim facts and express their opinion on a fact, this freedom of speech is not unlimited. Art. 51 CV provides that citizens may not, in exercising their freedoms and rights, violate the interests of the state, society and the collective or the legitimate freedoms and rights of other citizens. Thus, the rights of other citizens are a constitutional barrier to all fundamental rights,[11] including freedom of speech and other freedoms of communication. Therefore, the citizen may not violate the honour of the citizens under the guise of freedom of speech, which is also documented as a fundamental right of Art. 38 CV. Confidential and intimate personal information, e.g. about illnesses, may not be passed on either. This restriction is immanent to the freedom of speech of Art. 35 CV.

Moreover, the recognition of personal data as property would not lead to an unacceptable impediment to normal communication between citizens. The protection of personal data as property only has the result that the economic interests arising from the use of personal data are in principle wholly or partly the property of the owner of such data. If personal data is not used for commercial purposes, protection of ownership is not activated. The usual communication, whereby personal data is typically not used commercially, remains unaffected from the outset.

For these reasons, the protection of personal data as property would be compatible with the constitutional guarantee of freedom of communication, including freedom of speech.

3.7 *Interim Conclusion: Recognition of Personal Data as Property Within the Meaning of Art. 13 CV*

An overall view of the various perspectives outlined above shows that ownership of personal data should be attributed to the citizen rather than to the company. This is legitimized by the fact that the citizen produces personal data with an asset with his own behavior. This ownership is guaranteed by Art. 13 CV.

---

[10] Jessica Litman, Information Privacy/Information Property, 52 Stan. L. Rev. 1283.

[11] Jiao Hongchang (Hrsg.), Xianfaxue, 5th ed., Verlag Peking Universität 2013, p. 369.

4 Simple Legal Implementation

The constitutional property guarantee for personal data must be implemented simply by law. This does not mean that the legislator necessarily has to take action. First of all, it must be examined whether the protection of personal data can be implemented by existing legal institutions, for example by extending existing protection mechanisms to personal data. Only if this path is not feasible should the legislator create a new legal institution. In this sense, it makes sense to first clarify whether the tort protection mechanism already offers a suitable solution.

4.1 Sufficient and Suitable Protection by Tort Law?

Tort law offers comprehensive protection for all kinds of legal interests. This legal protection also applies to subjective rights which are not traditionally recognised as proprietary positions. For example, the body and personal honour are not regarded as property, but are of course protected by tort law. In the case of infringement of such rights, damages for pain and suffering may be considered. At first glance, this protection mechanism also appears to be applicable to the protection of personal data. If companies misuse personal data of individuals in order to maximize profits, they are to pay damages and in particular damages for pain and suffering for the violation of personal rights. Thus, the asset of personal data is ultimately realized in the interest of victims. In this way, the law of torts at first glance represents a practical, simple implementation of the constitutional protection mandate.

However, the protection of tort law has two major disadvantages. First, such an institutional arrangement leads to a gap in legal protection. As long as personal data are not recognised as property, there is no infringement if the use of personal data produces economic value but does not constitute an infringement of personal rights. In practice, companies are granted a "licence" to use personal data for commercial purposes free of charge and without violation of personal rights. It is precisely because personal data are not recognised as property that the person concerned cannot claim the asset created in the process and possibly enforce these—non-existent—claims in tort. Secondly, tortious protection is backward-looking and does not promote any future-oriented freedom of action. Only the protection of personal data as property enables individuals and companies to regulate their behaviour ex ante by means of an agreement. This gives both sides greater freedom and legal certainty. This freedom would not be possible if the legal system was limited to prosecuting ex post violations of the law through tort law.[12]

[12] See Lawrence Lessig, Code, Basic Books, 228–230 (2006).

4.2 An Intellectual Property Right to Personal Data

Now that tort law has been eliminated as the protection model for the property components of personal data, there are no other existing legal institutions in sight that could close this gap in legal protection. There is no alternative but to construct an intellectual property right to personal data. This does not contradict the concept of the right of personality or the concept of the offence, but complements it. This procedure is also compatible with two paragraphs of the Chinese BGB-AT passed in 2017: § 111 of this law already provides that personal data of natural persons are legally protected. This provision serves as a fundamental decision for the right to personal data. In the same spirit, Section 27 of this Act states: "Legal provisions protecting data and virtual property positions on the Internet shall remain unaffected". It would be logical if the legislator were to pass a law on the protection of personal data in the near future, as is urgently recommended by many authors.[13] Such a future data protection law could also regulate the commercial use of personal data.[14] It is also possible to regulate this problem by means of a separate law.

Irrespective of the concrete legislative approach, the following two points must be taken into account in the conception of legal policy. Firstly, the intellectual property rights to personal data must be designed as exclusive property rights. Thus, the right holder can prohibit third parties from collecting, processing, exploiting and marketing his personal data. He is entitled to a reservation of consent. Only when a corresponding consent has been granted may a company collect, store, collect, process, combine, exploit and market the personal data of the consenting party for business interests. Companies must provide comprehensive information in advance on what activities are intended and for what purposes in connection with personal data. On the basis of such information, citizens can decide autonomously whether to grant consent. The information made transparent indicates the extent to which the consent given is sufficient. The requirement for consent does not depend on whether or not there are special circumstances of a specific legal personality protection worthiness. Because it is not about the protection of personality. Instead, it is a matter of protecting the intellectual property rights of individuals in personal data as an economic good. Consequently, a company may not evade the consent requirement by anonymizing personal data. A violation of the right of personality can be avoided by anonymising personal data. This has no effect on the property rights of personal data.[15]

Secondly, a wealth compensation is necessary if a company wants to use personal data of citizens. This follows from the fact that the intellectual property right to personal data is, by its very nature, a property right. Such an asset comparison can

[13] See eg. Wang Liming, Lu Geren Xinxi de Falv Baohu, in: Xiandai Faxue 2013 Nr. 4, S. 70; Yu Zhigang, "Gongmin Geren Xinxi" de Quanli Shuxing zu Xingfa Baohu Silu, in: Zhejiang Shehui Kexue 2017 No. 10, p. 9.

[14] Yang Weiqin, Jjiazhi Weidu zhong de Geren Xinxi Quanshu Moshi Kaocha, in: Faxue Pinglun 2016 No. 4, p. 74.

[15] In relation to the German legal position, see Fezer, Dateneigentum der Bürger, ZD 2017, 98.

be regulated individually or collectively. In principle, an individual settlement of assets is preferable to a collective settlement in order to meet the specific needs of the individual as far as possible. If this proves to be technically impossible or disproportionate, a collective settlement of assets is also justified. In return for the use of personal data by companies, it could be agreed that the owner of the data used would receive appropriate remuneration, digital content or a service free of charge.

The Collision of Values in Thai Constitutional Law

Torpong Kittiyanupong

1 Introduction

The "value of democracy" and "the defence of democracy" are the subject of discussion in the Western countries.[1] The important theoretical problem in the political order is the connection between value, democracy and fundamental rights. However, the value of democracy can collide with other values in a political order that existed before democracy was established. The collision of values in a political or legal order can also influence the interpretation of the constitution and the law. It should be noted from the outset that the application and interpretation of law associated with the value of democracy and those based on other non-democratic values concern two different levels of protection of fundamental rights. It is therefore first necessary to ask what the values are in a political order. The answer then leads to the question of whether this order is democratic.

[1] The value of democracy is much discussed in German-language literature. The most important examples are three statements by Hans Kelsen, Carl Schmitt and Robert Alexy. In two papers by Hans Kelsen, "Vom Wesen und Wert der Demokratie (1920 und 1929)" and "Die Verteidigung der Demokratie (1932)", it is mainly clarified how the value of democracy can be maintained and defended against other political ideologies. In "Die Tyrannei der Werte (1960)" by Carl Schmitt it is noted that after the Second World War the concept of "value order" was conceived in the German legal system. However, Carl Schmitt regarded it as a false tendency. Ultimately, Robert Alexy's work "A Theory of Constitutional Rights (1994)" stresses that value is very important for the application and interpretation of law. Through value orientation, the goal of the constitution can be achieved.

The main idea of this article was already published in Thai language in the Thammasat Law Journal, Vol. 48, No. 3 (September 2019), pp. 439–466.

T. Kittiyanupong (✉)
Faculty of Law, Thammasat University, Bangkok, Thailand
e-mail: ktorpong@tu.ac.th

M. Deguchi and K. Yakushiji (eds.), *Europe and Asia as a Legal Area for Fundamental Rights*, https://doi.org/10.1007/978-981-19-7542-4_9

However, it is not so easy to decide which value is the highest in a political order, because in a political order there is always "the collision of values". In other words, the different parts of society are guided by different values and have their own "highest value". Therefore, the "collision of values" in a political order is the collision of interests, of beliefs and conceptions, of traditions and cultures, and of worldviews, etc. The discussion and the struggle for value in a society shows in which political-ideological direction the citizen wants to lead the state. In Thailand the situation is very interesting. The Thai democracy has completely failed since the revolution in 1932 in which the absolute monarchy came to an end. The reason for the failure of democracy in Thailand is not only the military coup, but also the collision of values in the Thai legal system. This collision of values causes a lack of orientation in politics and is an important obstacle in the defence of democracy and the constitution. The application and interpretation of the law, which are not compatible with the fundamental values of democracy, lead to endless political disputes.

2 Value, Legal Interpretation and Democracy

In Far Eastern countries the value has not only the dimension of goodness, custom and morality or of traditions and cultures. The values directed by the citizens are, moreover, the orientation for the policy on the determination of the political structure and on the development of democracy. But value also plays an important role in the interpretation of the law by the courts. It is therefore necessary to explain what the value is. It can then be further analysed how value can play a role in politics and law.

2.1 The Importance of Value

In a society there are different norms that set commandments and prohibitions for people. But the most important norm is the legal norm. The legal norms are the "should" determined by the act of will, which is intentionally directed at human behavior.[2] They are an "objective scheme of interpretation" which is brought to that fact. The legal norms, however, are not the only norm directed at human behavior.[3] Norms are also customs, traditions and cultures as well as values directed by human beings.

In the nineteenth century the talk of values became common and thinking in values became common. However, it was not until Nietzsche's writings became widespread

---

[2] *Dreier, Ralf*, Sein und Sollen: Bemerkungen zur Reinen Rechtslehre Kelsens, JZ 27 (1972), 239, 331.

[3] *Kelsen, Hans*, Reine Rechtslehre, Studienaufgabe 1st edition 1934, hrsg. v. Matthias Jestaedt, Tübingen 2008, pp. 18–19.

that the talk of values became popular.[4] After that, people often talk about life values, cultural values, eternal values or spiritual values. This doctrine of values continues to develop into a philosophy of values that influences life in Far Eastern countries.[5] From a social science point of view, the values are "basic attitudes of people who stand out due to a special firmness, conviction of correctness and emotional foundation"[6] Then one comes to the question "what should I do?" and "what is valuable in life, yes in the world at all?"[7] The values which guide people's lives are, for example, freedom from state paternalism, respect for the industrious and contempt for the idle, with marriage, family and children as a normal model of life, recognition of hard and socially indispensable family work, fundamental respect for the Christian Churches and moral authority, etc.[8] Values are therefore standards. "They stand between being and should. They are normative, but are subject to change through social factuality, they stand between right and morality, between commitment and appeal, between universalism and pluralism, and not least between hot emotion and cool intellect.[9] An important example of the collision of values in legal disputes is the crucifix decision of the Federal Constitutional Court. [10] In this case, the fundamental rights, which are regarded as a principle and a value, collide with the religious value, which is also protected and maintained by the citizen. Such a dispute is not only a legal dispute, but also a collision of values in which the values represented by many sections of the population are in conflict and competition. This collision of values can continue to

---

[4] *Schmitt, Carl,* Die Tyrannei der Werte, 3rd, corrected edition, Berlin 2011, p. 38.

[5] *Schmitt, Carl,* ebd.

[6] *Di Fabio, Udo,* Grundrechte als Werteordnung, JZ 59 (2004), 1, 3.

[7] *Pfordten, Dietmar v.d.,* Sein, Werten, Sollen, Archiv für Rechts- und Sozialphilosophie, Vol. 79, No. 1 (1993), 48, 52.

[8] *Di Fabio, Udo,* JZ 59 (2004), 1, 4.

[9] *Alexy, Robert,* Theorie der Grundrechte, Baden-Baden 1994, pp. 84–85.

[10] BVerfGE 93, 1 ff. The crucifix decision of the Federal Constitutional Court of 16 May 1995 is an important example of the collision of values in constitutional disputes and of the weighing of fundamental rights. The content of the decision is presented below: Art. 13 of the School Regulations for Elementary Schools in Bavaria (VSO) stipulates that a cross shall hang in the classrooms of all schools in the State of Bavaria. The Federal Constitutional Court has declared this Art. 13 VSO invalid. Art. 13 VSO, which determines that all pupils must learn "under the cross", contradicts the freedom of religion and faith of the pupils after art. 4 exp. 1 GG. Freedom of belief and religion protects not only the freedom of choice of the religion of citizens, but also the freedom of the citizens in which they can do or refrain from doing according to their own will and faith. The cross is a symbol for the particular religion and a particular faith. It is not only a cultural symbol of Western countries. The hanging of the cross in the study room is not in harmony with the religious freedom of pupils who are not Christians. This decision by the majority vote of the Federal Constitutional Court was much criticized by the public at the time for destroying the role of the Church as a historical and cultural symbol of Germany. This case represents a constellation of the conflict of values in constitutional law, in which the judge is demanded to bind the application and interpretation of law with the values. In the decision the court must make a value judgement and weigh the conflicting values against each other, which value can claim a fundamental priority, see Kittiyanupong, Torpong, Die politische Stellung des Bundesverfassungsgerichts, *Thammasat Law Journal*, Volume 45 No. 3 (2016), pp. 759–761.

lead to a collision of the interests of citizens.[11] Who decides this collision of values, can be asked therefore for neutrality, because the decision or a "value judgement" can affect many humans.[12] Therefore, the judge must perform his "integration work", [13] i.e. bind his application and interpretation of the law to values. [14] The judge has to note that he is a representative of all citizens for this value judgement. Therefore he is not allowed to decide in the litigation according to his own value. However, he must observe all conflicting values and weigh them against each other.[15]

2.2 The Values and Democracy

When we explain the concept of value together with democracy, we come to the conclusion that "the value of democracy" is the basis accepted by people in a democratic-political order together. In addition, the value of democracy is the basic attitude that must be protected and promoted by people in a political order. In literature, the fundamental values of democracy are "the freedom and equality of man".[16] It can be said that, unlike other ideologies, democracy enables a higher degree of individual and collective freedom.[17] The defence of democracy is therefore closely linked to the protection of fundamental rights. Hans Kelsen explained well, in his democratic-theoretical paper "Vom Wesen und Wert der Demokratie" (On the Nature and Value of Democracy)[18] that freedom is the reaction against the coercion flowing from the social state, the protest against the foreign will, to which one's own must bow, against the agony of heteronomy[19] „The burden of foreign will, imposed by social order, is felt all the more oppressively, the more directly the primary feeling of one's own value is expressed in the rejection of any added value of another, the more elementary the experience of what is forced to obedience to the Lord, the very one

[11] *Schmitt, Carl*, Die Tyrannei der Werte, p. 49.

[12] *Czermak, Gerhard*, Der Kruzifix-Beschluß zwischen Neutralität und Glaubensförderung sowie als Spielball der Emotionen, ZRP 29 (1996), 201, 201.

[13] *Di Fabio, Udo*, JZ 59 (2004), 1, 2.

[14] Carl Schmitt has expressed quite interestingly that "the value is almost longing for updating. It is not really, but it is reality-based and lurks for execution and enforcement"; see Schmitt Carl, Die Tyrannei der Werte, p. 37. It is remarkable that the value itself is not a legal norm. But it has to be considered in the application and interpretation of the law as "supra-legal values" or "valuation standards", see Larenz, Karl, Methodenlehre der Rechtswissenschaft, 5th edition, Berlin, Heidelberg, New York, Tokyo 1983, p. 118.

[15] See *Zippelius, Reinhold*, Rechtsnorm und richterliche Entscheidungsfreiheit, JZ 25 (1970), 241, 244.

[16] See *Rinderle, Peter*, Werte und Mechanismen der Demokratie, Zeitschrift für philosophische Forschung, vol. 65, H. 1 (2011), 74, 74.

[17] *Rinderle, Peter*, Zeitschrift für philosophische Forschung, vol. 65, H. 1 (2011), 74, 74.

[18] See *Kelsen, Hans*, Vom Wesen und Wert der Demokratie (2nd ed. 1929), in: Hans Kelsen, Verteidigung der Demokratie, hrsg. v. Matthias Jestaedt und Oliver Lepsius, Tübingen 2006, pp. 149–228.

[19] *Kelsen, Hans*, ebd., p. 154.

who commands.[20] These insoluble conflicts between the idea of individual freedom and the idea of social order can only be resolved by appropriate mechanisms of domination.[21]

The discussion about the value of democracy continues with the question of the best state. According to Rousseau, this question is literal: "How to find a form of society that defends and protects each member and in which each individual, although united with all, obeys only himself and remains as free as before?"[22] Such a question is a fundamental problem in the defence of democracy. The important theoretical question about the defense of democracy is which form of government is best for the citizen, between the rule of the majority and the rule of the best.[23] This question refers to the value. The citizens of a political order must make a basic decision as to the direction in which they want to lead political life. Therefore the basic decision for a suitable form of government is a "value judgement". Hans Kelsen[24] further explains that the various political ideologies have made accusations against each other in the struggle for the dissemination of political convictions. Above all, the dictatorship accused democracy that its principle, the principle of the majority, was completely unsuitable to guarantee the factually correct formation of the will of the community. "The majority should not decide, which offers no guarantee whatsoever for the goodness of the order thus created, since the majority principle provides only a method of forming the will, not a determination of the content of the will. Rather, the best should govern". Kelsen made a comment that this accusation against democracy was made unreasonably by supporters of the dictatorship. "The rule of the best only means that the social order should have the best, the right content. But everyone is in complete agreement on this. What matters is the answer to the question: Who is the best, which is the method that leads with absolute certainty to the best and only the best coming to power and asserting power—against the onslaught of the bad.[25] The rule of the best also means that the best should be a "God-given leader. After that, the best changes as "the highest value" of the political order and will replace the belief in the equality of people. Carl Schmitt,[26] in his essay "The Tyranny of Values", expressed in a very similar way that there are always different values in a political order. Therefore, comparative value judgements are inevitable.[27] In some situations the citizen must choose between God and humanity or between person

[20] *Kelsen, Hans*, ebd.

[21] *Groß, Thomas*, Hans Kelsen, Vom Wesen und Wert der Demokratie, in: Kritische Justiz, Vol. 40, No. 3 (2007), 306, 307.

[22] See *Kelsen, Hans*, in: Hans Kelsen, Verteidigung der Demokratie, hrsg. v. Matthias Jestaedt und Oliver Lepsius, Tübingen 2006, p. 156.

[23] *Kelsen, Hans*, Verteidigung der Demokratie, in: Hans Kelsen, Verteidigung der Demokratie, hrsg. v. Matthias Jestaedt und Oliver Lepsius, Tübingen 2006, p. 234.

[24] *Hans Kelsen*, ebd.

[25] *Hans Kelsen*, ebd.

[26] *Schmitt, Carl*, Die Tyrannei der Werte, pp. 18–19.

[27] see *Alexy, Robert*, Theorie der Grundrecht, p. 128 f.

and freedom.[28] The value chosen by the citizen is therefore the highest value in the political order. Such a value judgement is not easy because it is an emotional game ball and can affect many people. A value judgement in politics can therefore lead to infinite conflicts.

But now that we are talking about the values of democracy, we can come to the conclusion that the fundamental values of democracy are the freedom and equality of people. Freedom and equality are also the historical starting point of all democratic aspirations.[29] In the case of a collision of values, i.e. the collision between fundamental rights and other values, fundamental rights should have a greater weight. A political order in which a person is abolished as "the highest value" or a person is regarded as "an absolute value" is not a democracy. It is an autocracy in which people are not equal. But the best is regarded as a higher value or the highest value. And to protect this absolute good, it is inevitable to give it grateful and unconditional obedience.[30] On this point Kelsen[31] explained well in the following: "Only he who believes in the existence of an absolute value, who knows himself or another in possession of this value has the right to condemn democracy, has the right to enforce his will against that of all others, to impose his convictions, even by force, on all others. But the one who knows that only relative values are accessible to human knowledge can only justify the compulsion necessary for its realization by having the consent, if not of all, then at least of the majority of those to whom the coercive order claims validity. That is the principle of democracy". This principle thus guarantees the greatest possible freedom for the citizen. One can thus be of the opinion that in a democratic-political order there can be no absolute value or the highest value, but only a relative value. Therefore, one value can be weighed against the other value. The value that exists in a democratic order must have its validity reduced so that other values can also claim its validity. In my opinion, the balancing and harmonisation of values is a fundamental principle of democracy.

3 The Collision of Values in Thai Constitutional Law

Thai democracy has failed from the time of the Great Revolution in 1932[32] to the present. The reasons for the failure of Thai democracy are widely analysed in the

[28] *Schmitt, Carl*, Die Tyrannei der Werte, p. 19.

[29] *Köttgen, Arnold*, Kelsen und Demokratie, Zeitschrift für die gesamte Staatswissenschaft, Bd. 90, H1 (1931), 97, 97.

[30] *Kelsen, Hans*, Verteidigung der Demokratie, in: Hans Kelsen, Verteidigung der Demikratie, hrsg. v. Matthias Jestaedt und Oliver Lepsius, Tübingen 2006, p. 236.

[31] *Kelsen, Hans*, ebd.

[32] On 24 June 1932, a political party called "Khana Ratsadon" (People's Party) revolted against King Prajadhipok (Rama VII). Thailand's first temporary constitution came into force on 27 June 1932 with the signing of King Prajadhipok. After the revolution and the foundation of the first constitution, an era dawned in which sovereignty belonged to the people, see Mewongukote, Boonsri, Constitutional Law, Bangkok 2006, p. 208 (Thai).

literature of law and political science. Among other things, the military coup plays a major role. But I would like to present another problem of Thai democracy. It is the problem of the conflict of values in the Thai political order that I see as an important reason for the failure of democracy in Thailand.

3.1 "The Values in the Thai Constitution" and "Thai Democracy as a Value-Bound Democracy"

In Thai society people are different in terms of origin, religion and political convictions. These differences often lead to conflicts of interest between different groups of people. In many cases such conflicts also appear as a collision of values. First of all it should be emphasized that most Thai people are brought up to be humble human beings. They must feel solidarity and be proud of their ancestors. They must have respect for Buddhism and be absolutely grateful to the King.[33] These facts give the appearance of being the important values in the Thai political order. These basic attitudes of the Thai people are important prerequisites for the success and functioning of democracy. If the basic attitudes of the citizens are compatible with the value of democracy, namely freedom and equality, democracy could succeed. On the other hand, democracy fails from the outset if the basic attitudes of citizens are not consistent with the value of democracy. In the latter political order, people are indifferent to the constitution and democracy. Then the elites, the military and senior officials can seize the opportunity to abolish the constitution and democracy. This is particularly the case in Thailand. The basic attitudes of the citizens and the value of democracy are therefore the most important prerequisites for the success of Thai democracy.[34]

In the Thai political order today there is a hard struggle between the attempt to make a step forward in the democratic idea and the preservation of customs. According to the idea of democracy, people believe in the ability and reason of the people as well as in freedom and justice. In Thailand, however, the tradition, culture and nationalism must also be strictly upheld.[35] These two political movements in Thailand are on the verge of a climax and a major collision. On the one hand, in democratic society the fundamental rights of the individual are the fundamental values or principles. In other words, the protection of fundamental rights and human dignity is the ultimate goal of the Constitution.[36] In this sense, fundamental rights are the optimisation imperatives,[37] which are to be realised to the greatest possible extent relative to the legal and actual possibilities. The fundamental rights can claim

[33] *Vinichakul, Thongchai*, Royal nationalism: Thai History, 1st ed. Bangkok 2016, p. 19 (Thai).

[34] *Mektrirat, Nakarin*, Gedanke, Wissen und politische Macht in der thailändischen Revolution von 1932, 3. Aufl., Nonthaburi 2017, p. 24 (Thai).

[35] *Mektrirat, Nakarin*, ebd., p. 81.

[36] *Kittiyanupong, Torpong*, Grundrechtstheorie, Bangkok 2018, p. 18 (Thai).

[37] *Alexy, Robert*, Theorie der Grundrechte, p. 75.

their validity as high as possible, as far as they are not limited by the constitutional reservation or by other constitutional principles. Although fundamental rights are explicitly guaranteed by the Thai constitution, they are only regarded to a limited extent as fundamental values of democracy. What are the reasons for this? The exercise of fundamental rights and other values, namely political culture and tradition, can conflict and collide with each other, so that fundamental rights cannot fully claim their validity. Kasetsiri has correctly explained this constellation[38] namely that Thai society is a society that does not have enough innovative power to struggle with the old social tradition and culture. Therefore, it is difficult to develop the country according to the Western democratic idea. Such a society could be called a hierarchical society, in which every member is not really the same. These social conditions clearly favour the conservatives of Thai society. Society stands still and has no forward movement.[39] This problem is a major obstacle to the development of democracy and the protection of fundamental rights in Thailand. In order to solve this problem, the social structure must be changed. Compared to the Weimar Republic, which is called a value-neutral democracy or value relativism,[40] Thai democracy is a value-bound democracy. The value-bound democracy in this sense, however, is the binding of democracy to traditions, culture and the hierarchical social structure of the people. But it can also be described as an unfinished democracy.

3.2 *The King as the Political Highest Value?*

In recent years, the status and political position of the king has become a central discussion in Thailand. In my opinion, this discussion is an important example of the conflict of values in the Thai legal system. This collision of values is shaking up Thai society and it cannot yet find a result. It is generally accepted in Thailand that the King is both a constitutional body and an important social institution. The strong political position of the Thai king can be seen as a constitutional value. The value of the king is in the consciousness of the people, in the constitution as well as in laws. But the important question is whether the king can still be the highest value in politics and the constitution in a democratic society. This question is very important for the interpretation of the Constitution and the law. The majority of historical literature is of the opinion that after the revolution of 1932 the value of the king and the idea of democracy are competing for the highest position in the constitution.[41] The political position of the king has gradually become dynamic in the various constitutions of

---

[38] *Kasetsiri, Charnvit*, A Political History of Thailand 1932–1957, 7th Ed. Bangkok 2017, p. 23 (Thai).

[39] *Kasetsiri, Charnvit*, ebd.

[40] *Michaelis, Lars Oliver*, Aufgaben, Befugnisse und Kontrolle der Ämter für Verfassungsschutz im streitbaren Parteienstaat, KritV 85, No. 2 (2002), 188, 194.

[41] *Prichasilpakul, Somchai*, Die Diskussion über den Status des Königs im Prozess der Verfassungsgründung zwischen 1932–2007, 1. Aufl., Bangkok 2018, p. 8 (Thai).

Thailand. The reason for this is the ambiguity about whether the Thai constitution was founded by the social contract between king and people or whether it was given alone by the king.[42] The tendency, however, is to observe that the status of the king is made stronger again and again in the constitution. Although the status of the king should be devalued after the revolution, in fact the importance of the king is not seriously challenged.[43] The position of the Thai king was thus more highly appreciated in the last 30 years than in the time of absolutism.[44] The Thai king is sacred and untouchable today.[45]

I call the constellation explained above "the collision of values" in Thai constitutional law. In my opinion it is a fundamental problem of our constitutional law. Theoretically, the constitution is an objective order of values.[46] It consists of values, goodness, traditions and cultures. These values are theoretically the "supra-legal values" and "valuation standards" for constitutional and legal interpretation.[47] It is remarkable, however, that the values that are present in the constitution and the political order can collide with each other. This conflict of values calls for a comparative value judgement. The Thai constitution is a clear example of the need for a value judgement to guide the interpretation of the constitution and the law. There are competing values in the Thai constitution, but science cannot yet judge which value prevails. In my opinion, the most important conflict in the Thai constitution is the conflict of values between the status of the king and democracy and fundamental rights. The interpreter of the constitution is challenged and asked what value the interpretation of the constitution is based on. According to the wording of the Constitution,[48] it is not human dignity that is sacrosanct, but the king. By this norm of the constitution one understands the highest value of the king from constitutional as well as from traditional point of view.[49] The concept of the inviolability of the king in constitutional law is completely unclear. This can lead to legal uncertainty. In the literature it is partly explained that no one may vehemently reprimand or criticise the king.[50] Due to the principle "The King can do no wrong" no one may sue

[42] *Mektrirat, Nakarin*, Gedanke, Wissen und politische Macht in der thailändischen Revolution von 1932, p. 11 (Thai).

[43] *Vinichakul, Thongchai*, Royal nationalism: Thai History, p. 19. (thai); vgl. *Kasetsiri, Charnvit*, A Political History of Thailand 1932–1957, p. 102 (Thai).

[44] *Vinichakul, Thongchai*, ebd., p. 14.

[45] *Prichasilpakul, Somchai*, Die Diskussion über den Status des Königs im Prozess der Verfassungsgründung zwischen 1932–2007 p. 6.

[46] *Kommers, Donald P/Miller, Russell A.*, The Constitutional Jurisprudence of the Federal Republic of Germany, p. 57.

[47] *Larenz, Karl*, Methodenlehre der Rechtswissenschaft, p. 118.

[48] Art. 6 of the Thai constitution of 2017 states: "The king is to be respected and he is untouchable. No one may sue him in court".

[49] Vgl. *Saenguthai, Yud*, Lehrbuch der thailändischen Verfassung von 1968 und von 1972 über die Stellung des Königs, hrsg. Worachet Pakeerut, Bangkok 2008, p. 14.

[50] *Saenguthai, Yud*, ebd., pp. 17–19.

him in court neither in civil nor criminal proceedings.[51] This principle of the Thai constitution has established the highest value of the king in the constitution and the political order. However, this value structure in the constitution is very questionable. As stated above, no value in democratic society can be regarded as the highest value or the absolute value. Because the highest value or the absolute value demands from the other values always grateful and unconditional obedience.[52] In the constitution of a democratic society, however, other values must also be able to exist. The values of the democratic order are, in particular, human dignity and the free development of people's personalities.[53] If human dignity is to be regarded as the highest value, it is also the central fundamental right of the Constitution. [54] As a person in the political order one can claim that one can live without fear of arbitrary actions of the state, that one has the freedom of reasonable action, and that one can demand equal treatment by the state. In addition, man can claim for himself that he can freely do or refrain from doing according to his own faith and opinion. Freedom of expression is ultimately a central value of democracy. Finally, in view of the constitutional guarantee of fundamental rights, it can be summarised that a person cannot be regarded as the highest political value in democracy. This is a fundamental problem of Thai democracy that has not yet been resolved.

3.3 Freedom of Expression and the Monarchy as an Important Case of Collision in the Thai Legal System

An important example of a conflict of values in Thai constitutional law is the conflict between freedom of expression[55] and the value of the king. Fundamental rights are an important value of democracy. If the Constitution is seen as an objective order of values and fundamental rights are seen from their objective side, the fundamental rights guaranteed in the Constitution are not only a subjective right to a certain act or omission of the State. Fundamental rights also have a meaning in terms of value. More specifically, fundamental rights have an important meaning for the interpretation of the Constitution and the law in a legal order. That is why the interpretation must be constitutional. The aim of constitutional and legislative interpretation is to protect the greatest possible freedom of the citizen. For example, freedom of expression protects individuals, the press and newspapers against attacks by the state. At the

[51] *Prichasilpakul, Somchai*, Die Diskussion über den Status des Königs im Prozess der Verfassungsgründung zwischen 1932–2007, p. 104.

[52] *Kelsen, Hans*, Verteidigung der Demokratie, in: Hans Kelsen, Verteidigung der Demokratie, 229, 236.

[53] *Schapp, Jan*, Über die Freiheit im Recht, AcP 192, Bd., H5 (1992) 355, 356; *Rüfner, Wolfgang*, Grundrechtskonflikte, FG BVerfG (1976). vol. II, 453, 463.

[54] *Di Fabio, Udo*, JZ 59 (2004), 1, 6.

[55] Freedom of opinion is guaranteed in Art. 34 of the Thai Constitution of 2017.

same time, freedom of expression is a value of democratic society. The state must therefore not only refrain from unconstitutional attacks on freedom of expression. It must also create favourable conditions for the effective exercise of freedom of expression.[56] On the other hand, the protection of freedom of expression is also a promotion of the political life of the citizen.[57] The interpretation of the norms of fundamental rights must therefore be compatible with the form of government and the idea of democracy.

Today, there is strong criticism in Thailand that the interpretation of the law by the administration and the judiciary is incompatible with the value of fundamental rights and democracy. The most important example of this is the interpretation problem of Art. 112 of the Thai Penal Code.[58] The interpretation of this provision represents a clear collision of values in constitutional law. Worachet Pakeerut[59] has stated that Art. 112 of the Thai Criminal Code (ThStGB) has at least three important problems. The first problem is the scope of this regulation. This majesty insult regulation protects not only the special status of the king, but also that of the queen, the crown prince and the regent. However, there was no justification for this. Secondly, the determination of the minimum custodial sentence in this provision is problematic. The minimum sentence of three to fifteen years for an insult was too high and found no democratic legitimacy. The last problem is that this provision does not provide any justification for honest and fair expression of opinion and criticism.

Although Art. 112 ThStGB has at least the three problems mentioned above, the main problem of this provision is its application and interpretation. This problem indicates whether the interpreter of the law, namely the administration and courts, has a liberal-democratic attitude.[60] It has been observed that the police, prosecutors and courts have interpreted this penal provision extensively. According to this, not only insult but also disrespect is punishable. This provision, which is widely interpreted by the administration and the courts, clearly leads to legal uncertainty among citizens. Many people have consequently decided not to enjoy their freedom of expression and to censor their own thoughts.[61] Pakeerut[62] has summed up well that the interpretation of Art. 112 ThStGB must be consistent with the ethos of democracy and the constitutional monarchy. The interpretation of the constitution and the law, which serves the idea of the absolute monarchy, is outdated. I would like to explain this point in more detail. The interpretation problem of Art. 112 ThStGB

---

[56] *Kommers, Donald P/Miller, Russell A.*, The Constitutional Jurisprudence of the Federal Republic of Germany, p. 58.

[57] *Kommers, Donald P./Miller, Russell A.*, ebd., p. 58; see also *Alexy, Robert*, Grundrechte als subjektive und als objektive Normen, Der Staat 29 (1990), 49, 59.

[58] Article 112 of the Thai Penal Code states: "Anyone who has offended the King, Queen, Crown Prince or Regent shall be punished with a term of imprisonment of three to fifteen years".

[59] *Pakeerut, Worachet*, Recht und Gesinnung—Die Versammlungen von Diskussion und Interviews, Bangkok 2015, pp. 363–365 (Thai).

[60] *Pakeerut, Worachet*, ebd., p. 365.

[61] *Saengkanokkul, Piyabutr*, Putschgericht, Richter, Diktatur und Rechtsstaat,1st edition, Nonthaburi 2017, pp. 44–45 (Thai).

[62] *Pakeerut, Worachet*, Recht und Gesinnung, p. 366 (Thai).

is in my opinion a problem of the value judgement by the constitutional and law interpreter.[63] This need for a value judgement in the decision-making of the court arises from a collision of constitutional values: the inviolability of the king and the fundamental rights of the people. In individual cases, the court must interpret the law with the help of additional evaluations and find a solution to the problem through comparative value judgements.[64] The competing values must be weighed against each other. Finally, it should be noted that the solution must take account of both values, which can never be the case, if one is completely ignored, he may also step back in concreto.[65] The court must therefore interpret the laws in such a way as to ensure that fundamental rights and other values are realised to the greatest extent possible in terms of legal and factual possibilities.[66]

3.4 Balancing and Harmonising Values: The Way Out of the Political Crisis in Thailand

As Carl Schmitt[67] quite rightly said, in a political order there is always a collision of values. These competing values can always lead to a conflict of interest. Although a comparative value judgement is conceivable to solve this collision case, a person must not be regarded as the highest value or an inviolable value in politics. According to Carl Schmitt, the "tyranny of values" is an inviolable value in politics. Kelsen is similarly of the opinion: "Only those who believe in the existence of an absolute value, those who know themselves or someone else in possession of this value have the right to condemn democracy, have the right to enforce their will against that of all others, their conviction, even by force, to impose it on all others".[68] The absolute and inviolable value in the Constitution and in politics can therefore attack fundamental rights and other values in their core area. In a democratic society, different values must have their own political sphere so that they have the chance to develop their political convictions. This problem is scientifically referred to as "the balancing of values and fundamental rights" and as "the harmonisation of values".

The fundamental rights guaranteed in the Constitution are principles and values. They are legal norms, but their application is not a definitive one, but only a prima facie one. They can claim their validity to the greatest extent possible, as long as

---

[63] Karl Larenz explained well in the following: "It is evident that in many cases the judge is not able to take the decision solely from the law, not even from the judgments of the legislator to be recognized from him. This is the case where the law uses so-called indefinite legal terms or general clauses. Here there is only a very general framework which the judge must fill in the individual case by an additional evaluation", see Larenz, Karl, Methodenlehre der Rechtswissenschaft, p. 118.

[64] See *Alexy, Rob*ert, Theorie der Grundrechte, pp. 128–129.

[65] See. *Rüfner, Wolfgang*, Grundrechtskonflikte, FG BVerfG, Vol. II (1976), 453, 468.

[66] See. *Alexy, Robert*, Theorie der Grundrechte, p. 75 & 81.

[67] *Schmitt, Carl*, Die Tyrannei der Werte, p. 49.

[68] *Kelsen, Hans*, Verteidigung der Demokratie, in: Hans Kelsen, Verteidigung der Demokratie, 229, 236.

they do not conflict with other rules, principles and values that are also valid in the legal order. In a collision constellation one of the colliding values may not be regarded as the highest or the absolute value. They are exclusively a prima facie or a value that can be weighed up. The Court must interpret the Constitution and laws in accordance with the principle of constitutional unity and the principle of practical concordance, so that all conflicting fundamental rights and values can apply uniformly and harmoniously.[69] On a case-by-case basis, the court must weigh up fundamental rights and values and decide which value has greater weight. However, fundamental rights or values, which have to be overridden in individual cases, must not be attacked in their core area.[70] This solution to the problem is referred to in science as a "comparison of fundamental rights" or "the weighing of the merits of different fundamental rights and values of equal rank".[71]

The doctrine of balancing and harmonising fundamental rights and values, which has been developed very intensively in the German legal system, can be introduced into the Thai legal system. The organs of state, which should realize these principles, are the administration and the jurisdiction. A court can defend a value in the political order, but it must ensure that its interpretation of the Constitution and the law is compatible with the value of democracy. The value defended by the administration and the courts shall not entirely require grateful and unconditional obedience from other values, in particular fundamental rights.[72] More specifically, in the event of a conflict between the status of king and the exercise of freedom of expression, the court must interpret the laws in such a way that both the traditional and cultural value of the king and the fundamental rights of the citizen can simultaneously claim their validity in the legal order. If it is still completely unclear that the expression of opinion disproportionately undermines the value of the King in politics and in the Constitution, freedom of expression must be respected. Thus, freedom of expression, which is an important value of democracy, can also be present in the Thai political order. Finally, it is also remarkable that the balancing and harmonisation of values is not only useful for the protection of fundamental rights and the defence of democracy. They can also maintain the honour and value of the King. The absolute and inviolable value in politics can certainly lead to endless conflicts and resistance. Harmonising

---

[69] *Fischer-Lescano, Andreas*, Kritik der praktischen Konkordanz, Kritische Justiz, Vol. 41, No. 2 (2008), 166, 171.

[70] See *Fehn, Karsten*, Grundrecht versus Grundrecht—Die Problematik der Grundrechtskollision anhand von Fällen, VR 40 (1994), 413, 420; *Bethe, Herbert*, Grundrechtskollision, in: Handbuch der Grundrechte, Volume III, Grundrecht in Deutschland, Allgemeine Lehren, Heidelberg 2009, § 72 Rn. 86 et seq.; *Bleasing, Heiner*, Grundrechtskollision, simultaneously Diss. iur. (Bochum 1974), p. 5; *Britz, Gabriele*, Prozedurale Lösung von Grundrechtskollisionen durch "grundrechtliches Vorverfahren", Der Staat 42 (2003), 35, 36.

[71] *Fehn, Karsten*, VR 40 (1994), 413, 420; *Jansen, Nils*, Die Abwägung von Grundrechten, Der Staat 36 (1997), 27, 27 ff.,; *Vosgerau, Ulrich*, Zur Kollision von Grundrechtsfunktionen, Ein zentrales Problem der Grundrechtsdogmatik, AöR 133 (2008), 346, 350.

[72] See *Kelsen, Hans*, Verteidigung der Demokratie, in: Hans Kelsen, Verteidigung der Demokratie, 229, 236.

constitutional and political values through constitutional and legislative interpretation is therefore the best way to defend the Constitution, democracy and the monarchy.

4 Outlook

The problem of conflict of values is still a central discussion in the Thai legal system. The present collision cases are emotionally charged and have not yet been completely solved by jurisprudence. The obstacle for the scientific discussion is the taboo character of this problem. The situation is desperate and the conflict is waiting for its climax. The call for jurisdiction to solve the problem is becoming more and more urgent. The court is expected to make a value judgement through its decision-making power. Jurisdiction should balance conflicting values, namely fundamental rights and traditional and cultural values. The most important thing, however, is that the judiciary has a democratic attitude. Finally, the jurisdiction must interpret the laws in such a way that the fundamental rights are to be realised to the greatest possible extent, relative to the legal and actual possibilities. In the constellations of conflicting values, jurisdiction is expected not only to assume responsibility, but also to have the courage to make democratic decisions.

The European Convention on Human Rights: A Constitution for Europe?

Angelika Nußberger

1 Hope and disillusionment—The Drafting Process

It was not a great moment for Europe.

After two and a half years of deliberations, the wording of the European Convention on Human Rights (ECHR) was finally approved on 4 November 1950. However, the members of the Consultative Assembly who had been eager to create an effective mechanism for the protection of human rights and to restrict the hitherto absolute concept of State sovereingty were not in a celebrating mood. The words of the President of the Consultative Assembly, the Belgian Paul-Henri Spaak, at the beginning of the signing ceremony speak for themselves: "[I]t is not a very good Convention, but it is a lovely Palace!"[1] With the latter, he referred to Palazzo Barberini in Rome where the ceremony took place.

Why was the mood so bad, what did they find so lamentable?

The first phase of the drafting of the Convention, which had been enthusiastically launched and involved mainly experts, was followed by a second phase in which government representatives brought the overly lofty and hopeful passages back into political reality. The first draft (drawn up by consensus) was discarded and a fresh start was made. Political considerations became more important than content. In particular,

[1] See *Bates*, The evolution of the European Convention on Human Rights. From its Inception to the Creation of a Permanent Court of Human Rights, Oxford 2010, p. 99.

The text was first published in German in the Juristenzeitung: Nußberger, Die Europäische Menschenrechtskonvention-eine Verfassung für Europa, JZ 74 (2019)/ Heft 9, 421–428, the – slightly adapted – text was translated into English by Prof. Dr. Michael Pils.

The original version of this chapter was revised: Chapter note has been modified. The correction to this chapter is available at https://doi.org/10.1007/978-981-19-7542-4_14

A. Nußberger (✉)
Faculty of Law, University of Cologne, Cologne, Germany
e-mail: angelika.nussberger@uni-koeln.de

M. Deguchi and K. Yakushiji (eds.), *Europe and Asia as a Legal Area for Fundamental Rights*, https://doi.org/10.1007/978-981-19-7542-4_10

the control mechanism for compliance with the ECHR, which had originally been considered particularly important, was watered down. The idea of a Court competent not only to pronounce binding judgments but also to order enforcement measures was abandoned; individual complaints and judicial review were made optional and judicial review was based on a political filter.[2]

At the same time, the individual legal guarantees were made more specific and more detailed than in the first versions. However, due to seemingly insurmountable controversies, important rights such as the right to property and the right to education had been excluded. This was necessary in order to conform to the political will and bring the treaty negotiations to an end as quickly as possible. In view of the beginning of the Cold War, this was motivated by the desire not only to commit to fundamental rights but also to document this commitment externally. Thus, the Italian politician Count Sforza, the Chairman of the Committee of Ministers, declared that it was important to send a clear message and to demonstrate, by signing the treaty, that there was a great difference between a—literally—"free world and an enslaved world, whether the slaves were aware of their enslavement or not".[3]

Many issues of these initial misgivings continued to exist. The Parliamentary Assembly and the Committee of Ministers did not cooperate. The former felt treated by the latter like "an assembly of schoolboys". The representatives of the different countries accused each other of having given priority to national interests over the interests of the community. According to the French chief negotiator Pierre-Henri Teitgen, the British had "bullied" the Committee of Ministers and achieved only "the shadow of a guarantee of rights and fundamental freedoms".[4] Realists and idealists continued to fight.

In short, they had been out for much, but had achieved little.

Legal history, however, teaches us that the success of a constitution or a treaty cannot be measured by the mood of the so-called "fathers" or "mothers" at the conclusion of their work. Apparently, some had been out only for little, but have achieved much – the best example is the German Constitution (Grundgesetz). It has been conceived only as a provisional solution. Yet, in 2019 we proudly celebrated its 70th birthday. Still, it serves as a reference model worldwide.

Conversely, 100 years ago, already during the negotiations, it was obvious that the expectation the Treaty of Versailles would serve as the basis for a long-lasting peace was bound to fail. Indeed, this was proven only a few years later.

It was with the following words that Eleonor Roosevelt opened the final vote on the Universal Declaration of Human Rights: "We stand today at the threshold of a great event both in the life of the United Nations and in the life of mankind… This Declaration may well become the international Magna Carta of all men everywhere."[5] However, many did not share this pathos. For at the same time, the so-called "raisin

---

[2] *Bates* (f.n. 2), pp. 118–131.

[3] *Bates* (f.n. 2), p. 99.

[4] *Bates* (f.n. 2), p. 100.

[5] Statement by Mrs. Franklin D. Roosevelt, Department of State Bulletin, December 19, 1948, pp. 751–752, cited in Glendon, A World Made New. Eleanor Roosevelt and the Universal Declaration of Human Rights, New York 2001, p. 166.

bombers" (Rosinenbomber) were already flying to Berlin at three-and-a-half minute intervals, the Cold War had begun. The Universal Declaration of Human Rights could have a real impact only decades later, if at all. Moreover, more had been hoped for—especially a binding treaty—and had to be put on hold in the course of the treaty negotiations.

In retrospect, the situation was similar to the European Convention on Human Rights, apart from the fact that, as mentioned above, even the fiction of pathos was missing. The "biographer" of the Convention, the English legal scholar Ed Bates, reports that in the scientific literature in the 1950s the ECHR was virtually hushed up. Even David Maxwell-Fyfe, one of the main protagonists during the negotiations, dedicated only a short paragraph to it in his memoirs because of its apparent insignificance.[6] Nevertheless, just seven decades later, we are discussing whether it might not be the secret constitution of Europe.

All beginnings may be difficult—wasn't the ECHR nevertheless born under a good star?

2 Patience and Innovative Ideas—The Slow Maturation Process of the ECHR

2.1 The Early Years

As a rule, international agreements are not concluded for a distant future, but for the present times. As soon as they come into force, they are effective. Borders are drawn, customs duties abolished, legal duties are carried out. A characteristic feature of human rights treaties seems to be, however, that they take a long time to mature, even after their entry into force. This would not mean that nothing is happening. Only—what happens takes time.

Thus, in the case of the ECHR as well, the main actors were hesitant, their attitude was ambivalent. This was particularly true for the British. They had been the ones providing the political inspiration—linked to the name of Churchill– as well as the innovative ideas for legal implementation; without Lauterpacht as mastermind[7] and Maxwell-Fyfe as co-author, the ECHR would hardly have developed in what it is today. Nonetheless, and this is almost reminiscent of the British attitude towards international judicial human rights protection today, it was a British Labour MEP who was the only one to vote against the first draft, which was driven by initial enthusiasm, arguing that the Convention would do absolutely nothing to protect human rights, but rather "create an expensive and encroaching machinery".[8] And although the United Kingdom was the first to ratify the ECHR, it refused to accept the individual complaints procedure and the jurisdiction of the Court. The British

---

[6] *Bates* (f.n. 2), pp. 11, 12.

[7] See *Lauterpacht*, An International Bill of the Rights of Man, New York 1945.

[8] TP Vol. II at 256, cited from *Bates* (f.n. 2), p. 74, f.n. 143.

had also previously blocked all attempts to ensure compliance with the obligations of the ECHR through compulsory judicial review.[9] The French had pushed for it, but in turn refused to ratify the ECHR later on. They only acceded to it in 1974, when President Georges Pompidou succeeded to President Charles de Gaulle. And it was not until 1981, under the socialist Minister of Justice Badinter, that France ratified the Individual Complaints Protocol of the ECHR.

But even if the political process was slow, it was steady and always led in one direction. In the 1950s and 1960s the ten founding members—including Turkey—were joined step by step by other States from different geographical regions of Europe, excluding the East. The only setback in the development was the temporary withdrawal of Greece due to the military coup by the colonels.

It was also a slow process of finding legal solutions. At the beginning, there was a—little known—drumbeat. Greece filed the first interstate complaint against the United Kingdom because of the methods used to quell an uprising in the then British crown colony of Cyprus. The complaint was declared admissible. An investigation report identified unacceptable practices such as flogging and collective punishment. However, no conviction was handed down because the United Kingdom abolished the controversial legislation in time before a conviction could be handed down. The case was subsequently closed, albeit not unanimously. The relevant resolutions of the Committee of Ministers together with the relevant documents were only published in 1997 and 2006.[10] At least this first early case has shown that control from outside can have a positive effect.

Moreover, the decisive organs, the Commission and the Court, were created in the 1950s. The first major cases, Lawless v. Ireland,[11] the Belgian Language Dispute[12] and Golder v. the United Kingdom,[13] were landmark cases in the development of the case law. Early on the Court showed innovative approaches, demanded unwritten rights beyond the guarantees contained in the text of the treaty such as “access to court”, and began to interpret the Convention guarantees in the light of the principle of the rule of law.[14] Nonetheless, nobody in the 1960s and early 1970s would have thought of speaking of a “Constitution of Europe” with regard to the ECHR. On the contrary—at best, the convention was known to a narrow circle of insiders. If it was mentioned at all, it was rather compared to a “Sleeping Beauty”.[15]

---

[9] *Bates* (f.n. 2), pp. 457 ff.

[10] *Bates* (f.n. 2), pp. 195 ff.

[11] *ECtHR*, 14.11.1960, no. 332/57 – Lawless v. Ireland.

[12] *ECtHR*, 23.07.1968, no. 1474/62; 1677/62; 1691/62; 1769/63; 1994/63; 2126/64—Case Relating To Certain Aspects of the Laws on the Use of Languages in Education in Belgium.

[13] *ECtHR*, 21.02.1975, no. 4451/70 - Golder v. United Kingdom.

[14] *Nußberger*, in: Nolte/Krieger (eds.), The International Rule of law, Oxford 2019.

[15] *Frowein*, European Integration Through Fundamental Rights, Michigan Journal of Law Reform 18 (1984), 5, 8.

2.2 1979 as the Turn of an Era?

The American historian Samuel Moyn has written a book on the history of human rights with the beautiful title "The Last Utopia". According to his main thesis, contrary to what is generally assumed, human rights were not a formative political factor immediately after Word War II and the Holocaust. Rather, it was only in the 1970s that a genuine social movement based on human rights emerged.[16] He sees a number of catalysts for what he calls an "explosion" of human rights—the search for an European identity defined not only in the categories of the Cold War, the encounter of politicians, journalists and intellectuals with Soviet and later on Eastern European dissidents, and the moralization of American foreign policy after the trauma of the Vietnam War. One might think of Jimmy Carter's keynote speech at Notre Dame University on 22 May 1977, in which he attempted to put American foreign policy on a new basis of legitimacy and to raise America's standing in the world by advocating a renewed US commitment to human rights.[17] All these were signs of the collapse of the utopias that had been in place until then, based on the communist or capitalist model.[18]

Thus, it was only in the 1970s that the reference to human rights became common knowledge, not only in politics, but also in the general discourse.

The historian Frank Bösch called the year 1979 "Turning Point" (Zeitenwende). The subtitle of his book is: "When the world of today began".[19] His thesis is that we have to look for the "sources of the present time" in precisely that year, in 1979, a year which for Peter Sloterdijk is also "the key date of the twentieth century".[20] Key points of history in the national and international context are the opening of China, the Islamic revolution in Tehran, the foundation of the green ecological parties and their entry into the first state parliaments, the reactor accident in Harrisburg, the election of Margaret Thatcher as Prime Minister, the visit of Pope John Paul to Poland, the Vietnamese boat people, the revolution in Nicaragua, the hostage-taking at the US Embassy in Tehran, the NATO double-trackdown and finally the invasion of Afghanistan. All this happened in one year.

It may be a coincidence, but it is significant that it was in 1979 that the two judgments of the ECHR were handed down, which also marked the beginning of a new era in European human rights law: Tyrer v. United Kingdom[21] and Marckx

---

[16] *Moyn*, The Last Utopia. Human Rights in History, Cambridge (USA) 2012, p. 8.

[17] Carter's keynote speech at University of Notre Dame on 22 May 1977, in: Public Papers of the Presidents of the United States: Jimmy Carter, 1977, Vol. 1. Washington D.C.: GPO 1977, pp. 954–962.

[18] *Moyn* (f.n. 17), p. 8: "These were belief systems that promised a free way of life, but led into bloody morass, or offered emancipation from empire and capital, but suddenly came to seem like dark tragedies rather than bright hopes. In this atmosphere, an internationalism revolving around individual rights surged, and it did so because it was defined as a pure alternative in an age of ideological betrayal and political collapse".

[19] *Bösch*, Zeitenwende 1979. Als die Welt von heute begann, 2019.

[20] *Sloterdijk*, Zorn und Zeit. Politisch-psychologischer Versuch, 2016, p. 336 f.

[21] *ECtHR*, 25.04.1978, no. 5856/72 – Tyrer v. United Kingdom.

v. Belgium.[22] The case of Tyrer was about the prohibition of corporal punishment for children, the case of Marckx about discrimination against children born out of wedlock.

In three respects, these two cases before the European Court of Human Rights have set the tone for the future and - without exaggeration - have created the conditions for what we now describe as 'constitutionalisation of Europe' or 'European public order': Firstly, the "living-instrument doctrine" was invented, thereby liberating the Convention, which was already roughly 30 years old at the time, from its historical corset; secondly, the "margin-of-appreciation doctrine" that made the intertwining of national and international human rights jurisdiction negotiable; and thirdly, the intrusion into national legislation from outside.

It was thus a court, an international, but still a rather little-known court that used at the end of the 1970s an international treaty as a spring board for giving politics a new - and since then often reconsidered, discussed and criticized - understanding of State sovereignty. The Luxembourg court had done so in a similar vein a decade and a half earlier and invented what was further on called "supranational law".[23] Strasbourg no longer accepted the self-containedness and complacency of nation-states - at least in human rights issues. One may see in the Court's new interpretive approach invented in the 1970s a consistent and logical development of the concept of "control" already laid down in the Convention from the very beginning. Or, one may speak of an "ultra vires act", of self-empowerment not covered by any norm of competence. Be that as it may – in the year 1979 when the European Court of Human Rights had to decide on the rights of illegitimate children and on the rights of young people being beaten for "educational purposes", the basis was laid down for far-reaching future developoments, e.g. cases of transsexuals giving birth to a child as a woman and wanting to register as a father and not as a mother,[24] cases of refugees knocking at the doors of consulates abroad in order to be given a flight ticket to a safe country,[25] and cases of convicted criminals who feel treated in an "inhuman manner" because of the size of their cells.[26] When the doors of an international court are opened wide, it must decide. On everything. This has important consequences for State and society.

---

[22] *ECtHR,* 13.06.1979, no. 6833/74 – Marckx v. Belgium.

[23] *CJEU,* 05.02.1963 – 26/62, *van Gend en Loos,* ECLI:EU:C:1963:1.

[24] *ECtHR,* pending before the Chamber, no. 53568/18 and 54,941/18, O.H. and G.H. v. Germany.

[25] *ECtHR,* 0505.2020, no. 3599/18 – M.N. et al. v. Belgium.

[26] Landmark case *ECHR,* 20.10.2016, no. 7334/13 - Mursic v. Croatia.

3 Approaches to Constitutionalisation[27]

Why did the decisions in the cases of Marckx and Tyrer herald a new era? What was new?

3.1 *From Piecemeal to Comprehensive Control*

In his dissenting opinion in the case of Marckx v. Belgium, not just anyone, but the British judge Sir Gerald Fitzmaurice - former member of the International Law Commission, judge at the ICJ and so famous that even a headland on the east coast of the Antarctic Peninsula bears his name – invokes literally, "the small voice of juridical conscience" which opposes the "eagerness for specific results – however meritorious they may be in themselves".[28] The fine British humour does not weaken the fundamental criticism expressed in the judge's words. In his view, the majority opinion in Marckx is not legally justifiable, the boundaries between political and legal decisions are shifted. One would go too far.

"Within certain limits almost anything can colourably be represented as connected with or related to some other given thing" he writes.[29] Somehow everything has to do with everything. Therefore, everything could theoretically be considered protected under one of the provisions of the Convention, especially under "private or family life". However, the rules of interpretation do not allow such a broad reading of the terms. Otherwise it would distort the basic idea of the ECHR, i.e. granting protection against encroachments of a totalitarian or dictatorial State into the private sphere. Fitzmaurice argued that, in comparison with "family life", a regulation on descent were a completely different legal category and could not be subsumed under it. The interpretation of the majority is

> "... little else but a misguided endeavour to read—or rather introduce—a whole code of family law into Article 8 (art. 8) of the Convention, thus inflating it in a manner, and to an extent, wholly incommensurable with its true and intended proportions".[30]

This discussion is ultimately about the fundamental question of whether human rights cover every aspect of human existence or whether only certain parts of it are protected. In the end, the idea of comprehensive protection leaving open only a few white spots has prevailed. "Possible repercussions on family life are not enough to make a thing part of it", Fitzmaurice writes.[31] But, as shown by the fact that the

---

[27] On the process of what is called "constitutionalisaton" see *Walter* ZaöRV 1999, 962–983 and ZaöRV 2015, 753–770; *Schaefer* EuR 2017, 80–106; *Tomuschat* EuGRZ 2003, 95–100.

[28] *Fitzmaurice*, dissenting opinion to *ECtHR*, 13.06.1979, no. 6833/74 – Marckx v. Belgium, para. 5.

[29] *Fitzmaurice* (f.n. 29), para. 5.

[30] *Fitzmaurice* (f.n. 29), para. 15.

[31] *Fitzmaurice* (f.n. 29), para. 15.

majority has won: "possible repercussions" are sufficient. Thus, human rights control is no longer carried out only from a bird's eye view. It is rather through the magnifying glass that the Court watches what is happening inside the member States. National legislation such as family law can be controlled before the ECtHR. And thus - and this is the beginning of a miraculous transformation - the role of the ECHR suddenly resembles that of a constitutional court. This is all the more true as the consequences of the decisions of the European Court are similar to those of constitutional courts. Even if the the ECHR does not act as a court of cassation, the national authorities are obliged to adapt the law in conformity with the Convention if they do not want to be condemned again.[32] This is a duty under international law monitored by the Committee of Ministers.[33]

By now, Art. 8 ECHR can be called a catch-all fundamental right. However, there is still a dispute about where the boundaries lie. An illustrative example is the case of di Trizio v. Switzerland,[34] where the majority interprets a social benefit as an aspect of "family life", while the minority argues that social benefits are exclusively covered by "property" under Article 1 of Protocol 1.[35] Is "more family" possible with more money, or, conversely, does it restrict family life when less money is provided by the State? Is – as in the case Parrillo v. Italy[36] – embryo donation for scientific research stemming from an in vitro fertilization also part of private life? Such examples show how far Fitzmaurice's "repercussions" can go. Let me repeat his sentence: "Within certain limits almost anything can colourably be represented as connected with or related to some other given thing". His doubts are not simply "checked off" and historical rubbish, but return and lead us directly to the question of whether and, if so, how an international treaty can be transformed into a constitution or a near-constitution.

3.2 *Turning Away from Historical Interpretation*

The methodological approach to the interpretation of an international treaty attaches far less importance to historical interpretation than the interpretation of ordinary laws. According to the Vienna Convention on the Law of Treaties, recourse may be had to supplementary means of interpretation, including the preparatory work of the treaty and the circumstances of its conclusion, in order to confirm the meaning resulting from the interpretation obtained by other methods of interpretation or to clarify an interpretation which would otherwise be ambiguous or unclear, absurd or

---

[32] See Art. 46 (1) ECHR: „The High Contracting Parties undertake to abide by the final judgment of the Court in any case to which they are parties".

[33] See Art. 46 (2) ECHR: "The final judgment of the Court shall be transmitted to the Committee of Ministers, which shall supervise its execution".

[34] *ECtHR*, 02.02.2016, no. 7186/09 – Di Trizio v. Switzerland.

[35] *Keller, Spano, Kjølbro*, dissenting opinion concerning ECtHR, 02.02.2016 (f.n. 35).

[36] *ECtHR*, 28.05.2013, no. 46470/11 – Parrillo v. Italy.

unreasonable.[37] However, the two decisions Marckx and Tyrer go further than what the Vienna Convention prescribes. It is argued that an interpretation which does not only disregard the historical intention, but explicitly contradicts it, may be necessary under certain circumstances, especially if otherwise the zeitgeist, e.g. the zeitgeist of the 1940s and 1950s, would remain dominant, thereby depriving the treaty of its topicality and relevance. The ECHR is a "living instrument".[38] Theoretically, this approach can be traced back to another provision of the Vienna Convention on the Law of Treaties, Article 33(3) (b), according to which any subsequent practice in the application of the treaty that shows the agreement of the parties on its interpretation must be taken into account. A "subsequent practice" is also a new consensus in society.

In 1979, this approach was used to justify the qualification of corporal punishment as "inhuman treatment" and the interpretation of the disadvantaged position of children born out of wedlock as "discriminatory" and thus incompatible with the Convention, although it can hardly be denied that both would have been in line with the consensus in society in the 1940s and 1950s. In the words of former court president Sir Niklas Bratza, the living-instrument doctrine allows "to breathe life into the words of the instrument so as to make it relevant to contemporary European society".[39]

It was an (unheard-of) novelty to regard obligations under international law, which are to be realized in the framework of intergovernmental relations, as adaptable to social change. This approach in some way compensated for one of the essential deficits of multilateral international treaties - their rigidity due to the unanimity requirement for changes. In the 70 years of its existence, the German Constitution has been modified 62 times, but the substantive provisions of the ECHR have not been adapted once; the Convention has only been supplemented by protocols. For example, the death penalty is still part of Article 2 ECHR; the catalogue of prohibitions of discrimination does not contain criteria such as "sexual orientation". But with a "living instrument", one can generously ignore such historical remnants and gaps. However, it has to be admitted that, if equal rights between men and women and the abolition of the death penalty are considered as "fundamentals", as *sine qua non* conditions for the membership in the Council of Europe, then, in 1953, some of the founding States would have had difficulties in meeting these requirements at the time of ratification.

---

[37] Art. 32 of the Vienna Convention on the Law of Treaties.

[38] *ECtHR*, 13.06.1979 (Fn. 23), para. 41: „interpreted in the light of present-day conditions "; CJEU, 05.02.1963 (f.n. 23).

[39] *Bratza*, European Human Rights Law Review 2 (2014), 116, 118.

3.3 Margin of Appreciation

Finally, the Marckx judgment contains a reference to the notion of "margin of appreciation", although not in the majority opinion, but in Judge Fitzmaurice's dissent. He defends the Belgian legal regulation according to which mothers of children born out of wedlock are not *ex lege* mothers of their children; such a regulation would be "well within the margin of appreciation or discretion that any Government, acting *bona fide*, ought to be accorded".[40] And further: "… in any event, States must be allowed to change their attitudes in their own good time, in their own way and by reasonable means".[41] The recourse to the "margin of appreciation" is an argumentation pattern that has been used before in judgments of the Court, but it has not yet been developed into a "doctrine". Later on, it would run like a red thread through the Court's case law.[42]

Judges' opinions on the margin to be granted to member States in specific cases often differ; those who argue for a violation of the Convention deny that there might be any "margin", those who argue against it tend to grant a wide margin. Probably the most famous example in this context is the judgment on the "crucifix in the classroom", the Lautsi judgment, where the different outcome of the case before the Chamber[43] ("violation") and before the Grand Chamber[44] ("no violation") is essentially due to the different interpretation of the margin of appreciation to be given to member States in deciding on questions of religion. The decisive question is how much unity or how much diversity is desired or accepted. Ultimately, the answer to this question is a premise of deciding on human rights cases. Decisions are "objectivized" by using certain criteria developed in the case-law. Nevertheless, they are not calculable. Convention case-law thus ressembles a traffic-light-model – "red", "yellow", "green". Between compatible with the Convention ("green") and non-compatible with the Convention ("red") there is an area in which the Court may accept different solutions. Stopping and driving on is equally permitted. Whether, for instance, incest between siblings is punished or not,[45] whether criminal convictions of a naked rambler are tolerated,[46] whether euthanasia is allowed[47] – all these are questions of the "margin". If a European consensus exists, it may lead the way, but

---

[40] *Fitzmaurice* (Fn. 29), para. 29.

[41] *Fitzmaurice* (Fn. 29), para. 29.

[42] *Asche*, Die Margin of Appreciation, 2018; *Binder*, JRP 2015, 1; *Greer*, UCL Human Rights Review 3 (2010), 1; *Legg*, The Margin of Appreciation in International Human Rights Law: Deference and Proportionality, Oxford 2012; *Letsas*, in: Etinson (ed.), Human Rights: Moral or Political?, Oxford 2018; *Rozakis*, in: Titiun (ed.), La conscience de droits, Mélanges en l'honneur de Jean-Paul Costa, Paris 2011, 527.

[43] *ECtHR*, 03.11.2009, no. 30814/06 – Lautsi v. Italy.

[44] *ECtHR* (GC), 18.03.2011, no. 30814/06 – Lautsi v. Italy.

[45] *ECtHR*, 12.04.2012, no. 43547/08 – Stübing v. Germany.

[46] *ECtHR*, 28.10.2014, no. 49327/11 – Gough v. United Kingdom.

[47] *ECtHR*, 05.06.2015, no. 46043/14 – Lambert v. France.

even that is not mandatory.[48] Exceptions to mainstream approaches may be allowed if they are well reasoned.

All these thoughts are, for the first time, condensed in Marckx v. Belgium. It is not exaggerated to claim that Marckx was a ground-breaking case.

That brings us back to the functions of a Constitution. Such a judgment helps to build up a system of values. A system of values may bring about a new identity, a "constitutional identity".

4 Constitution or Aliud?

After the little detour into history it is necessary to ask if the revolutionary approach to interpretation developed in 1979 has built the basis for transforming the ECHR into a Constitution.

To put it bluntly: no, the ECHR is not a Constitution. It is missing three things: First, a State. Second, regulations on State organisation (in addition to human rights). And third, the final word.

Let me explain in detail:

4.1 Community of Treaty Partners vs. State

First, the community of the 46 member States to the Convention does not form a State. According to international law theory, three elements are required for statehood: territory, people ("Volk") and government. There is no "Volk", there is no territory, there is no government within the Convention system. The well-established criteria do not fit. Instead of a people there are "the Europeans", very broadly understood as all those living temporarily or permanently in the 46 member States. There is something like an "European legal space". But this is an abstract concept not necessarily ending at Europe's borders. It is based on the Court's jurisdiction, and may be understood broadly; it cannot be compared to a well-defined territory.[49] Finally, there is the obligation under international law to abide by treaties, an obligation that can only be

---

[48] *Dzehtsiarou*, European consensus and the legitimacy of the European Court of Human Rights, Cambridge 2015; *Dothan*, Chicago Journal of International Law 18 (2018), 393; *Kleinlein*, European Journal of International Law 28 (2017), 871; *Nußberger*, ReWiss 2012, 197; *Unger-Sternberg*, AVR 2013, 312.

[49] *Besson*, Leiden Journal of International Law 25 (2012), 857; Bhuta (ed.), The Frontiers of Human Rights: Extraterritoriality and its Challenges, Oxford, 2016; *Jankowska-Gilberg*, Extraterritorialität der Menschenrechte, 2008; *Milanovic*, Extraterritorial Application of Human Rights Treaties, Oxford 2011; *Milanovic*, Human Rights Law Review 2008, 412; *Milanovic*, Papic, International and Comparative Law Quaterly 67 (2018), 779; *Nußberger*, Current Legal Problems 65 (2012), 241.

enforced to a limited extent. A "treaty government" - in contrast to the government within a State - does not exist and should not exist.

4.2 *Rules on State Organisation vs. Definition of a Role Model for Society*

While every national full-fledged constitution contains detailed provisions on the organisation of the State, nothing comparable can be found in the Convention. In the German Constitution, e.g., while Articles 1 to 19 are dedicated to human rights, Articles 21 to 146 provide detailed regulations on the competences of State organs as well as their limits. Such regulations are missing in the Convention.

Nevertheless, the Convention is more than just a catalogue of fundamental rights. In Article 20 of the German Constitution basic principles such as rule of law, democracy, welfare State and federal State are defined. Similar ideas can be deduced from or read into the Convention.

4.2.1 The Idea of Democracy

This applies first and foremost to the idea of democracy. The formula "necessary in a democratic society"[50] is enshrined in many Convention articles such as Article 8, Article 9, Article 10, and Article 11. Democracy is thus the yardstick, the basis for balancing rights and interests in human rights conflicts. In its case law on Articles 10 and 11 the European Court of Human Rights has paved the way for pluralism and tolerance as foundations for a democratic society. Moreover, democratic elections are prescribed by Article 3 of Protocol 1.[51] Democracy is also the guiding principle in the "proceduralisation" of rights—the more intensively and openly a matter has been discussed in the legislative process, the more leeway is left to the national legislature.[52] Last but not least, separation of powers is underlying Convention articles such as Article 6 on fair procedure which, among other things, defines the scope of control of the decisions of the executive.[53]

---

[50] See Art. 8 (2), Art. 9 (2), Art. 10 (2), Art. 11 (2) ECHR.

[51] "The High Contracting Parties undertake to hold free elections at reasonable intervals by secret ballot, under conditions which will ensure the free expression of the opinion of the people in the choice of the legislature.".

[52] *Nußberger*, in: Gerards, Brems (eds.), Procedural Review in European Fundamental Rights Cases, Cambridge 2017, p. 161.

[53] *ECtHR*, 06.11.2018, no. 55391/13, 57,728/13 and 74,041/13 – Ramos Nunes de Carvalho e Sá, paras. 204 ff.; see also Concurring Opinion by Raimondi, Nußberger, Jäderblom, Mose, Polackova, Koskelo.

4.2.2 The Idea of Rule of Law

The idea of rule of law also plays a central role in the Convention system. Although it is only mentioned in the preamble and not in the text of the Convention itself, there is consensus that the individual guarantees have to be interpreted in the light of the principle of the rule of law. Since restrictions of fundamental rights are allowed only when they are "in accordance with the law", the European Court of Human Rights has defined notions such as foreseeability and legal certainty in a detailed manner. Guarantees such as fair trial, *nulla poena sine lege*, *ne bis in idem* and independence of the judiciary are basic components both of the Court's jurisprudence and the general understanding of rule of law.[54]

4.2.3 The Idea of the Welfare State

Furthermore, the idea of the welfare State is an element underlying the Court's approach to the interpretation of various Convention guarantees. That is especially true for the interpretation of Article 3, the prohibition of inhuman treatment.[55] While "inhuman treatment" is primarily understood as interference with the bodily or psychological integrity of a person, i.e. an active intrusion, it is also possible to understand it as "not enough" State action. This applies to cases where vulnerable persons are left without any help and shelter. The interpretation of Article 1 of Protocol 1 is also relevant in this context. According to the Court's view, it is not only property in the narrow sense of the word that is to be protected, but also social rights laid down in the legislation, such as pension rights, be it an invalidity pension or an old age pension.[56] The idea of "positive obligations" derived from human rights guarantees transforms the State from a purely liberal State into a State responsible for the well-being of its population.[57] It is true that there are no social rights in the ECHR. Yet, the protection of social rights by the ECHR is more effective than the protection provided by toothless treaties such as the European Social Charter.

---

[54] *Nußberger*, in: Zubik (ed.), Human Rights in Contemporary World. Essays in Honour of Professor Leszek Garlicki, Warschau 2017, pp. 162–173.

[55] *ECtHR*, 23.04.2002, no. 56869/00 - Larioshina v. Russia; *ECtHR*, 21.01.2011, no. 30696/09 - M.S.S. v. Greece and Belgium; *ECtHR*, 24.05.2018, Nr. 6882/13 - N.T.P et al. v. France.

[56] See the development of the case-law from *ECtHR*, 06.09.1996, no. 17371/90 – Gaygususz v. Austria to *ECtHR (GC)* 13.12.2016, no. 53080/13—Belane Nagy v. Hungary.

[57] *Dröge*, Positive Verpflichtungen der Staaten der Europäischen Menschenrechtskonvention, 2003; *Klatt*, ZaöRV 2011, 691; *Krieger*, ZaöRV 2014, 187; *Mowbray*, The development of positive obligations under the European Convention on Human Rights by the European Court of Human Rights, 2004; *Stoyanova*, Nordic Journal of International Law 87 (2018), 344; *Xenos*, The positive obligations of the state under the European Convention of Human Rights, 2013.

4.2.4 Federalism

Even elements of federalism can be detected in the Convention. With the entry into force of Protocol 15 on 1 August 2021, the principle of subsidiarity has been explicitly included in the preamble to the Convention. Already before, it has been dominant in the Court's case law. Thus, the Court emphasizes repeatedly that the national authorities are, in principle, better placed than an international court to evaluate local needs and conditions. It would only intervene when really necessary to protect the Convention guarantees.[58] If national courts apply the ECHR in accordance with the case-law and arrive at certain conclusions, the European Court of Human Rights would need "very good reasons" to decide the case differently.[59] The former President of the Court, Robert Spano, has coined in this respect the notion of the "new age of subsidiarity".[60]

The ECHR thus works on the basis of a model of society where the main coordinates are clear, even if they can be implemented in very different ways. This is nicely summarized in the judgment Shindler v. United Kingdom: "There [are] a wealth of differences, inter alia, in the historical development, cultural diversity and political thought within Europe which it is for each contracting State to mould into its own democratic vision".[61] Thus, the ECHR does not only allow different understandings of what is a "democratic and social constitutional State", but even requests them; the Convention system lives from the wealth of alternative models. In contrast to a national, but federal State such as Germany, there is, however, no provision for "the establishment of equivalent living conditions throughout the federal territory" or for "the maintenance of legal or economic unity".[62] The federal bracket is very soft.

In 60 years of jurisprudence, the Court has moulded the human rights guarantees enshrined in the Convention into a specific model of society based above all on rule of law and democracy. Nevertheless, in comparison to national constitutions, what is missing are detailed provisions on legislation, on the organisation of the executive power or on financial flows. Such deliberate omissions cannot and must not be filled.

---

[58] "The Convention leaves to each Contracting State, in the first place, the task of securing the rights and liberties it enshrines. The institutions created by it make their own contribution to this task but they become involved only through the contentious proceedings and once all domestic remedies have been exhausted", *ECtHR*, 07.12.1976, no. 5493/72 - Handyside v. United Kingdom, para. 48.

[59] "Where the balancing exercise has been undertaken by the national authorities in conformity with the criteria laid down in the Court's case law, the Court would require strong reasons to substitute its view fort hat of the domestic courts, ECtHR, 07.02,2012, no. 40660/08, 60,641/08—von Hannover v. Germany, para. 107.

[60] *Spano*, Human Rights Law Review 18 (2018), 473, 474.

[61] *ECtHR*, 07.05.2013, no. 19840/09 - Shindler v. United Kingdom.

[62] See Art. 72 (2) of the Basic Law for the Federal Republic of Germany.

4.3 The Last vs. The Penultimate Word

According to the famous *dictum* of the German Federal Constitutional Court in the so-called Görgülü decision the Basic Law "does not waive the sovereignty contained in the last instance in the German Constitution".[63] The ECHR, as an international treaty, in principle also claims this "last word", since no norm of national law, not even constitutional provisions, justify breaking an international treaty. Article 27 of the Vienna Convention on the Law of Treaties is clear in this respect: "A contracting party may not rely on its domestic law to justify the non-performance of an international treaty". Here, however, the logic of one system collides with the logic of another system, since constitutional law must equally claim ultimate validity in order to fulfil its role as a "Constitution". In European law, the European Court of Justice in its decision Gend van Loos[64] tried to solve the dilemma inventing "supranationality" and thus trumping national constitutional law.[65] This came, however, at a high price.[66] The Court claimed the existence of a rule that was never negotiated. The fault lines can be seen many years later in the growing number of national constitutional courts judgments openly contradicting this assumption. The counter-model is based on "identity control" and "ultra vires control"[67]; it is not far fetched to interpret the "Brexit" as a follow-up to this unsolved conflict about "who's first".

The European Court of Human Rights has followed suit and asserted the primacy of the Convention over national constitutional law, for example in the judgment Gladkov and Anchugov v. Russia.[68] It is a case concerning prisoners' right to vote. The interpretation of the Convention contradicts a provision contained in a part of the Russian Constitution that cannot be changed.[69] The fact that the Görgülü *dictum* has been so influential and was followed by a large number of constitutional and supreme courts of the member States shows that the dispute over the last word is not yet solved.[70] The European Court of Human Rights responds to the calls for a duel with an offer of diplomatic dialogue.[71] It avoids the discourse on the "last word"; what is the point of arguing about something that cannot but lead to a dead end. Even the Federal Constitutional Court has never played the Görgülü card, but has

---

[63] BVerfGE (Decisions of the FCC) 111, 307, 319.

[64] *CJEU* (f.n. 24).

[65] See concerning the development *Terhechte*, Konstitutionalisierung und Normativität der europäischen Grundrechte, Tübingen 2011, pp. 41 ff.

[66] *Grimm*, Europa ja- aber welches?, in: Rüttgers/Decker (eds.), Europas Ende, Europas Anfang. Neue Perspektiven für die Europäische Union, 2017, p. 42.

[67] BVerfGE (Decisions oft he FCC) 140, 317.

[68] *ECtHR*, 04.07.2013, no. 11157/04 and 15,162/05- Anchugov and Gladkov v. Russia, paras. 50–53; see *Fleig-Goldstein*, CJTL 2017, 172.

[69] See concerning the conflict and its consequences *Hartwig*, EuGRZ 2017, 1; *Malksöö*, European Constitutional Law Review 12 (2016), 377, 379.

[70] See *H. Keller, R. Walter*, The Bell of Görgülü Can't Be Unrung—Can it?, Global Community Yearbook of International Law and Jurisprudence 2019.

[71] *Biaggini*, EuGRZ 2014, 29; *López Guerra*, in: Müller (ed.), *Judicial Dialogue and Human Rights*, Cambridge 2017, 401; *Spano*, Nordic Journal of Human Rights 33 (2015), 1.

rather tried to ensure a lively exchange within the constitutional court network.[72] As long as the controversy is not "fundamentalist", but is fought out only with a view to individual cases, dialogue can work, even if sometimes the keyboards of legal argumentation tend to strike a dissonant accord. One prominent example is a decision of the British Supreme Court,[73] in which the majority rejects the European Court of Human Rights' case law on the presumption of innocence.[74] To say that the Strasbourg argument reflects "hopeless and probably irretrievable confusion", akin to "a boat which, once severed from its moorings, floats out to sea and is tossed hopelessly this way and that"[75] is, commenting with British understatement, not really friendly.

For the Convention model these three central differences – no State in the background, no rules on State organization, no last word – demonstrate that the Convention is an *aliud* in comparison to a Constitution. It is like a Gothic vault without a keystone. Nevertheless, miraculously, it does not collapse. The Convention takes over many functions of a Constitution - the function of legitimation, the function of integration, the function of limitation, the function of organisation, the function of identity - without becoming a Constitution and without wanting to become a Constitution. The Convention works together with the 46 national constitutions and does not replace them.[76]

Then what is it? It is not a hybrid form such as the "Treaty establishing a Constitution for Europe" - this model failed in two referenda in France and the Netherlands in 2005 - but, referring to Rousseau's "Contrat social", a "Treaty on a 'Contrat social'", a hybrid and yet successful construction, something like a "shadow Constitution".[77]

5 The European Court of Human Rights as a Constitutional Court or "Contrat Social"-Court?

This raises the question about the status of the Court. Is it a constitutional court or a "'Contrat social' Court"? It resembles a constitutional court, but it is a constitutional court without a Constitution. "Constitutional court" is, however, not a protected trademark. There are very many different models, constitutional courts work differently and have different control competences. The European Court of Human Rights is a new species of constitutional court. With its final decision-making competence in human rights issues on the basis of the Convention, with a case-law comprising thousands of cases, with decisions influential in 46 European legal systems, the Court designs a certain human-rights-centered model of society and adapts it to new social

[72] *Voßkuhle*, Der Europäische Verfassungsgerichtsverbund, NVwZ 2010, 1.

[73] Hilary Term [2019] UKSC 2, 30.1.2019.

[74] *ECtHR (GC)*, 12.07.2013, no. 25424/09- Allen v. United Kingdom.

[75] Lord Wilson (f.n. 75), para. 85.

[76] See *Keller/ Kühne*, ZaöRV 2016, 245–307, *Walter* (1999), ibid. 31, 966 ff.

[77] See *Stone Sweet, Keller*, in: *Stone Sweet/Keller* (eds.), A Europe of Rights, 2008, 3, 13.

developments. Thus, even if it is no constitutional court for Europe, it assumes its function. It is more visible and its judgments have more long-lasting effects than many constitutional courts working on the basis of genuine constitutions.[78]

6 Crisis and Future

If we understand the Convention as a treaty based on a specific model of society, we cannot but see that this model is threatened. Even if the development has been going in one direction for a long time and the Court has been successful in contributing to the acceptance and implementation of common standards in Europe, there are increasing signs that there is no guarantee that such linear process will continue. There can be a turn-around leading in the opposite direction. Let's get back to the decisive year of 1979 and the path chosen at that time, not by consensus, but on the basis of a majority decision. In retrospect, we can discern the first fault lines already at that very point.[79]

Is the Convention a "living instrument"? No, say the critics. They point to the principles of democratic decision-making, and argue that judicial law-making without political debate is incompatible with real democracy. Another danger is that progress might be turned into regress – using the same methods, arguing on the basis of consensus, it is at least not theoretically excluded to lower the standards already achieved.

Do the vague terms of the Convention allow a broad interpretation? We recall the sentence of Fitzmaurice: "Within certain limits almost anything can colourably be represented as connected with or related to some other given thing". No, say the critics, a broad interpretation of the Convention is not justified even if it might make human rights protection more effective as it would inevitably restrict State sovereignty.

Is the "margin of appreciation" an instrument helping to accommodate a progressive jurisprudence with the principle of State sovereignty? Again, the critics' answer is in the negative based on the argument that the result when deciding on the basis of the margin of appreciation would not be foreseeable.

All these are signs of what has recently been called "principled resistance".[80] But "principled resistance" goes even further and calls into question the very model of society that is underlying the Convention. Breaking taboos has become fashionable not only in politics but also in law. Basic credos of human rights philosophy are attacked. This is true for the credo of freedom of opinion, based on the famous formula that all opinions, even those that "that offend, shock or disturb the State

---

[78] also*Keller/Kühne* (f.n. 78), 293.

[79] See *Breuer*, Principled Resistance Against ECtHR Judgments—A New Paradigm?, Springer 2019; *Popelier/Lambrecht/Lemmens* (eds.), Criticism of the European Court of Human Rights: Shifting the Convention System: Counter-dynamics at the National and EU Level, 2016.

[80] See *Breuer* (f.n. 81).

or any sector of the population"[81] have to be generally accepted. It is also true for the credo of freedom of religion based on tolerance and pluralism.[82] The Court increasingly sees itself in the defensive and has to draw red lines, especially with its case law on Article 18, the prohibition of the abuse of political power.[83] The Committee of Ministers has also taken a different course and in 2018 for the first time initiated the procedure under Article 46 (4) ECHR against Azerbaijan. This is referred to as the "nuclear option", a procedure in which the Court was called upon to determine whether a breach of the Treaty continues even after the Court has handed down a judgment finding a violation.[84]

In fact, the European Court of Human Rights as the guardian of a human-rights-focused model of society is more than ever called upon to send out clear messages.

It seems as if debates about the dichotomy between State and society were being revived and, once again, undecided.[85] When the Convention was drafted, the ideological clash of two systems – the communist one and the liberal one – was already visible. The liberal States were keen to nail down the standards they considered to be essential. The dividing lines between the different systems were clear. After the fall of the wall there was hope the different systems might merge. This turned out to be an illusion. New dividing lines are to be seen.

The European Convention on Human Rights is not a Constitution. Still, it is meant to hold together what starts floating away in different directions.

---

[81] *ECtHR* (Fn. 60), para. 49.

[82] "As enshrined in Article 9, freedom of thought, conscience and religion is one of the foundations of a "democratic society" within the meaning of the Convention. This freedom is, in its religious dimension, one of the most vital elements that go to make up the identity of believers and their conception of life, but it is also a precious asset for atheists, agnostics, sceptics and the unconcerned. The pluralism indissociable from a democratic society, which has been dearly won over the centuries, depends on it. That freedom entails, inter alia, freedom to hold or not to hold religious beliefs and to practise or not to practise a religion" *ECtHR*, 25.05.1993, no. 14307/88 – Kokkinakis v. Greece, para 31.

[83] See *ECtHR*, 28.11.2017, no. 72508/13 - Merabishvili v. Georgia; *ECtHR*, 15.11.2018, no. 29580/12 – Navalnyy v. Russia.

[84] *Committee of Ministers*, Interim Resolution, 25.10.2017, Az. CM/ResDH (2017) 379; ECtHR, 29.05.2019, no. 15172/13– Ilgar Mammadov v. Azerbaijan.

[85] See *Voßkuhle*, in: *Stock/ Markschies/Hauer* (eds.), Zukunftsort: EUROPA 2015, 135.

The European Fundamental Rights' Protection System: The General Protection System—and the Specific Problem of the European Union Accession to the European Convention on Human Rights (The Lisbon Treaty and its Follow Up)

Jean-Paul Costa

1 A Foreword

First of all, I would like to express two feelings. The first one is a feeling of gratitude for having been invited to Japan in order to deliver lectures. I am very grateful towards the Faculty of Law of Ritsumeikan University, and particularly to Professor Masahisa Deguchi, who has conceived and organised my visit. My second feeling is pride. Indeed, I am proud to address this international and learned audience, with participants from Asian and European countries, and to give the so-called keynote speech. I measure this honor and shall do my best to be worth of it.

I add an observation. I am convinced that international comparisons, especially in the field of human rights, are extremely useful. World globalization is not only economic and commercial. It is also, and should be, legal and judicial. That is why I am glad to participate to this seminar.

My speech, after a short historical introduction, will be divided into three parts:

First, I shall give a general, wide description of the European system or systems of protection of fundamental rights.

Secondly I'll deal with the specific issue of the accession of the European Union to the European Convention on Human rights.

Thirdly and finally I would like to look forward to the European future, from the legal and political points of view.

J.-P. Costa (✉)
Former President of the European Court of Human Rights, Honorary President of the Foundation René Cassin-International Institute of Human rights, Paris, France

M. Deguchi and K. Yakushiji (eds.), *Europe and Asia as a Legal Area for Fundamental Rights*, https://doi.org/10.1007/978-981-19-7542-4_11

2 Introduction

For historical reasons, there are two main different Europe, as regards organization and also fundamental rights.

Since the beginning of the years 1950, two different legal and political European systems have been created and have developed:

On one hand, the "big" Europe: it started with the adoption of the Status of the Council of Europe, signed in London in May 1949, gathering at the beginning 10 States, with its seat in Strasbourg, France. It was having the long-term ambition to cover the whole European continent; the objective of the creation of the Council was rather political. The aim was to reunify the continent, which had been profoundly divided during the First and the Second World Wars, with as a consequence millions of dead and injured persons and huge material destructions. The main mottos were peace, the rule of law, and human rights.

However, due to the climate of the then Cold War, the Soviet Union, as well as the Eastern and Central European States, which were generally under the Moscow influence, decided not to join the system. It will not be before the fall of the Berlin Wall (November 1989) and the disappearance of the Soviet Union (at the end of 1991) that all those States progressively entered the Council of Europe, with the support of the traditional member countries of the organization.

On the other hand, it exists a "smaller" Europe: it started with the Paris Treaty in 1951, establishing the European coal and steel community (CECA), and gathering at the time just six States (Belgium, Germany, France, Italy, Luxembourg and the Netherlands, but not the United Kingdom, which joined in 1972 only), with its seat in Brussels, and the ambition to create a unified market, first by a coal and steel "pool», then later on, in the middle run, enlarging itself to the whole economy. The first and main objective was clearly economical, but not without a political hidden agenda, namely to foster the reconciliation of countries through economy, and economic integration. The CECA was followed and accompanied by the Common Market (set up by the Treaty of Rome in March 1957), and they eventually became the European Communities.

To be complete, three countries, not members of the European Union (but of the Council of Europe) compose another set, namely the European Free Trade Area or EFTA. They are Norway, Iceland and Liechtenstein. They themselves have a Court, the EFTA Court of Justice, also located in Luxemburg. With all respect, it plays a marginal role, due to the small number of cases it has to adjudicate, and to the fact that it inspires itself narrowly of the ECJ case-law. Therefore I will not insist on the EFTA Court.

Both main systems have gone on and grown up, parallelly, without formal connections between themselves. To give you just an example, the European Parliament, an E.U. important organ, sits in Strasbourg, but without any real link with the Council of Europe. The common feature of the history of the two main organizations has been a continuous geographical enlargement.

Currently, the first and eldest system is still based on the Council of Europe, but its member States are now 47 (instead of 10), covering practically all Europe, including countries such as the Russian Federation, some ex-members of the former Soviet Union, the Eastern and Central European States and Turkey, whilst the second system has changed its name. Its title is now the European Union (E.U.), with, instead of six, gathers 28 member States, now potentially 27, since the referendum in the UK in June 2016 gave a majority to the so-called Brexit, i.e. the decision to leave the European Union. As one knows, the concrete consequences of the Brexit are still subject to a negotiation process. All the 27 countries are also members of the Council of Europe, but 20 States of the latter are not members of the E.U. Those 20 include the Russian Federation, Turkey, Ukraine, Norway, Switzerland...and some other States, including of course the UK.

Later on I will add a few sentences about Brexit.

3 The Global Protection of Fundamental Rights in Europe

1. The necessity to protect rights and freedoms in Europe appeared since the beginning as a priority of the young Council of Europe. The adoption by the United Nations, as early as in December 1948, of the Universal Declaration of Human rights, an extremely important instrument—even if with no legal binding effect—has obviously had a strong influence over the young Council of Europe organization. The idea was indeed to adopt at a regional level a system of protection inspired by the world-wide Declaration and it started with the European continent. Let me recall that a man, René Cassin, was one of the main darters of the Universal Declaration, before becoming in 1959 the First French judge, and in 1965 the first French President of the European Court of Human rights. In 1968, Cassin was granted the Nobel Prize for Peace, and in the following year he created the International Institute of Human Rights, a training and research institution, which I am the President of.

In fact, a treaty was rapidly drafted within the Council of Europe, and signed in November, 1950, namely the Convention for the protection of human rights and fundamental freedoms, more commonly titled the European Convention on Human rights (hereinafter "the Convention"). It was the first instrument elaborated within the Council of Europe. At the material time, two States, the United Kingdom and France, took an especially active part in the drafting of the Convention.

In the following decades, other regional and subregional instruments were adopted, in America, Africa, the Arab World or south-East Asia.

The European Convention, as an international treaty, has a double character and content. It is both a catalog of rights, principally civil and economic rights, which the States parties to the Convention undertake to guarantee to the persons within their jurisdiction, and a judicial, binding mechanism. This one has changed several times in its organization since its setting up. The changes have been brought by the means of several amendments to the Convention (14 in force), adopted by the member States.

Fundamentally, the mechanism is now consisting of a supranational tribunal, the European Court of Human rights ("the ECHR"), created by the Convention itself, which is unique and permanent. It is located in Strasbourg, with 47 States (or High contracting parties), and 47 Judges. The judges, working full-time and residing in Strasbourg, are appointed according to a complex mechanism. Each member country submits a list of three candidates, men and women, to the Parliamentary Assembly of the Council of Europe, which after having heard the candidates, elects one out of the three by secret ballot, for a term which is presently a 9-year, non-renewable term.

Two main other Council of Europe organs take a part in this system of protection: the Parliamentary Assembly, which elects the Judges, and also adopts important soft law instruments, and the Committee of Ministers, which supervises the execution of the Court's judgments; without forgetting the Secretary General of the Council. According to the Convention, the persons living in Europe have a right of individual petition before the Court, against each and every of the 47 States. Some inter-State cases also exist; they are very few; however they are of an outstanding importance, legally and politically. But the normal procedure is the right of individual petition, or application. The States always constitute the defending party. The judgments of the Strasbourg Court are obligatory and legally binding. The number of cases has enormously increased with the lapse of time. In the current years, more than 50,000 new applications are sent each year to the Registry; but a large majority of them are rejected by the court as inadmissible, for various legal reasons.

2. At the level of the European Union ("the E.U."), the initial idea was not at all to protect fundamental rights. And the Communities or E. U. treaties had no provisions specifically relevant as regards human rights.

Nonetheless, it is true that, since the first period, a judicial mechanism had been put into force, namely the Court of Justice, located in Luxembourg, currently called the European Court of Justice, or ECJ (with 28 Judges and 11 advocate generals). The judges and Advocate Generals are directly appointed by the member countries.

Another court, the Tribunal of the E.U., is subordinate to the E.C., with a specific jurisdiction. It is composed of 44 Judges, with no Advocate Generals. Until 2016, there was also a Tribunal of the Civil service of the E.U. But it disappeared last year; its competences were then transferred to the Tribunal.

In reality, the original and still principal task of the ECJ has been to protect the law of the E. U., and to harmonize the economic, social and commercial regulation of the Common market. This is mainly achieved through the procedure called preliminary ruling: whenever a piece of European legislation is challenged or must be interpreted during the process of a trial before a national court, because this has an influence on the outcome of the litigation, the domestic judges may (and in some cases have to) send the question in debate to the ECJ, which settles the question and refers it back to the domestic court (which is bound by the ECJ's answer).

Progressively, since the beginning of the 70ies, the case-law of the ECJ has introduced and developed the idea that it had to protect some fundamental legal principles of the E.U., including the protection of human rights, which belong to the common constitutional traditions of its member States or to the human rights treaties to which they are parties, including (mainly) the European Convention on Human rights itself and its case law. This is facilitated by the fact that each Member State, individually, is also a member party to the Convention.

Moreover, the European legislation, as it is produced by the E.U. treaties and their bodies (the Council, the European Parliament, and the European Commission) has extended its scope, no longer merely to economic and financial matters, but also to political, new fields, such as security, justice, asylum right, immigration rights etc. The result is that more and more fundamental rights may be breached by the decisions made by the E.U., obliging the ECJ. to more apply the fundamental legal principles.

4 The Problem of a Unique or at Least Unified European Protection of Fundamental Rights

Both courts, the ECJ and the ECHR, have made efforts to make their respective case laws converge, when interpreting the Convention and/or the "fundamental legal principles" of the E.U. This is not at all a formal obligation, rather a wise way of avoiding contradictions and better protecting the rights and freedoms of the European citizens, at least of the ones living in the 28 (or 27 after the Brexit vote) States belonging to both the E.U. and the Council of Europe. This is achieved by the watch and knowledge of their respective case-laws, and by a deliberate intention, and in most of the cases convergence does exist (but not always).

Nevertheless, in order to strengthen and unify (or at least more formally harmonize) the protection, three avenues have been explored in the last twenty years:

4.1 The First Attempt of Having the European Communities Becoming a High Contracting Party to the Convention

This attempt, probably premature, did fail. Actually, the Commission and the Council, in 1994, requested the opinion of the Court of Justice in Luxembourg about the legal feasibility of such an important political and legal move. However, in March 1996, the opinion provided by that Court resulted as negative. Its legal reasoning was based on the fact that the then Communities had no competence, under international law and their own status, to become a party to an international treaty such as the Convention.

4.2 The European Charter of Fundamental Rights ("the Charter")

This new instrument was drafted at the end of the 1990ies, within the E.U. The objective was to adopt a new catalog of fundamental rights, applicable to the E.U. countries and inside the E.U. organs, It is more or less similar in its content to the Convention, but a little wider (for instance, by the inclusion in the text of some social rights, not explicitly guaranteed under the Convention—they are protected under another Council of Europe instrument, the European social Charter, signed in 1961); and also more modern (for instance, by the introduction of some "new" rights, such as the rights in relation with Information technology or new technologies at large, or bioethics). Obviously, the 1950 Convention could not foresee technological or societal changes due to take piece fifty years after. The Charter was signed and proclaimed in December, 2000 at the European Summit in Nice, but without any legal binding effect at that time. Anyway it started to influence both the European Union and the Strasbourg court itself (by example in the case of transsexuals: *Christine Goodwin and others v.UK*, 2002).

4.3 The Lisbon Treaty

It is also a treaty of the E.U, the most recent for the time being. It was drafted in the years 2008–2009, after the failure in 2005 of the draft European Constitutional Treaty, and it entered into force on 1 December 2009.

It has had, in the field of human rights hereto concerned, two major effects: first, it gives a legal binding force to the Charter; and secondly it provides for the adhesion or accession of the E.U. to the Convention (the text of its Article 7 seems very clear "The Union shall accede to the European Convention on Human rights"). It is really an obligation.

Why is it so? What is the rationale of the accession?

To strengthen the protection of all European citizens, to avoid any contradiction when interpreting the Charter and the Convention—two instruments that are close, but different, —finally in order to get a unique, harmonized interpretation of Human rights in Europe. This was already the scope of the project in 1994–1996; the lack of competence founding the 1996 opinion is no longer an obstacle, due to the ulterior changes in the European treaties. It has to be reminded that, without a formal accession of the E.U., as such, to the Convention, any petition against the Union or its organs before the Strasbourg Court is rejected as inadmissible *ratione personae* under international law, especially under the Vienna Convention on the law of treaties. Even, if an individual challenges before the Strasbourg Court a decision of a State party to the Convention, and if this decision has been made following a compulsory ruling of the E.U., the application is in principle ill-founded. This has been ruled out several times by the ECHR case-law, by example in the famous judgment of 2005,

Bosphorus v. Ireland, and recalled, a contrario, in a judgment of 2012, *Michaud v. France*. However, the legal reasoning of the Court in Strasbourg is based on a presumption of "equivalent protection" under the E.U. legal system, a presumption which is rebuttable and can be rebutted in some concrete circumstances, due to a manifest lack or insufficiency of protection.

Unfortunately, the accession process- supposedly transforming the E.U. in a 48th high contracting party to the Convention—has started slowly, and eventually was stopped.

After lengthy negotiations following the entry into force of the Lisbon Treaty, a draft agreement between the Council of Europe and the E.U. was finally signed in April 2013 (more than three years after the entry into force of the Lisbon Treaty) in order to make the accession effective; but it had to be submitted for legal advice to the ECJ. And in December 2014 the ECJ, by its advisory opinion, raised several objections to the draft agreement and finally gave a negative advice to the acceptance of it, and to the accession itself. It is a somewhat surprising outcome, notably because the conclusions on the case of the ECJ's Advocate General, Ms Julian Kokott (German), expressed in June 2014, were in favor of a positive answer of the Court (with some reservations). Admittedly, an Advocate General's opinion is not binding, but is usually very influential.

5 The Possible Prospect

For the time being at least, the accession process of the E.U. to the Convention seems blocked. Admittedly, it's possible to imagine in the future another, revised agreement, able to overcome the ECJ Judges' objections (which are perhaps more psychological than purely legal…). But Europe is facing a period of doubt and skepticism, and the accession, despite the clear provisions of the Lisbon Treaty, seems not any more a priority for European leaders and decision-makers.

Some member States of the ECHR. or their supreme courts are rather critical, or even hostile, towards certain judgments of the ECHR. To give you just an example, by the *Hirst v. UK* judgment of 2005, several times confirmed by the Court, for instance by *Scoppola v. Italy* (2009), the Court considered as a violation of the Convention, not any prohibition of the right of vote of detainees, but a blanket (i.e.) an absolute prohibition of this right. Still U.K. and other States such as Russia want to maintain an absolute prohibition.

What is worse is that some countries which dislike a judgment of the Court contrary to an Act of their Parliament, or to a decision of a superior national court, despite the efforts of the Committee of Ministers of the Council of Europe, refuse to abide by the judgment and to execute it, which is discouraging, and could have a contagious effect towards other States.

Insofar as the ECJ is concerned, the problem exists much less. The main reason is that the most frequent way of making recourse to Luxembourg, as already said, is that a national judge sends a request for preliminary ruling. Logically, this judge will eventually follow the ECJ's opinion.

Is the current situation a desperate one? Not completely.

As regards the relationship between the ECHR and the ECJ, both Courts are still striving to avoid the worst risks of contradiction between themselves.

Moreover, it would be possible to the ECHR to exert a stricter judicial review over the decisions made by the organs of the E.U. Notions like equivalent protection, rebuttable presumption or manifestly insufficient protection are flexible and depend on Strasbourg Court's own appreciation.

Furthermore, as a follow up of the Brighton conference on the future of the ECHR, which took place in 2012, two new Protocols to the Convention, n° 15 and n° 16, were signed. They are not yet in force, but they contain interesting reforms. Among other provisions, the former decides the introduction of the Preamble to the convention of the principles of subsidiarity and of the national margin of appreciation, thus reminding the Court about its judicial obligations. And the latter creates an optional mechanism, somehow analogous to the preliminary ruling, enabling the superior domestic courts to send a request for advisory opinion to the ECHR, not binding but very influential; the aim is double: to prevent useless ill-founded applications to Strasbourg, and to harmonize the case-law in the States parties to the Convention.

As regards now the relations between States and the two courts, judicial diplomacy—a term which I was a user of when President of the ECHR- is more necessary. Misunderstandings maybe, and have often been, avoided by establishing a dialog with the national stakeholders (the courts and the political bodies).

However, the situation generated at the level of the E.U. by the *Brexit* decision is very worrying. With the only exception of Greece, that left the Council of Europe between 1967 and 1974, during the dictatorship of the Colonels, no State has abandoned the Council or the E.U. in the past. The British popular decision, which reflects a deep distrust of the people towards the European institutions (but also perhaps towards the elites), might inspire other nations, and will anyway not facilitate the protection of fundamental rights at European level. There are two main dangers: within the E.U., the risk is to have other countries, in particular those having joined the organization more recently, drawing argument from the Brexit to decide to do the same, through a referendum or not. Within the Council of Europe, the risk is that countries often condemned by the Strasbourg Court (such as Turkey or Russia) decide to apply a "leave" decision to the Council. I simply mention that the risks may even be double. For instance, a reestablishment of the death penalty in Turkey should lead to a frontal conflict with both the E.U., to prevent Turkey's accession, and the Council of Europe, to expose Turkey to a possible exclusion.

As a **conclusion**, I should say that it is very desirable that in the middle term, on one hand the Lisbon Treaty be finally implemented, which means the accession of the European Union to the Convention; and on the other hand the legal/political construction of Europe be resumed.

The main obstacles are not technical, but political. For instance, the development of the plague of *terrorism* has spread over the continent fear, the need for safety more than for freedom, and a general spirit of nationalism and populism. It is of course the duty of the States to protect their populations and to fight against terrorism, which constitutes a terrible violation of human rights; but one of the traps of the terrorists consists of obliging the States to put aside the usual tools of democratic societies and make recourse to exceptional ways of action. This is dangerous and requires wide changes and a profound reflection in Europe and in the whole World.

Thank you very much for your attention.

Jean-Paul Costa, 9 January 2017

Jean-Paul Costa, a French national, is a former Judge (1998-2006), and President (January 2007–November 2011), of the European Court of Human Rights. He is right now President of the International Institute of Human rights (founded by René Cassin).

Protection of Human Rights by National and International Courts: A Comparison

Jean-Paul Costa

1 Introduction

The notion of human rights has become universally well-known in 1948, when the United Nations (created in October 1945) solemnly proclaimed the Universal Declaration of Human rights, eventually adopted by its General Assembly, in its meeting in Paris on 10 December 1948. The Declaration was drafted within the UN Commission of Human rights, presided by Ms Eleanor Roosevelt (the late President Franklin Roosevelt's widow); one of the most active drafters was the French René Cassin, who eventually was granted the Nobel Prize for Peace in 1968.

Of course, the very idea of human rights was not completely new. In some Western countries, the notion appeared beforehand. In England, the Magna Carta was granted by the King as early as in 1215; then the Habeas corpus law and the Bill or Rights were adopted in 1679 and 1689, respectively. In the United States of America, the Declaration of independence of 1776 (drafted mainly by Thomas Jefferson) insisted on the importance of the protection of human rights, which was confirmed after the 1787 Constitution by the first amendments to it in 1791, still in force; whilst in France the first piece of legislation—and the first symbolic political act—of the newborn French Revolution was the Declaration of the rights of man and the citizen, adopted by the Constituante (the Constituting Assembly) in August 1789. But again, though important, those legal acts were far from being universal. And the emergence of the notion of human rights and freedoms or of fundamental rights at the more recent period finds its origins in the disaster of the Second World War, with its consequences

President of the René Cassin Foundation and former President of the European Court of Human Rights. This paper was lectured as Visiting Professor of Ritsumeikan University, Law Faculty on 23rd March 2017 in Kyoto.

J.-P. Costa (✉)
Former President of the European Court of Human Rights, Paris, France
e-mail: costajeanpaul3@gmail.com

M. Deguchi and K. Yakushiji (eds.), *Europe and Asia as a Legal Area for Fundamental Rights*, https://doi.org/10.1007/978-981-19-7542-4_12

in terms of millions of dead and injured persons, and of huge material destructions, without forgetting the high number of refugees and displaced populations.

Since that period, most national Constitutions in the world, and many international instruments, have defined and enumerated catalogs of human rights and freedoms, giving them a legal protection at either constitutional or international level. Moreover, the strong movement of decolonization and accession to independence, in the forties, fifties and six- ties, has contributed to the multiplication of States in the world (to give you an indication, there were 58 States within the UN Organization in 1948, when the Universal Declaration was adopted: they are 193 right now). Accordingly, the number of Constitutions has also considerably grown up, and the constitutional protection of human rights in the world has equally increased. And the impressive rise and development of international public law has led to many new tools of protection in the field of human rights.

However, such protection is completely effective only if legal mechanisms, especially judicial ones, guarantee the rights and freedoms against infringement by various stakeholders, including the States themselves and their agents. This will be more completely explained later on.

My lecture will describe first the national tools of protection (Constitutions and courts), secondly the international tools (Treaties and courts or quasi- jurisdictions), and finally will compare the two categories and analyze their combination, if any.

2 The National Tools of Protection

2.1 The Constitutions

They are the most important legal texts in a country, at the top of the "hierarchy of norms" (see the inventor of that legal doctrine, the famous Hans Kelsen from Austria, 1881–1973, and its books, particularly the "General theory of norms", a book published after his death in 1979).

A wide majority of States does have a written Constitution (the oldest one is the American Constitution, 1787); a few States, such as United Kingdom and Israel, have not: their constitutional traditions and principles, in this case, are of a customary character. This does not mean a lack of importance.

In particular, the hierarchy of norms is a common feature in practically all countries. As a matter of principle, the constitutional norms, either written or unwritten, are hierarchically superior to all the other legal norms, such as the Acts of Parliament or the administrative rules and regulations. Whenever two categories of legal norms are conflicting between them, the superior shall prevail.

Sometimes, there is coexistence of written provisions and of unwritten principles. By example, in my own country, France, the present Constitution dates back to 1958 (the "Fifth Republic"). The constitutional lawyers utilize often the notion of "block of constitutionality", composed of the articles of the current Constitution, of some other older written provisions, including the 1789 Declaration as well as the Preamble to the 1946 Constitution, and some unwritten fundamental principles. All of those rights have a constitutional value, and a high proportion of them deal with human rights. This means that human rights are provided for and guaranteed at a constitutional level.

Most Constitutions, at least since the end of World War II, contain a list of fundamental rights, which belong to the people. That is the case, for instance, for Japan, where more than 30 articles of the 1946 Constitution deal with Human rights and their protection.

2.2 *The National Courts*

Every country has a specific judicial system.

Sometimes, the courts belong to a unique category, and they have jurisdiction for disputes between private individuals and for disputes between private persons and public powers as well (for instance, United States, UK, "common law" countries, Japan…).

In other cases, the judicial system is dual or dualistic, with "ordinary courts" on one hand and administrative courts on the other hand (for instance, France, Belgium, Italy, and many European States, the so-called "continental law" countries).

Sometimes, the structure of the judicial system is more complex. For instance, in Germany, they are five orders of jurisdictions. Another element of complexity affecting the judicial organization is connected with federalism. Many countries in the world are Federal States (opposed to unitary States). They do not constitute the majority but many very populated countries, such as India, the United States, Brazil, Mexico, the Russian Federation, Germany, are federal. This means that there are usually two sets of judicial bodies and of judicial hierarchy, at the level of the States composing the Federation (such as the Lander in Germany or the cantons in Switzerland) and at the level of the Federation itself.

In all hypotheses, usually, those tribunals have no competence or jurisdiction to review the conformity of the legislation with the Constitution: the result is, or was, the sovereignty of the legislation and of the Parliament.

On the other hand, mainly since the end of the First World War, and even more after 1945, there appeared Constitutional courts, established with the special aim, among other tasks, of reviewing whether the legislation adopted by Parliament is in conformity with the Constitution, or not. If not, the acts of Parliament are or become invalid: they are either quashed or simply put aside and anyhow not enforceable.

Many examples can be given of such Courts. The oldest one is the Supreme Court of the United States, created by the 1787 Constitution; its role in the sense of a constitutional review dates back to its famous judgment in the case of Marbury v. Madison in 1803.

Roughly, there are about one hundred Constitutional courts in the world. This is more than the majority of the current number of States members of the United

Nations. The most populated countries have got a constitutional court: China, India, the USA, Indonesia,

Brazil, Pakistan, Nigeria, Bangladesh, the Russian Federation, Japan…And most European countries, including Germany, France, Italy, or the UK as well.

This power of Constitutional courts puts an end to the sovereignty of the legislation and the Parliament, and ensures the primacy of the constitutional provisions, including the fundamental rights, whenever they are included in said provisions. In other words, the legislator must respect the fundamental rights.

3 The International Tools of Protection

Before the Universal Declaration of human rights, no real protection of human rights did exist at international level. Even the Declaration itself provides just an indirect protection, insofar as it has no legally binding effect. Its scope is rather political and moral.

3.1 The International Treaties

But, as a follow up, many **international treaties** have been drafted in the field of human rights, several of which have a binding effect.

Most of them are regional treaties: the European Convention on Human Rights (1950), the American Convention on Human rights (1959), the African Charter of Human and Peoples' rights (1986), the Arab Charter of Human rights (2004).

Some other treaties are worldwide, but they constitute "soft law" rather than binding instruments: for instance the UN Covenants on civil and political rights, and on economic, social and cultural rights (1966) both derived from the universal Declaration, or the UN Convention on the rights of the child (1990), and many others.

More precisely, such treaties may be binding at national level, depending on the law of each country; but they lack international courts able to protect and enforce them at international level. The dream of a World Court, shyly expressed by a few persons at the time of the drafting of the Universal Declaration, has never been made concrete. Actually, the International Court of Justice (ICJ) in The Hague is a worldwide Tribunal, and even is one the permanent organs of the United Nations. But its judicial activity is dedicated to conflicts between States, and not between people and States: furthermore, it is only indirectly and seldom that the ICJ touches upon human rights issues.

3.2 *The International Courts*

<u>**The international courts**</u> specialized in the protection of Human rights:

The oldest and most important is the European Court of human rights (ECHR), created by the European Convention (signed in 1950), which started its operations in 1959 and is located in Strasbourg, France. Other regional or subregional international courts are important, especially the Interamerican Court of Human rights, created by the American Convention: it started in 1979 and is located in San José, Costa Rica. One should also mention the African Court of human and peoples' rights, which sits in Arusha, Tanzania; and other mechanisms at a subregional level, including the Commission of human rights of ASEAN (ASEAN has ten member countries), and the future Arab court of human rights, under the aegis of the Arab League, which will sit in Bahrain. They are more embryos of international tribunals.

Moreover, the European Court of Justice (created in 1954 and located in Luxemburg), which functions within the European Union, ensures an important, complementary role of protection of human rights at the level of the European Union, notwithstanding the fact that it is not a truly specialized "human rights court".

Besides, some "quasi-courts" do exist, usually in the framework of the United Nations such as the important Committee of Human rights of the UN, or its Committee against torture, or the Committee of the rights of the child….

The difference is that whilst the Courts issue binding judgments that the States must abide by, the quasi-tribunals issue simply reports and recommendations (sometimes very influential, as instruments of "soft law", reflecting the interests of the international com- munity, but not binding stricto sensu). The States can and should implement those decisions, but legally they are not bound to do so.

4 Comparison and Combination of National and International Protections

4.1 *The Usual Process Before National Courts, Ordinary or Constitutional*

There are various ways and means of protecting human rights and fundamental freedoms at a national judicial level.

Before the judiciary as such, usually the way consists of pursuing the liability of the persons responsible of a breach of one's human rights. This liability can be pursued even against the State or the State's agents, either by a direct action in torts, or by challenging the legality of any administrative regulation on the basis of which the State's action has been undertaken.

Before the Constitutional courts, the ways are various as well. In some countries, there is a concrete or direct way of action, based on the argument that the State has directedly violated the human rights by its doings or its omissions. This is for instance the case in Germany with the Federal Constitutional Court in Karlsruhe.

More often, the proceeding will consist in an abstract constitutional review, based upon the alleged lack of conformity with the Constitution of a piece of legislation able by its application to violate the applicant's rights. The most common procedure is, like in the USA, to utilize the so-called exception procedure. If the Supreme Court does rule that the challenged legislation is unconstitutional, it will not be applied to the applicant, but on the basis of the principle of stare decisis (the precedent), it won't be applied either to any other person (or company) in the same situation. In reality, the legislation will be left out.

4.2 The Process Before International Courts

An important principle of international law is the principle of subsidiarity. Even if the international courts are willingly set up by the States—who thus accept the powers and role of the international machinery, this one remains subsidiary, i.e. the States' mechanism remains entitled to offer the primary guarantee and judicial protection to the individuals; the review by international courts is ultimate.

This is translated in procedural terms into the obligation for the applicant of exhausting domestic remedies. If an individual (or a legal person) does not provide the domestic system and its judiciary with a chance to redress the alleged violation of his or her human rights, the individual's complaints before the international court shall be rejected as inadmissible. Only in exceptional cases, when it's clear that the domestic remedies don't exist or are not effective, they are admissible. Normally, the recourse to the domestic system must be done first.

The importance of the subsidiarity principle cannot be under estimated. In the case of the European Convention on human rights, as a follow up to the Brighton high-level conference in 2012, a new Protocol (n°15) to the Convention —not yet in force-foresees that the subsidiarity principle (and the doctrine of the national margin of appreciation as well) will be introduced in the Preamble to the Convention, in order to oblige the Strasbourg court to practice a judicial restraint.

In terms of procedure, the most important and active international tribunal, in the field of human rights, is precisely the ECHR in Strasbourg. Its system of judicial protection lies on two pillars: the right of individual petition, which has become general and compulsory since 1998, and the obligatory character of the Court's judgments when they find a violation of the Convention by the defending State. The execution of the judgment, according to the Convention itself, is supervised by the Committee of Ministers of the Council of Europe.

Thus, admittedly subject to the respect of the exhaustion of domestic remedies (and to other procedural prerequisites), the protection by the ECHR of human rights, as they are guaranteed by the Convention, is rather simple. This explains the huge number of cases brought to Strasbourg (more than 50,000 each year!—but a wide proportion are inadmissible).

4.3 *The Effectiveness of the National Protection*

It very much depends on various possible situations and factors:

First of all, the existence of the rule of law in the specific country, and of a tradition or a culture of respect for the rule of law and of avoiding arbitrariness.

Another element is the existence there of effective remedies, and in particular of a judicial system independent, impartial, honest (the danger being corruption of the judges), efficient, which includes a reasonable delay in the adjudication of the cases.

René Cassin used to say that the rule of the right to a fair trial, as it is expressed in Article 6 of the European Convention on human rights, is crucial and central. No other right can be respected if the trail is unfair.

Finally, the possibility of a constitutional review of the legislation is also increasingly extremely important; otherwise the legislation could be enforced against freedom.

Sometimes, such possibility simply does not exist, like in France before 1958, or is not open to the ordinary citizen, like in France before 2010. This is why an advisory body such as the Venice Commission (which operates within the Council of Europe but has extended its competence to extra-Europeans countries), insists on the necessity of the rule of law and on the creation of an effective constitutional judicial review.

Facing all those criteria, the records of the various States (by example of the 47 members of the Council of Europe, under the European Convention on Human rights) are quite different one from each other.

4.4 *The Effectiveness of the International Protection*

As a matter of principle, this way of protecting human rights, even if subsidiary, is even better, since its aim is to correct the misgivings and shortcomings of the national protection. This is well reflected in the wording of Article 19 of the European Convention: "To ensure the observance of the engagements of the high contracting parties to the Convention and the Protocols thereof, there shall be set up a European Court of human rights". The overlook of the case-law of courts such as, by excellence, the Strasbourg, San Jose and Luxemburg Courts, shows that they have been very effective in protecting human rights and freedoms, even against the States, and very influential in shaping a continental or subregional legal order, in spite of several serious difficulties met in the past.

But some serious obstacles remain and hinder the effectiveness of the systems.

One should mention the lack of sufficient financial and human means compared with the big number and complexity of the cases. Also, the difficulty, at least in the case of Strasbourg and San José (the things are easier for the ECJ), to achieve a prompt and complete execution of judgments by the defending State, especially in sensitive trials, which take place more often than not. One may add the political skepticism, criticism and even open attacks from a few countries; criticism sometimes is expressed by domestic supreme and constitutional courts, hence the necessity of an international dialog between judges, an attitude that I qualified of "judicial diplomacy" when I was president of the ECHR.

A long-lasting obviously negative influence comes from the existence of situations amounting to potential or even real armed conflicts (look in Europe at the more or less frozen wars in some zones like in Cyprus, Transnistria, Chechnya, Nagorno Karabakh, Georgia, Ukraine…). They could revive, and in the meantime they don't facilitate the settlement of legal cases. The background is problematic.

A last element, which appeared some years ago, particularly with the World Trade center attempt in New York in 2001, and has spread over many parts of the world, is the terrorism phenomenon. Whilst the States are obliged to fight against these terrible violations of human rights, and to protect their populations from this plague, the danger still exists of sacrificing freedom for security's sake, and to endanger human rights.

4.5 The Combination Between National and International Protection

All in all, and I must be optimistic, in the last 30 or 40 years or so, there has been a sort of virtuous circle; I mean by that a positive interaction between national courts, including the constitutional one, and international courts.

Fundamental rights have been more and more guaranteed and protected—at least legally—, either at national level, thanks to their inclusion in the Constitutions and the appearance of constitutional Courts, or at international level, through international conventions and treaties and international Courts. It happens that an international catalog of hu man rights is very similar to a constitutional catalog. Both ways of protection add to each other, not without conflicts sometimes.

Politically democracy has globally improved, at least in some regions of the World, such as Latin America and Central and Eastern Europe and some parts of Africa, in spite of worrying recent shortcomings and ways backwards. And the link between democracy, the rule of law and human rights is quite strong.

In the more traditional democracies, the legal influence of a tribunal like the Strasbourg court or the Luxembourg court has spread over many national systems, thus promoting useful reforms, not only procedural, but also substantive. Reciprocally, the most "advanced" domestic courts have also influenced by their examples the international case-law, enabling it to benefit all countries concerned.

Admittedly, a mutual positive influence has not to be taken for granted and implies sometimes mutual concessions; but all in all, I repeat, convergence efforts have produced, even to an extent improvable, a win–win relationship.

However, things are not always that simple and positive. In theory like in practice, combination of national and international laws may be conflictual. In theory many legal systems refuse the superiority of the treaties over the constitutions and constitutional principles. Despite the point of view of Kelsen, who claimed the founding principle of international Law, Pacta sunt servanda, implies the primacy of the treaties, many Constitutions say the contrary. For instance, the French.

Constitution admits the primacy of the treaties over the legislation, but asserts the primacy of the Constitution over the treaties.

In practice, this controversy may have negative effects, whenever a country does not accept to implement an international judgment if the condition of the implementation is a change in the Constitution. Fortunately, examples also exist of a willing acceptance of such international ruling. Paradoxically, in some cases, legislation considered at international level as in conformity with the treaty (by example the European Convention), can even be afterwards quashed by the national Constitutional court. This happens, admittedly more seldom than the reverse.

5 As a Conclusion

I should simply say that the universal dimension of human rights is a relatively recent phenomenon, that their protection becomes more and more sophisticated, and finally more effective. But I make an important reservation, namely that the world has become increasingly dangerous and human rights unfriendly. The struggle between the threats and the efforts of protection may be permanent. However it is the duty of human rights defenders and lawyers to go on fighting against the threats and in favor of all means of protection.

Thank you very much for your attention.

Jean-Paul Costa

The European Court of Human Rights and the Courts of the High Contracting Parties—Specifically Regarding the Consequences of the Imminent Accession of the European Union to the European Convention on Human Rights

Birgit Daiber

1 Introduction

The relationship between a constitutional court and the ordinary, administrative, financial, social and labour courts (courts) contains certain particularities. By establishing the European Court of Human Rights (ECHR),[1] an international court to supervise the compliance with the European Convention on Human Rights,[2] the High Contracting Parties to the Convention set up a further court which has a special relationship with the courts of the High Contracting Parties.[3] This relationship I undertake to develop in the following. I will pursue this in three steps: Firstly, the direction from the ECHR to the courts is considered (2.). This is followed by the opposite view from the courts to the ECHR (3.). Finally there shall be a look at the consequences of the imminent accession of the European Union (EU) to the ECHR (4).

[1] Art. 19 et seqq. of the Convention for the Protection of Human Rights and Fundamental Freedoms as amended by Protocols No. 11 and No. 14. Articles without any further specification refer to the Convention.

[2] S. https://rm.coe.int/1680a2353d.

[3] Concerning the relationship between the ECHR and the German Federal Constitutional Court (Bundesverfassungsgericht – BVerfG) s. *O. Klein*, Straßburger Wolken am Karlsruher Himmel, Zum geänderten Verhältnis zwischen Bundesverfassungsgericht und Europäischem Gerichtshof für Menschenrechte seit 1998, Neue Zeitschrift für Verwaltungsrecht (NvwZ) 2010, p. 221 et seqq.

B. Daiber (✉)
Seoul National University, Seoul, South Korea
e-mail: bdaiber@snu.ac.kr

M. Deguchi and K. Yakushiji (eds.), *Europe and Asia as a Legal Area for Fundamental Rights*, https://doi.org/10.1007/978-981-19-7542-4_13

2 From the ECHR to the Courts

1. Judgments of the ECHR have an impact on the courts, because the ECHR revises judgments of these courts. It is competent to rule on Inter-State Cases opposing two High Contracting Parties[4] or on applications from any person, non-governmental organisation or group of individuals.[5] As the ECHR may only deal with a matter after all domestic remedies have been exhausted[6] and the High Contracting Parties have an obligation to provide access to a court,[7] it will normally deal with judgments of the courts of the High Contracting Parties when fulfilling its duty.

Judgments of the Court are binding.[8] But they are only declaratory in nature[9] and cannot set aside the revised judgment of the courts.[10] They can only state if a violation of at least one provision of the Convention by the High Contracting Party concerned took place or not. In case a violation of the Convention was found, the High Contraction Parties have discretion in assessing how to implement the judgment.[11]

---

[4] Art. 33.

[5] Art. 34.

[6] Art. 35.

[7] Art. 13.

[8] Art. 46 I.

[9] *J. Meyer-Ladewig*, EMRK, 3rd ed., Baden-Baden 2011, Art. 46 para. 23; *Chr. Grabenwarter/K. Pabel*, Europäische Menschenrechtskonvention, 5th ed., München et al. 2012, § 16 para. 3; *K. Rohleder*, Grundrechtsschutz im europäischen Mehrebenen-System Unter besonderer Berücksichtigung des Verhältnisses zwischen Bundesverfassungsgericht und Europäischem Gerichtshof für Menschenrechte, Baden-Baden 2009, p. 45; *A.-Chr. Zoellner*, Das Verhältnis von Bundesverfassungsgericht und Europäischem Gerichtshof für Menschenrechte Unter Berücksichtigung der Rolles des EuGH, Hamburg 2009, p. 94 et seq.; *Chr. Gusy*, Wirkungen der Rechtsprechung des Europäischen Gerichtshofs für Menschenrechte in Deutschland, Juristische Arbeitsblätter (JA) 2009, p. 406, 408; *J. Meyer-Ladewig/H. Petzold*, Die Bindung deutscher Gerichte an Urteile des EGMR, Neues aus Straßburg und Karlsruhe, Neue Juristische Wochenschrift (NJW) 2005, p. 15, 16; *W. Schaller*, Das Verhältnis von EMRK und deutscher Rechtsordnung vor und nach dem Beitritt der EU zur EMRK, Europarecht (EuR) 2006, p. 656, 658; *F. Tulkens*, La protection des droits fondamentaux avant et après l'adhésion de l'Union européenne à la Convention européenne des droits de l'homme: Le point de vue de la Cour européenne des droits de l'homme, in: J. Iliopoulos-Strangas/V. Pereira da Silva/M. Potacs (ed.), Der Beitritt der Europäischen Union zur EMRK - The Accession of the European Union to the ECHR - L'adhésion de l'Union Européenne à la CEDH, Die Auswirkung auf den Schutz der Grundrechte in Europa - The impact on the protection of fundamental rights in Europe - L'impact sur la protection des droits fondamentaux en Europe, Baden-Baden 2013, p. 159, 174.

[10] *J. Meyer-Ladewig* (fn. 9), Art. 46 para. 23; *Chr. Grabenwarter/K. Pabel* (fn. 9), § 16 para. 3; *I. Karper*, Reformen des Europäischen Gerichts- und Rechtsschutzsystems, Baden-Baden 2010, p. 181; *K. Rohleder* (fn. 9), p. 45; *A.-Chr. Zoellner* (fn. 9), p. 94 et seq.; *Chr. Gusy* (fn. 9), p. 408; *J. Meyer- Ladewig/H. Petzold* (fn. 9), p. 16; *R. Passos*, The Protection of Fundamental Rights in Europe before and after the Accession of the European Union to the European Convention on Human Rights: A View from the European Parliament, in: J. Iliopoulos-Strangas/V. Pereira da Silva/M. Potacs (ed.) (fn. 9), p. 125, 156; *W. Schaller* (fn. 9), p. 658; *F. Tulkens* (fn. 9), p. 174.

[11] *J. Meyer-Ladewig* (fn. 9), Art. 46 para. 25; *Chr. Grabenwarter/K. Pabel* (fn. 9), § 16 para. 3; *I. Karper* (fn. 10), p. 181; *Chr. Gusy* (fn. 9), p. 408; *F. Tulkens* (fn. 9), p. 174; *R. Uerpmann-Wittzack*, Rechtsfragen und Rechtsfolgen des Beitritts der Europäischen Union zur EMRK, EuR

2. As far as Germany is concerned, the courts have to take these decisions into account, as the German Federal Constitutional has stated in its Görgülü decision.[12] To explain this result of only having to take it into account, this Court relies on the level of the European Convention on Human Rights within the German legal order. As an international treaty entered into by Germany, the Convention needs the consent of the federal legislative bodies which is given by a federal statute.[13] For this reason, the German Federal Constitutional Court concludes that "within the German legal system, the European Convention on Human Rights and its protocols … have the status of a federal statute."[14] It follows that the courts—in relying on an ECHR judgment—may not violate "fundamental principles of the constitution."[15] Besides, the courts must confine themselves to the limits of their competences[16] and of "methodically justifiable interpretation."[17]

Of course, the German Federal Constitutional Court cannot reduce the binding force of an ECHR judgment *on* the Federal Republic of Germany. Based on a dualistic concept of the relationship between the international and the internal legal order,[18] the Court only rules on the (possible) impact of an ECHR judgment *within* the latter one. In limiting the possible effects of an ECHR judgment there, it accepts the risk that Germany could violate its international obligations stemming from the European Convention on Human Rights it has entered into when reducing the effect of an ECHR judgment *within* the internal legal order.

3. Comparing the ECHR to a Constitutional Court, it can be found that the Court is competent for applications by any person, like the German Federal Constitutional Court is, for example.[19] It also reviews court judgments only after the exhaustion

2012, Beiheft, p. 167, 177. S. also *K. Rohleder* (fn. 9), p. 51 et seqq.; *A.-Chr. Zoellner* (fn. 9), p. 104 et seqq.

[12] BVerfGE 111, 307, 315, 323 et seqq. Thereto s. *K. Rohleder* (fn. 9), p. 164 et seqq., 196 et seqq.; *A.-Chr. Zoellner* (fn. 9), p. 179 et seqq.; *L. Hummel*, Internationales Steuerrecht (IStR) 2005, p. 35 et seq.; *J. Meyer-Ladewig/ H. Petzold* (fn. 9); *M. Sachs*, Juristische Schulung (JuS) 2005, p. 164 et seqq. An English translation of the decision can be found here: http://www.gesetze-im-internet.de/englisch_gg/englisch_gg.html.

[13] Art. 59 II 2 of the Basic Law for the Federal Republic of Germany (Grundgesetz - GG). An English translation of the Basic Law (unfortunately not the current version) can be found here: http://www.gesetze-im-internet.de/englisch_gg/englisch_gg.html.

[14] BVerfGE 111, 307, 315, 317; 128, 326, 367. Concerning the status of the Convention within the German legal order s. also BVerfGE 120, 180, 200; *K. Rohleder* (fn. 9), p. 51 et seqq.; *A.-Chr. Zoellner* (fn. 9), p. 136 et seqq.

[15] BVerfGE 111, 307, 319, 323 et seq, 329.

[16] L.c., p. 323 et seq, 326 et seq.

[17] L.c., p. 323, 329.

[18] L.c., p. 318.

[19] Art. 93 I No. 4 a GG in connection with § 90 I of the Law on the German Federal Constitutional Court (Bundesverfassungsgerichtsgesetz – BVerfGG). An English translation of the BVerfGG can be found here: http://www.gesetze-iminternet.de/englisch_bverfgg/englisch_bverfgg.html.

of all available remedies.[20] And, finally, it also limits its review to compliance with human rights.[21]

On the other hand, the ECHR cannot set aside a judgment, like the German Federal Constitutional Court can,[22] for example. It also cannot claim supremacy *within* the legal order of the High Contracting Parties.

3 From the Courts to the ECHR

1. As far as the opposite view—not *to* the courts, but *from* the courts—is concerned, they have the possibility to directly contact the German Federal Constitutional Court in the German federal constitutional order. By introducing a concrete judicial review, the courts can stay proceedings before them in order to obtain a decision on the constitutionality of a federal statute by the German Federal Constitutional Court in cases where they deem this statute on which they have to base their decisions to be unconstitutional.[23]

The courts also have the possibility of directly contacting the European Court of Justice (ECJ), which rules on the EU legal order. Like the German Federal Constitutional Court, it can be requested by the courts to rule on the validity of acts of the institutions, bodies, offices or agencies of the Union.[24] In addition, the courts can also ask the ECJ to give a (preliminary) ruling on the interpretation of such acts or the EU Treaties themselves.[25] This possibility is linked to the necessity of an answer to that question for the proceedings before the courts.[26] It even turns into an obligation, if the decision of the courts cannot be challenged before a higher instance.[27]

2. Before the ECHR there exists no such procedure at the moment.[28] This can be explained on the one hand by the fact that this court does not have the power

---

[20] For the German Federal Constitutional Court s. § 93 II BVerfGG.

[21] For the constitutional complaint to the German Federal Constitutional Court s. Art. 93 I No. 4 a GG in connection with § 90 I BVerfGG. For the ECHR s. Art. 33 et seq.

[22] § 95 II BVerfGG.

[23] Art. 100 I GG.

[24] Art. 267 I lit. b 1. alternative of the Treaty on the Functioning of the European Union (TFEU). The English version of the Treaty can be found here: https://eur-lex.europa.eu/legal-content/EN/TXT/?uri=CELEX%3A02016E%2FTXT-20200301.

[25] Art. 267 I lit. a and b 2. alternative TFEU.

[26] Art. 267 II TFEU.

[27] Art. 267 III TFEU.

[28] After its entry into force, Protocol No. 16 (https://rm.coe.int/1680084832) empowers the ECHR to give advisory opinions on request of the courts of the High Contracting Parties (Art. 1). But these opinions will not be binding (Art. 5). Which courts are competent to ask for such an opinion will be decided by the respective High Contracting Party (Art. 10). The Protocol shall enter into force on the first day of the month following the expiration of a period of three months after the date on which ten High Contracting Parties have expressed their consent to be bound by the Protocol (Art. 8 I). A chart of signatures and ratifications can be found here: http://conventions.coe.int/Treaty/Commun/ChercheSig.asp?NT=214&CM=7&DF=22/01/2014&CL=ENG.

to declare a law null and void. For this reason, a decision by the ECHR would not change the situation before the courts. Even if the ECHR were to find a violation of the Convention by a statute which the courts have to apply in the case pending before them, this statute would be valid after such a decision and therefore would have to be applied. In this context such a procedure is not compulsory.

On the other hand, there is no need for a uniform interpretation.[29] On the contrary, Art. 53 of the Convention explicitly allows the High Contracting Parties to guarantee a higher level of human rights protection. Therefore the courts do not necessarily apply the Convention. They only have to ensure that they do not go below the minimum guarantees of the Convention. Under these conditions it is not necessary to stay a procedure before a court of the High Contracting Parties in order to ask the ECHR for a preliminary ruling.

4 Consequences of the Accession of the EU to the ECHR[30]

1. At the moment, the EU itself is not a High Contracting Party to the Convention, but all its Member States are. However, an accession of the EU and its predecessor has been discussed since decades. After an ECJ opinion of 28 March 1996 stating that at

[29] Concerning the uniform interpretation as principal aim of the preliminary ruling procedure s. ECJ, Opinion 1/09 of 8 March 2011, ECR 2011, p. I-1137, para. 83.

[30] Concerning this accession and its consequences s. *K. Rohleder* (fn. 9), p. 385 et seqq.; *Chr. Schmidt*, Grund- und Menschenrechte in Europa, Das neue System des Grund- und Menschenrechtsschutzes in der Europäischen Union nach dem Inkrafttreten des Vertrags von Lissabon und dem Beitritt der Union zur EMRK, Baden-Baden 2013, p. 63 et seqq.; *B. Schneiders*, Die Grundrechte der EU und die EMRK, Das Verhältnis zwischen ungeschriebenen Grundrechten, Grundrechtecharta und Europäischer Menschenrechtskonvention, Baden-Baden 2010, p. 248 et seqq.; *J. Spiekermann*, Die Folgen des Beitritts der EU zur EMRK für das Verhältnis des EuGH zum EGMR und den damit einhergehenden Individualrechtsschutz, 2013, p. 7 et seqq.; *J. Ph. Terhechte*, Konstitutionalisierung und Normativität der europäischen Grundrechte, Tübingen 2011, p. 81 et seqq.; *J. Vondung*, Die Architektur des europäischen Grundrechtsschutzes nach dem Beitritt der EU zur EMRK, Tübingen 2012; *A.-Chr. Zoellner* (fn. 9), p. 252 et seqq.; *H.-P. Folz*, Der Beitritt der Europäischen Union zur Europäischen Menschenrechtskonvention: das Ende einer langen Reise und die Folgen, in: Chr. Vedder (ed.), Völkerrecht 2012, Richterliche Praxis und politische Realität, Beiträge zum 37. Österreichischen Völkerrechtstag 2012, Frankfurt a.M. 2013, p. 105 et seqq.; *C. Grewe*, Beitritt der EU zur EMRK und ZP 14: Wirksame Durchsetzung einer gesamteuropäischen Grundrechteverfassung?, EuR 2012, p. 285 et seqq.; *O. J. Gstrein*, Der geeinte

that moment the Treaties did not provide a competence for such an accession,[31] such a competence has been included in the Treaty of Lisbon, which entered into force on 1 December 2009. Art. 6 II 1 of the Treaty on European Union (TEU)[32] therefore now reads: The Union shall accede to the European Convention for the Protection of Human Rights and Fundamental Freedoms.[33]

As an international agreement concluded by the Union, the Convention will be binding both upon the institutions of the Union and on its Member States.[34] It becomes an integral part of the EU legal order.[35] As such it takes part in the precedence

Menschenrechtsschutz im Europa der Vielfalt-Zum Verhältnis der Luxemburger und Straßburger Gerichtshöfe nach Beitritt der Europäischen Union zur Europäischen Menschenrechtskonvention, Zeitschrift für europarechtliche Studien (ZEuS) 2012, p. 445 et seqq.; *A. M. Guerra Martins*, A Portuguese Perspective on the Accesion of the European Union to the European Convention on Human Rights, in: J. Iliopoulos-Strangas/V. Pereira da Silva/M. Potacs (ed.) (fn. 9), pp. 201, 219 et seqq.; *G. Heißl*, Happy End einer unendlichen Geschichte?, Der Beitritt der EU zur EMRK und seine Auswirkungen auf Österreich, in: M. Holoubek/A. Martin/St. Schwarzer (ed.), Die Zukunft der Verfassung – Die Verfassung der Zukunft?, Festschrift für Karl Korinek zum 70. Geburtstag, Wien 2010, p. 129 et seqq.; *E. Klein*, Das Verhältnis des Europäischen Gerichtshofs zum Europäischen Gerichtshof für Menschenrechte, in: D. Merten/H.-J. Papier (ed.), Handbuch der Grundrechte in Deutschland und Europa, vol. VI/1, § 167, para. 65 et seqq.; *Chr. Kohler/L. Malferrari*, Um letzte und vorletzte Worte: Zum geplanten Zusammenwirken von EGMR und EuGH nach dem Beitritt der EU zur EMRK, Europäische Zeitschrift für Wirtschaftsrecht (EuZW) 2011, p. 849 et seq.; *S. Leutheusser- Schnarrenberger*, Der Beitritt der EU zur EMRK: Eine schier unendliche Geschichte, in: Chr. Hohmann- Dennhardt/P. Masuch/M, Villiger (ed.), Grundrechte und Solidarität, Durchsetzung und Verfahren, Festschrift für Renate Jaeger, Kehl 2011, p. 135 et seqq.; *O. Mader*, Beitritt der EU zum Europarat, Institutionelle Aspekte der Entwicklung des europäischen Grundrechtsschutzes nach Lissabon, Archiv des Völkerrechts (AVR) 2011, p. 435 et seqq.; *W. Obwexer*, Der Beitritt der EU zur EMRK: Rechtsgrundlagen, Rechtsfragen und Rechtsfolgen, EuR 2012, p. 115 et seqq.; *E. Pache/F. Rösch*, Die neue Grundrechtsordnung der EU nach dem Vertrag von Lissabon, EuR 2009, p. 769, 779 et seqq.; *E. Pache/F. Rösch*, Die Grundrechte der EU nach Lissabon, Europäisches Wirtschafts- und Steuerrecht (EWS) 2009, p. 393, 398 et seqq.; *R. Passos* (fn. 10), p. 127 et seqq.; *O. Philipp*, EU-Beitritt zur Europäischen Konvention zum Schutz der Menschenrechte und Grundfreiheiten, EuZW 2010, p. 485; *F. de Quadros*, Rapport introductif: La protection des droits fondamentaux en Europe avant et après l 'adhésion de l'Union européenne à la Convention européenne des droits des l 'homme, in: J. Iliopoulos-Strangas/V. Pereira da Silva/M. Potacs (ed.) (fn. 9), pp. 111, 119 et seqq.; *N. Reich*, Beitritt der EU zur EMRK – Gefahr für das Verwerfungsmonopol des EuGH?, EuZW 2010, p. 641; *G. Ress*, Konsequenzen des Beitritts der EU zur EMRK, EuZW 2010, p. 841; *Th. Schilling*, Der Beitritt der EU zur EMRK, Verhandlungen und Modalitäten, Fast eine Polemik, Humboldt Forum Recht (HFR) 2011, p. 83 et seqq.; *V. Skouris*, Aspekte des Beitritts der Europäischen Union zur Europäischen Konvention für Menschenrechte, in: P.-Chr. Müller-Graff/St. Schmahl/V. Skouris (ed.), Europäisches Recht zwischen Bewährung und Wandel, Festschrift für Dieter H. Scheuing, Baden-Baden 2011, p. 208 et seqq.; *F. Tulkens* (fn. 9), p. 159 et seqq.; *R. Uerpmann-Wittzack* (fn. 11). S. also *S. Stock*, Der Beitritt der Europäischen Union zur Europäischen Menschenrechtskonvention als Gemischtes Abkommen?, Hamburg 2010.

[31] Opinion 2/94, ECR 1996, p. I-1759, para. 36.

[32] The English version of the Treaty can also be found here: https://eur-lex.europa.eu/legal-content/EN/TXT/?uri=CELEX%3A12008M.

[33] For the procedure to be followed s. Art. 218 TFEU, especially para. 6 subpara. 2 s. 1 lit. a) ii) and para. 8 subpara. 2 s. 2.

[34] Art. 216 II TFEU.

[35] ECJ, Judgment of 30 April 1974 in the case 181/73 (Haegeman), ECR 1974, p. 449, para. 5.

of the EU legal order as compared to the legal order—including the constitutional order[36]—of the Member States.[37,38]

This precedence has also been acknowledged by the German Federal Constitutional Court as the federal constitutional court of one of the EU Member States—but only in principle, because this court does not grant EU law precedence over the "inviolable core content of the constitutional identity of the Basic Law."[39]

After the accession of the EU to the Convention, the latter—as integral part of the EU legal order—will share this position of EU law within Germany. It will no longer be limited to the rank of a federal statute. This means that the basis on which the Görgülü decision of the German Constitutional Court[40] is founded will not—after the accession—be valid any more. The respective limitations enounced in the Görgülü decision will then change to those which apply to EU law.

2. This effect could be restricted to situations within the scope of application of EU law.[41]

a. Such a restriction would apply if the agreement on the accession of the EU to the Convention were a so-called mixed agreement. Such mixed agreements are concluded by the EU and its Member States on the one hand and a third party on the other hand if the EU does not have an external competence to enter into international obligations on each field covered by the agreement.[42] In such a case

---

[36] ECJ, Judgment of 17 December 1970 in the case 11/70 (Internationale Handelsgesellschaft), ECR 1970, p. 1125, para. 3.

[37] ECJ, Judgment of 15 July 1964 in the case 6/64 (Costa./.E.N.E.L.), ECR 1964, p. 585.

[38] Equally *K. Rohleder* (fn. 9), p. 411; *B. Schneiders* (fn. 30), p. 256; *S. Stock* (fn. 30), p. 207; *S. Bartole*, The Adhesion of the European Union to the European Convention for the Protection of Human Rights and Fundamental Freedoms: the Italian Perspective, in J. Iliopoulos-Strangas/V. Pereira da Silva/M. Potacs (ed.) (fn. 9), p. 193, 197.; *P. Gragl*, Der rechtliche Status der EMRK innerhalb des Unionsrechts, Zu den Auswirkungen auf die Rechtsautonomie der Europäischen Union nach ihrem Beitritt zur EMRK, ZEuS 2011, p. 409, 421; *E. Klein* (fn. 30). para. 68; *W. Obwexer* (fn. 30), p. 143; *W. Weiß*, Grundrechtsquellen im Verfassungsvertrag, ZEuS 2005, p. 323, 349 et seq. Differing *I. Karper* (fn.10), p. 181.

[39] BVerfGE 123, 267, 347, 353 et seq. An English translation of the judgment can be found here: http://www.bundesverfassungsgericht.de/entscheidungen/es20090630_2bve000208en.html. S. also BVerfGE 37, 271, 279 et seq.; 58, 1, 40; 73, 339, 376 et seq.

[40] S. above (2.2.)

[41] Supporting this *K. Rohleder* (fn. 9), pp. 398, 411 et seq.; *Chr. Schmidt* (fn. 30), p. 90; *B. Schneiders* (fn. 30), p. 256 et seqq.; *A.-Chr. Zoellner* (fn. 9), p. 255; *R. Arnold*, Der Schutz der Grundrechte in Europa vor und nach dem Beitritt der Europäischen Union zur EMRK: Auswirkungen auf Deutschland, in: J. Iliopoulos-Strangas/V. Pereira da Silva/M. Potacs (ed.) (fn. 9), p. 179, 188; *E. Klein* (fn. 30), para. 68; *W. Obwexer* (fn. 30), p. 119, 126 et seq.; *W. Schaller* (fn. 9), p. 663 et seqq. S. also *S. Stock* (fn. 30), p. 207, and *R. Uerpmann-Wittzack* (fn. 11), p. 176, 183, who act on the assumption of a mixed agreement. Tends to differ *W. Weiß* (fn. 38), p. 350 et seqq. S. also *S. Bartole*, (fn. 38), p. 198 et seq.

[42] *K. Schmalenbach*, in: Chr. Calliess/M. Ruffert (ed.), EUV/AEUV, 4th ed. 2011, Art. 216 AEUV para. 23.

only the provisions based on an external competence of the EU become an integral part of the EU legal order.[43]

As already mentioned,[44] the EU—since the entry into force of the Lisbon Treaty—has an (external) competence to accede to the Convention. Therefore there is no need for a mixed agreement and consequently the draft agreement on the accession is only conceived as an agreement between the High Contracting Parties to the Convention and the European Union.[45,46] As a result, a restriction of the Convention becoming an integral part of the EU legal order and therefore participating in its precedence over national law cannot be based on the fact that the agreement on the accession of the EU to the Convention is a mixed agreement.

b. Another reason for a limitation of the effect of the Convention within the Member States' legal order could be that the fundamental rights, as guaranteed by the European Convention for the Protection of Human Rights and Fundamental Freedoms and as they result from the constitutional traditions common to the Member States, which constitute general principles of the Union's law, also only apply to the Member States within the scope of application of EU law.[47] Enounced now in Art. 6 III TEU, fundamental rights as general principles of EU law were developed by the jurisprudence of the ECJ.[48] As a justification, the Court could rely on (the predecessor of) Art. 19 para. 1 subpara. 1 s. 2 TEU, which assigns to the Court the task of ensuring that in the interpretation and application of the Treaties the law is observed.[49] It is therefore the restricted role of the Court—to ensure the observation of the law only *in the application of the Treaties*—that causes the limitation of the binding force of fundamental rights as general principles of EU law on the Member States to the scope of application of EU law. The Convention, however, is not developed by the Court and hence not limited by the Court's responsibilities. For this reason this restriction of binding force of fundamental rights on the Member States to the scope of application of EU law does not equally apply to the Convention.

c. However the third instrument to guarantee fundamental rights on the EU level—the Charter of Fundamental Rights (CFR)—is also addressed to the Member States

[43] *S. Vöneky/B. Beylage-Haarmann*, in: E. Grabitz/M. Hilf/M. Nettesheim (ed.), Das Recht der Europäischen Union, vol. I, Art. 216 AEUV para. 52. S. also *K. Schmalenbach* (fn. 42), Art. 216 AEUV para. 43.

[44] S. above p. 124 et seq(4.1.).

[45] https://search.coe.int/cm/Pages/result_details.aspx?ObjectId=09000016805c7cccEN.pdf p. 4 (Appendix 1). Thereto J. *Polakiewicz*, Der Abkommensentwurf über den Beitritt der Europäischen Union zur Europäischen Menschenrechtskonvention, Europäische Grundrechte-Zeitschrift (EuGRZ) 2013, p. 472 et seqq.

[46] Equally *H.-P. Folz* (fn. 30), p. 108; *P. Gragl* (fn. 38), p. 419; *W. Obwexer* (fn. 30), p. 144 et seq. In contrast in favour of a mixed agreement *S. Stock* (fn. 30), p. 191 et seqq., *O. Mader* (fn. 30), p. 439 et seq., and *R. Uerpmann-Wittzack* (fn. 11), p. 183.

[47] ECJ, Judgment of 18 June 1991 in the case C-260/89 (ERT), ECR 1991, p. I-2925, para. 42.

[48] Judgment of 12 November 1969 in the case 29/69 (Stauder), ECR 1969, p. 419, para. 7; Judgment of 17 December 1970 (fn. 36), para. 4; Judgment of 14 May 1974 in the case 4/73 (Nold), ECR 1974, p. 491, para. 13.

[49] *F. C. Mayer*, in: E. Grabitz/M. Hilf/M. Nettesheim (ed.) (fn. 43), Grundrechtsschutz und rechtsstaatliche Grundsätze, para. 1.

only when they are implementing Union law. But this is explicitly laid down in the Charter—in Art. 51 I 1 thereof. Hence, one should expect that there would be a similar provision for the Convention, if its scope of application were limited.

d. Such a limitation could derive from Art. 6 II 2 EUV, which states that the accession of the EU to the Convention shall not affect the Union's competences as defined in the Treaties.[50] But the wording of this provision—competences—causes doubts: The binding force of the Convention on the Member States constitutes an obligation by a material provision. That is not the same as giving the EU a competence to legislate. And the latter, in fact, should be avoided, as can be seen from the preparatory documents for the European Convention, which deliberated the predecessor of the aforementioned provision. By precluding the affection of the EU's competences it should be rather prevented that "a general competence of the Union on fundamental rights [would be established or that] ... "positive" obligations of the Union to take action to comply with the ... [Convention] would arise ... [beyond] the extent ... [beyond] which competences of the Union permitting such action exist under the Treaty".[51]

The fact that the Treaties do not define the scope of application of a provision when they exclude the affection of the Union's competences can finally be seen when having a look on the provisions concerning the Charter of Fundamental Rights, which has the same legal value as the Treaties:[52] On the one hand, Art. 6 para. 1 subpara. 2 TEU and Art. 51 II CFR exclude—like Art. 6 II 2 TEU—the extension of the competences of the Union as defined in the Treaties. On the other hand, Art. 51 I 1 CFR indicates that the provisions of the Charter are addressed to the Member States only when they are implementing Union law. If the former provisions already restricted the scope of application of the Charter to cases where the Member States implement EU law, the latter provision would be superfluous. Therefore it must be assumed that Art. 6 para. 1 subpara. 2 TEU, Art. 51 II CFR and Art. 6 II 2 mean something different than limiting the scope of application to cases where the Member States implement EU law. Art. 6 II 2 FEU can hence not be regarded as limiting the binding force of the Convention on the Member States to cases within the scope of application of the Union's law.

e. A restriction could further derive from the Protocol (No 8) relating to Art. 6 II TEU on the accession of the Union to the European Convention on the Protection of Human Rights and Fundamental Freedoms, which forms an integral part of the Treaties.[53] The former's Art. 2 s. 2 states that the accession agreement shall ensure that nothing therein affects the situation of Member States in relation to the European Convention, in particular in relation to the Protocols thereto, measures taken by Member States derogating from the European Convention in accordance with Article

---

[50] Like this *K. Rohleder* (fn. 9), p. 398.

[51] CONV 354/02, https://data.consilium.europa.eu/doc/document/CV%20354%202002%20INIT/EN/pdf, p. 13. S. also *W. Obwexer* (fn. 30), p. 118.

[52] Art. 6 para. 1 subpara. 1 TEU.

[53] Art. 51 TEU.

15 thereof and reservations to the European Convention made by Member States in accordance with Article 57 thereof.

To assess the question of whether this implies the limitation of the binding force of the Convention on the Member States to situations within the scope of application of EU law, it has to be questioned what "situation of Member States in relation to the European Convention" means. The first approach thereto could be to have a look on the examples added to this phrase. But, protocols to the Convention, derogations and reservations are something different from the limitation of the scope of application thereof. However, the situation of Member States in relation to the European Convention could mean their being bound in every situation. But this is already the case now, as the Member States as High Contracting Parties to the Convention are already bound by Art. 1 thereof in every case within their jurisdiction. Therefore this would not be *affected* by an accession. Only if "situation of Member States in relation to the European Convention" also meant the level of the Convention *within* the Member States' legal orders could it imply the limitation of the binding force of the Convention as an integral part of the EU legal order on the Member States to situations within the scope of application of EU law. But is this a situation *in relation to*? Does a situation in relation to the Convention not mean the situation *under* public international law rather than the situation *within* the legal order of the Member States?[54] The examples which all belong to situations under public international law also point to that direction.

f. It is true that the preparatory documents for the European Convention[55] contain phrasings which could lead to a differing understanding. In one place there is said that according "to the Group's common understanding, the legal "scope" of the Union's accession to the … [Convention] would be limited to issues in respect of which the Union has competence".[56] But after only a semicolon the sentence continues that"it would thus not lead to any extension of the Union's competences".[57] Therefore the question remains whether the Group is not only talking about the competences—which, by the way, is the only point that has been entered into the legally binding Treaties.

In another place there is the phrasing that "accession by the Union would have legal effect only insofar as Union law is concerned."[58] This part of a sentence is based within the section dealing both with reservations made by Member States and by the Union in its own name. Therefore again the question arises whether they are talking only about the situation under public international law rather than the situation within the legal order of the Member States.

Two further points are to be noted: Firstly, the binding force of the Convention on the "Member States within the scope of application of EU law" is never explicitly

---

[54] Concerning the distinction between the obligation by public international law and by EU law respectively s. *K. Rohleder* (fn. 9), p. 410 et seq., and *A.-Chr. Zoellner* (fn. 9), p. 253.

[55] Fn. 51.

[56] L.c., p. 13.

[57] L.c.

[58] L.c., p. 15.

mentioned in the preparatory document. It only talks about the "Union's competence" and the "Union law." Secondly, Art. 216 II TFEU, which orders the binding force of an international agreement on the Member States, is also not cited therein either. Therefore there is no explanation why there should be a limitation of the binding force of an international agreement on the Member States.

g. With a view to the foregoing it could hence not convincingly be established that Art. 216 II TFEU does not constitute the binding force of the Convention on the Member States in every situation.

Of course, this time the EU only has an external competence and no related internal competence, while normally external and internal competence on the same subject belong to the same legislator: Either there is an explicit external competence which is accompanied by an internal competence[59] or the internal competence implies an external competence—with the same result of internal and external competence belonging together.[60]

But by conferring the external competence to the EU, the Member States have agreed that the former can enter into international obligations. Its institutions will conclude the agreement which will hence be an act of the institutions and therefore form an integral part of EU law, as can be seen from the Haegeman judgment of the ECJ.[61] Only as far as the *implementation* is concerned, the "measures ... are to be adopted, according to the state of ... [EU] law for the time being in the areas affected by the provisions of the agreement, either by the ... institutions or by the Member States."[62]

Obviously, for the Court it is sufficient that at least one institution acts based on an external competence to create EU law. Only insofar as the implementation is concerned, it relies on the internal competence.[63] Therefore, the institutions will—by concluding the accession agreement—integrate the Convention into the EU legal order and therewith determine its level within the EU and the Member States' legal order. Only if there should be a necessity for an implementation—which is generally

[59] Art. 79 III TFEU – Art. 79 II lit. c TFEU; Art. 186 II TFEU – Art. 180 TFEU; Art. 191 para. 4 subpara. 1 s. 2 TFEU – Art. 192 TFEU; Art. 207 III TFEU – Art. 207 II TFEU; Art. 209 para. 2 subpara. 1 TFEU – Art. 209 I TFEU; Art. 212 para. 3 subpara. 1 s. 2 TFEU – Art. 212 II TFEU; Art. 214 para. 4 subpara. 1 s. 2 TFEU – Art. 214 III TFEU; Art. 219 III TFEU – Art. 127 II, 140 III TFEU; Art. 8 II EUV – Art. 209, 212 TFEU (*K. Schmalenbach* (fn. 42), Art. 8 TEU para. 14); Art. 37 TEU – Art. 21 et seqq. TEU.

[60] ECJ, Judgment of 31 March 1971 in the case 22/70 (AETR), ECR 1971, p. 263, para. 30. The jurisprudence is now incorporated in Art. 216 I 4. and 5. alternative TFEU.

[61] Fn. 35, para 3 et seqq.

[62] ECJ, Judgment of 26 October 1982 in the case 104/81 (Kupferberg), ECR 1982, p. 3641, para.12.

[63] This approach is also advanced within the German constitutional order: When giving their consent to an international agreement pursuant to Art. 59 II GG, the German federal legislative bodies confer the status of a federal statute to the former—even if the agreement concerns matters which remain within the competences of the Länder. Only if a further implementation is needed will the question of whether the federal level or the Länder have the legislative competence arise. (*M. Nettesheim*, in: Th. Maunz/G. Dürig/R. Herzog/R. Scholz (ed.), Grundgesetz Kommentar, Art. 32 para. 70; Art. 59 para. 185).

not the case for fundamental rights—the EU, if lacking internal competence, could be banned from doing so.[64]

h. As material provisions of EU law, the provisions of the Convention—as was already decided in respect of the fundamental freedoms—are to be observed always. Material provisions enounced within EU law are not limited to situations within the scope of application thereof.

They themselves open the scope of application of EU law.[65] Even if the Member States act within their remaining competences, "it does not follow … that such decisions are bound to fall entirely outside the scope of … [EU] law."[66] Even in those situations "Member States must comply with EU law".[67] Therefore it does not form an exception if the Convention applies to the Member States in every situation—even if they act within their remaining competences.

i. The fact that, based on Art. 6 II 1 TEU and Art. 216 II TFEU, the EU can enter into legal obligations which are binding on the Member States even within their remaining competences, could finally explain why Art. 218 para. 2 subpara. 2 s. 2 TFEU was introduced into the Treaties. The necessity of the Member States' approving it in accordance with their respective constitutional requirements could be the compensation for their being bound even within their remaining competences.

3.After assessing the extent to which they are bound by the Convention, the judges of the courts have also to ascertain the status thereof within the EU legal order.

a. The fact that the Convention will become an integral part thereof after the accession of the EU thereto does not in itself reveal the status of the Convention within this legal order. On the one hand, an international treaty entered into by the EU is binding on the latter's institutions pursuant to Art. 216 II TFEU. Therefore it must rank higher than the law given by these institutions, which is the secondary law. On the other hand, such an international treaty is itself a measure of these institutions and is hence bound by primary law, which is especially shown by Art. 218 XI TFEU, which empowers the ECJ to rule on the question of whether an agreement envisaged is compatible with the Treaties. Therefore an international treaty entered into by the EU is deemed to be located between primary and secondary law.[68] For this reason, the Convention is also mostly considered to be situated between primary and secondary law.[69]

---

64 In contrast *K. Rohleder* (fn. 9), p. 411 et seq., who applies the jurisprudence on the implementation on the question of binding force.

65 This could have an impact on the scope of application of the CFR (s. Art. 51 I 1 thereof) and the fundamental rights as general principles (s. above (4.2.b.)) as well as that of the prohibition of discrimination, Art. 18 TFEU.

66 ECJ, judgment of 11 January 2000 in the case C-285/98 (Kreil), ECR 2000, p. I-69, para. 15.

67 ECJ, judgment of 27 October 2011 in the case C-255/09 (COM./.Portuguese Republic), ECR 2011, p. I-10547, para. 48.

68 *S. Vöneky/B. Beylage-Haarmann* (fn. 43), Art. 216 AEUV para. 41.

69 *Th. Kingreen*, in: Chr. Calliess/M. Ruffert (ed.) (fn. 42), Art. 6 EUV para. 27; *K. Rohleder* (fn. 9), p. 410 et seq.; *B. Schneiders* (fn. 30), p. 251 et seqq.; *S. Stock*, (fn. 30), p. 201 et seq.; *A.-Chr. Zoellner* (fn. 9), p. 253; *R. Arnold* (fn. 41), p. 188; *P. Gragl* (fn. 38) p. 415 et seqq.; *C. Grewe* (fn. 30), p. 291; *O. J. Gstrein* (fn. 30), p. 459; *H. Jarass*, Zum Verhältnis von Grundrechtecharta und sonstigem

b. Nevertheless the question is raised of whether Art. 6 II 1 TEU elevates the Convention to primary law.[70] Of course, the Convention is mentioned there, but this does not give it the status of primary law, which can be inferred from Art. 6 I TEU. This provision does not only refer to the Charter of Fundamental Rights but also states that the latter shall have the same legal value as the Treaties. Therefore a similar provision should be expected if the Convention were to be conferred the same status as the Charter.

Additionally, none of the goals to be reached by the accession of the Union to the Convention requires the latter to become primary law: This is first true for the binding force of the Convention on the EU and the possibility of a direct review of its acts and omissions by the ECHR,[71] as can be seen from the German situation.[72] Also, for the enhancement of the EU's credibility concerning its human rights policy[73]—especially with regard to the fact that it expects that every country wishing to become an EU Member State be(come) a Party to the Convention[74]—it is sufficient to just become a Party to the Convention. Finally, the coherence between the Convention and the jurisprudence of the ECHR on the one hand and especially the Charter and the ECJ on the other hand[75] cannot be guaranteed by giving both of the instruments the same legal status. It will rather be ensured by the binding force of the former's

---

Recht, EuR 2013, p. 29, 43; *B. Kizil*, EU-Grundrechtsschutz im Vertrag von Lissabon, JA 2011, p. 277, 278, 280; *E. Pache/F. Rösch*, Europäischer Grundrechtsschutz nach Lissabon – die Rolle der EMRK und der Grundrechtecharta in der EU, EuZW 2008, p. 519, 521 = *E. Pache/F. Rösch*, Die neue Grundrechtsordnung der EU nach dem Vertrag von Lissabon, EuR 2009, p. 769, 785 = *E. Pache/F. Rösch*, Die Grundrechte der EU nach Lissabon, EWS 2009, p. 393, 400; *W. Schaller* (fn. 9), p. 665; *E. Schulte-Herbrüggen*, Der Grundrechtsschutz in der Europäischen Union nach dem Vertrag von Lissabon, ZEuS 2009, p. 343, 363; *Ch. Tsiliotis*, Das Verhältnis zwischen den Europäischen Gerichtshöfen in Luxemburg und Straßburg vor und nach dem Beitritt der Europäischen Union zur EMRK, in: J. Iliopoulos-Strangas/V. Pereira da Silva/M. Potacs (ed.) (fn. 9), p. 51, 83 et seq.

[70] *St. Schmahl*, Grundrechtsschutz im Dreieck von EU, EMRK und nationalem Verfassungsrecht, EuR 2008, Beiheft 1, p. 7, 37.

[71] *B. Schneiders* (fn. 30), p. 249; *S. Stock* (fn. 30), p. 169, 174, 185 et seq.; *A. Stricker*, Die Bedeutung der Europäischen Menschenrechtskonvention und der gemeinsamen Verfassungsüberlieferungen für den Grundrechtsschutz der Europäischen Union, Frankfurt a.M. 2010, p. 99; *O. J. Gstrein* (fn. 30), p. 449; *S. O. Pais*, The Protection of Fundamental Rights in Europe before and after the Accession of the European Union to the European Convention on Human Rights – Some Questions concerning the Legal Impact of the Charter of Fundamental Rights, in: J. Iliopoulos-Strangas/V. Pereira da Silva/M. Potacs (ed.) (fn. 9), p. 95, 102; *V. Skouris* (fn. 30), p. 208; *F. Tulkens* (fn. 9), p. 165; *W. Weiß* (fn. 38), p. 348. S. also *R. Passos* (fn. 10), p. 133 et seq.

[72] S. above (2.2.). In contrast finding it "problematic" *C. Grewe* (fn. 30), p. 296.

[73] *B. Schneiders* (fn. 30), p. 249; *S. Stock* (fn. 30), p. 184; *O. J. Gstrein* (fn. 30), p. 449 et seq.; *S. O. Pais* (fn. 71), p. 102; *R. Passos* (fn. 10), p. 132; *J. Ph. Terhechte*, Autonomie und Kohärenz—Die Eigenständigkeit der Unionsgrundrechte im Zuge des EMRK-Beitritts der Europäischen Union, in: J. Iliopoulos-Strangas/V. Pereira da Silva/M. Potacs (ed.) (fn. 9), p. 23, 41; *F. Tulkens* (fn. 9), p. 161, 165, 174.

[74] *B. Schneiders* (fn. 30), p. 249; *S. Stock* (fn. 30), p. 184; *O. J. Gstrein* (fn. 30), p. 450; *S. O. Pais* (fn. 71), p. 102; *J. Polakiewicz* (fn. 45), p. 473; *F. Tulkens* (fn. 9), p. 161.

[75] *B. Schneiders* (fn. 30), p. 249; *S. Stock* (fn. 30), pp. 169, 185; *A. Stricker* (fn. 71), pp. 92, 99; *O. J. Gstrein* (fn. 30), p. 449; *S. O. Pais* (fn. 71), p. 102; *R. Passos* (fn. 10), p. 133; *J. Ph. Terhechte* (fn. 73), pp. 39, 42; *F. Tulkens* (fn. 9), pp. 162, 174; *W. Weiß* (fn. 38), p. 348.

jurisprudence on the latter's[76] and by Art. 52 III 1 CFR, which states that, insofar as the Charter contains rights which correspond to rights guaranteed by the Convention, the meaning and scope of those rights shall be the same as those laid down by the latter.[77]

c. Further, the status of primary law could be conferred upon the Convention because the decision concluding the accession agreement shall only enter into force after it has been approved by the Member States in accordance with their respective constitutional requirements.[78,79] This condition is the same as in one of the simplified procedures to revise the Treaties.[80] Therefore it is argued that the accession of the EU to the Convention is pursued according to a Treaty revision procedure, which would lead to the conclusion that the Convention becomes part of a Treaty revision and therefore part of the Treaties.[81]

One could argue that the accession procedure differs from the revision procedure envisaged because it demands a decision by the Council[82] and not by the European Council as the said revision procedure. Additionally, it necessitates the consent of the European Parliament,[83] while the said revision procedure does not. There are, however, other procedures to revise the Treaties where a decision of the Council[84] or the consent of the European Parliament[85] is needed. Therefore this cannot constitute an obstacle to the Convention becoming part of the primary law.

But, as we have already[86] seen, the necessity of the Member States' approval could also be understood as a compensation for their being bound even within their remaining competences. Also, the accession does not change the wording of the Treaties. Therefore it could be an additional part of the Treaties, but it need not to be. Even as a "regular" international agreement it will be binding on the institutions.[87] Therefore decisive regard can be held to the fact that the Treaties contain several provisions imposing conditions on the accession.[88] These conditions can only apply to the accession agreement if they are higher ranking than the aforesaid agreement.[89] Hence, the level between primary and secondary law seems to be envisaged by the Treaties for the Convention as it is for every other international agreement of the EU.

---

[76] S. below (4.4.).

[77] In contrast *G. Heißl* (fn. 30), p. 132.

[78] Art. 218 para. 8 subpara. 2 s. 2 TFEU.

[79] Raising the question *H.-P. Folz* (fn. 30), p. 117 et seq.

[80] Art. 48 para. 6 subpara. 2 s. 3 TEU.

[81] *R. Uerpmann-Wittzack* (fn. 11), p. 173 et seq.

[82] Art. 218 para. 8 subpara. 2 s. 2 TFEU.

[83] Art. 218 para. 6 subpara. 2 s. 1 lit. a) ii) TFEU.

[84] Art. 333 TFEU.

[85] Art. 48 para. 7 TEU.

[86] S. above (4.2.i).

[87] S. above (4.3.a).

[88] Art. 6 II 2 TEU, Protocol (No. 8).

[89] Differing *R. Uerpmann-Wittzack* (fn. 11), p. 174.

It is true that the ECJ held in its opinion on the accession of the EU to the Convention that that "would be of constitutional significance and … could be brought about only by way of Treaty amendment".[90,91] But the context shows that the "constitutional significance" only means that the agreement "therefore" cannot be based on (the predecessor of) Art. 352 TFEU.[92] It does not imply that the agreement has to be a Treaty amendment itself.[93] Otherwise the Court could not have concluded that "as … [EU] law now stands, the … [Union] has no competence to accede to the Convention".[94] If it were not only to be based on a Treaty amendment, but to be done itself by Treaty amendment, the EU could never have a competence to do so—and not only "as … [EU] law now stands." Therefore the said opinion, too, cannot lead to the Convention becoming primary law after the EU's accession thereto.

4. Finally, the fact that the Convention will become an integral part of EU law after the accession of the EU thereto entails a further consequence: The ECJ can be called upon to interpret it. Either this court is asked to verify if an act or omission of the Member States[95] or an act[96] or omission[97] of the EU institutions, bodies, offices or agencies is in compliance with EU law, which includes compliance with the Convention as its integral part. Or this court is asked by a court established in one of the EU Member States to give a preliminary ruling on the Convention as an act adopted by the institutions.[98]

Notwithstanding, the ECHR will remain competent to interpret the Convention. Such a role is also acknowledged by the ECJ: International agreement concluded by the Union can create or designate a court with jurisdiction to interpret and apply their provision.[99] The ECJ even accepts that "decisions of that court will be binding on … [EU] institutions, including" itself.[100]

As a consequence, there will be two courts which can interpret the Convention. The decisions of both of them will be binding on the courts of the High Contracting Parties. If the ECHR rules first and the ECJ accepts its interpretation and complies with it, there will be no problem for the courts. However, if the ECJ is the first to decide and the ECHR later gives a dissenting interpretation, the courts will face a contradiction between two judgments, both of which are binding on them.

---

[90] Fn. 31, para. 35.

[91] Therefore pleading for the status of primary law *C. Grewe* (fn. 30), p. 296.

[92] L.c.

[93] Differing *S. Stock* (fn. 30), p. 223.

[94] L.c., para. 36.

[95] Art. 258 TFEU.

[96] Art. 263 TFEU.

[97] Art. 265 TFEU.

[98] S. above (3.1.).

[99] Opinion 1/91 of 14 December 1991, ECR 1991, p. I-6079, para. 40, 70; Opinion 1/09 (fn. 29), para. 74.

[100] Opinion 1/91 (fn. 99), para. 39. S. also *G. Heißl* (fn. 30), p. 132.

In such a situation,[101] shall the courts ignore the first judgment of the ECJ on the ground that this court itself has acknowledged the binding force of a judgment of the ECHR? Or shall they introduce a (further) preliminary ruling to the ECJ in order to ask if this court will give up its former interpretation because of the ruling of the ECHR?[102] The ECJ has found another solution in cases where a change of the situation could occur: To show that its jurisprudence is based on the actual state of EU law, which can be amended in the future, it introduces in such a situation a reservation saying that something is in conformity with EU law or not "as … [EU] law now stands"[103]. Based on this, this article concludes with the suggestion that the ECJ, when interpreting the Convention, use a similar reservation, e.g., "subject to a prospective differing decision of the ECHR", when giving an interpretation of the Convention. On the one hand, this could give legal certainty to the courts which are bound by ECJ decisions, making clear that they are allowed to ignore the decision after a differing decision of the ECHR. And on the other hand, this could avoid the prolongation of legal proceedings before the courts and the enhancement of the workload of the ECJ by avoiding preliminary rulings of the ECJ where they are not really necessary because of the acknowledgement of the binding force of judgments of the ECHR by the ECJ.

Birgit Daiber was an Associate Professor at the Seoul National University School of Law. Currently, she is a visiting researcher at the University of Vienna and a visiting lecturer at the Human Rights Master Programme, offered conjointly by the University of Vienna and the Ludwig-Boltzmann-Institut für Grund- und Menschenrechte. Her article is based on a presentation she gave at the Joint Symposium of Ritsumeikan University, Ludwig-Maximilians-University Munich and Seoul National University on "The Role of Supreme Court and Constitutional Court in Japan, Korea and Germany" on 4 September 2013 at the Law Faculty of Ritsumeikan University. It was first published in the Ritsumeikan Law Review No. 31 (June 2014), pp. 119-135, and—besides the URLs which have been updated—it reflects the initial state of play. Since then, the European Court of Justice has given its opinion 2/13, declaring the initial agreement on the accession of the EU to the ECHR not to be in conformity with EU Law. But in the meantime, negotiations have restarted. Additionally, Protocol No. 16 mentioned in footnote 28 has entered into force on 1 August 2018.

---

[101] Concerning this situation s. also *P. Gragl* (fn. 38) p. 425 et seqq.

[102] Suggested by *G. Heißl* (fn. 30), p. 144, and Dr. *W. Michl* during the aforementioned symposium.

[103] S. e.g. Opinion 2/94 (fn. 31), para. 36.

Correction to: Europe and Asia as a Legal Area for Fundamental Rights

Masahisa Deguchi and Kimio Yakushiji

Correction to:
M. Deguchi and K. Yakushiji (eds.), *Europe and Asia as a Legal Area for Fundamental Rights*, https://doi.org/10.1007/978-981-19-7542-4

In the original version of the book, the following belated corrections have been incorporated:

In the last paragraph of Preface in Frontmatter, the name "Dr. Oshio Cho" has been changed to "Dr. Yoshio Cho".

In Chapter 10 the chapter note "The text was first published in German in the Juristenzeitung: Nußberger, Die Europäische Menschenrechtskonvention-eine Verfassung für Europa, JZ 74 (2019)/ Heft 9, 421–428." has been updated as "The text was first published in German in the Juristenzeitung: Nußberger, Die Europäische Menschenrechtskonvention-eine Verfassung für Europa, JZ 74 (2019)/ Heft 9, 421–428, the – slightly adapted – text was translated into English by Prof. Dr. Michael Pils".

The book has been updated with the changes.

The updated original version of this book can be found at
https://doi.org/10.1007/978-981-19-7542-4
https://doi.org/10.1007/978-981-19-7542-4_10

M. Deguchi and K. Yakushiji (eds.), *Europe and Asia as a Legal Area for Fundamental Rights*, https://doi.org/10.1007/978-981-19-7542-4_14

Afterword

Kimio Yakushiji

The title of this book is taken from the same title of the symposium held at Ritsumeikan University in February in 2019. As is explained in detail in the preface of this book by Professor Deguchi, this symposium is one of a series of comparative legal research programmes started by him in collaboration with scholars in European countries as well as Asian countries to study the following issue: whether and, if so, to what extent would the experience of European unification through the EU as well as the Council of Europe function as a model for economic, political, and legal integration in East and Southeast Asian regions? Based on the remarkable economic growth in many East and Southeast Asian countries in the 1980s and 1990s, demands for the free trade of commodities, services, and investments as well as migration of workers had increased much more than ever in this region. Many bilateral and regional free trade or economic partnership agreements have been concluded and ASEAN started to establish ASEAN economic, political-security, and socio-cultural communities. Economic globalization obliged many countries in this region to reform their traditional systems and introduce contemporary systems which coincided with common international standards not only in the field of economy but also in law and court systems. This was one of the reasons why the Government of Japan launched, in cooperation with related organizations including universities, a programme to provide legal technical assistance for Asian countries including drafting and amending basic laws, improving legal and judicial systems, and capacity building of legal professionals etc. The programme made use of Japan's past experiences and lessons in part gained by assimilating western Civil Law system in the late nineteenth and early twentieth centuries. Thus, for both Japan and other East and Southeast Asian countries, some EU laws and regulations such as civil, commercial, competition, and environmental ones have played and continue to serve as models for bringing about closer unity in laws and regulations as well as judicial systems in the region.

K. Yakushiji (✉)
Ritsumeikan University, Kyoto, Japan
e-mail: yakusiji@fc.ritsumei.ac.jp

M. Deguchi and K. Yakushiji (eds.), *Europe and Asia as a Legal Area for Fundamental Rights*,
https://doi.org/10.1007/978-981-19-7542-4

On the other hand, unlike the European countries, which have a common heritage of individual freedom, democracy, political liberty, independent judiciaries, and the rule of law, the heterogeneity of political and economic regimes as well as social and cultural traditions of the countries in these Asian regions have prevented and may continue to prevent the easy introduction of legal systems and institutions based on these ideals shared in Europe, especially since the Asian countries have respected principles such as sovereign equality, territorial integrity, and non-intervention. In these circumstances, chapters in this book throw light on various aspects of the development of legal theories and practice concerning European integration through the EU and Council of Europe, with their lessons and challenges, as well as Asian countries' approach to regional integration and the challenges of these countries. The chapters contributed to this book reflect the result of the discussions in a series of symposia and other academic programs. The introduction of the authors and the subject matters dealt with are introduced briefly in the preface by Professor Deguchi.

As the title of this book shows, it observes Europe and Asia as legal areas for "peace, fundamental rights, democracy, and the rule of law". Certainly, the book deals with the positive aspects of the European integration and Asian countries' moves toward regional integration, but also the difficulties and challenges that both regions have had to deal with, including such problems as Brexit and the mass influx of refugees. Although, owing to the time limit for publication, this book was unable to deal with recent issues such as serious violations of international human rights and humanitarian law by the Myanmar junta after its coup d'état, and the awful human rights violations and grave breach of international humanitarian law during the aggression by Russia against Ukraine, it does include chapters which cover some aspects of recent developments and challenges in the European Union.

Nowadays, to our regret, "peace, fundamental rights, democracy, and the rule of law" is facing crisis. On 24 February 2022, the Russian Federation, one of the five permanent members of the United Nations Security Council (UNSC) as well as one of the nuclear-armed States, carried out military operations declared as a 'special military operation' against Ukraine, and it continues to occupy several parts of territory of Ukraine. Though the UNSC could not adopt any effective resolution dealing with this issue because of the use of veto power by the Russian Federation, the UN General Assembly (UNGA) adopted resolution ES-11/1 entitled "Aggression against Ukraine" on 2 March 2022, which, among other things, demanded that the Russian Federation immediately cease its use of force against Ukraine (which was characterized as "aggression" in violation of article 2(4) of the Charter), and completely and unconditionally withdraw all of its military forces from the territory of Ukraine within its internationally recognized borders. The UNGA also adopted resolution ES-11/2 entitled "Humanitarian consequences of the aggression against Ukraine" on 24 March 2022, which, among other things, demanded an immediate cessation of any attacks against civilians and civilian objects, and suspended the Russian Federation from membership in the Human Rights Council. On 16 March 2022, the International Court of Justice ordered in its indication of provisional measures in the Allegation of Genocide under the Genocide Convention case that the Russian Federation shall: (1) immediately suspend the military operations that it commenced on 24 February

2022 in the territory of Ukraine; and (2) ensure that any irregular armed units which may be directed or supported by it, as well as any organizations and persons which may be subject to its control or direction, take no steps in furtherance of the military operations referred to in (1). The International Criminal Court has assigned the Situation in Ukraine to its Pre-trial Chamber II and started its investigation. In Europe, the Committee of Ministers of the Council of Europe decided, according to article 8 of the Statute of the Council of Europe, the cessation of membership of the Russian Federation in the Council. EU has responded to Russia's invasion of Ukraine by imposing a series of sanctions against Russia, adopting a temporary protection scheme for displaced persons and reception of refugees from Ukraine, providing support to the Ukrainian armed forces, granting EU candidate status to Ukraine, etc. However, the invasion and military occupation of Ukrainian territory by Russian troops has continued and more than eight million people crossed the border from Ukraine and over 7.1 million people remain displaced.

The crisis afflicting the legal area for "peace, fundamental rights, democracy, and the rule of law" also arose in Asian and East Asian regions. One example is the coup d'état in Myanmar that occurred on 1 February, by which civilian rule led by the National League for Democracy was displaced by the military, which vested power in a military junta. According to the statement of the UN Special Rapporteur on the situation of human rights in Myanmar on 23 June 2022, junta forces have killed more than 2000 civilians, arrested more than 14,000, and displaced more than 700,000, driving the number of internally displaced persons well over one million, and plunging the country into an economic and humanitarian crisis that threatens the lives and wellbeing of millions. Though ASEAN excluded Min Aung Hlaing of Myanmar from its summit meetings because the Myanmar military government had refused to allow the special envoy to meet with all parties concerned, which was a commitment through the Five-Point Consensus, ASEAN leaders have not yet achieved any tangible results for the improvement of the human rights situation in Myanmar.

Though "a legal area for peace, fundamental rights, democracy, and the rule of law" both in Europe and Asia faces some significant crises, the crises in the 2020s are not the same as the crises in 1920s and 1930s. Since then, the international community has built up the political, legal, economic, and social infrastructures for the maintenance and development of peace, fundamental rights, democracy, and the rule of law from the bottom of the destructive consequences including the enormous sacrifice of precious lives lost in World War II. I strongly hope that the international community shall overcome the current crises in a principled way based on justice, and advance one step further towards "a legal area for peace, fundamental rights, democracy, and the rule of law" for the world.

Finally, I feel much honored and grateful to be invited kindly by my friend Professor Deguchi to become a co-editor of this book, though my contribution is not so high. I would like to conclude my afterword by expressing again our heartfelt thanks to the Konrad-Adenauer-Foundation, Faculty of Law and Research Office of Ritsumeikan University, and the Kyoto Museum for World Peace for their generous financial and other support. I would like to extend my sincere gratitude to Professor

Jeffrey S. Lubbers of Washington College of Law, American University for his warm advice and our colleague Mr. Tha-Phuong Vo from Freiburg for his devoted assistance to the series of symposia and the editing work of this book. Please allow me to express our sincere thanks to our colleagues, staff and students at Ritsumeikan University for their support to the international symposia and seminars. I conclude my gratitude to express our thanks to Publishers for providing us the warm recommendation to publish this book and for giving us the necessary assistance to complete this work.

On behalf of coeditors,

Emeritus Prof. Kimio Yakushiji, School of Law, Ritsumeikan University.

The manufacturer's authorised representative in the EU is Springer Nature Customer Service Centre GmbH, Europaplatz 3, 69115 Heidelberg, Germany. If you have any concerns regarding our products, please contact ProductSafety@springernature.com

Printed and bound by CPI Group (UK) Ltd, Croydon, CR0 4YY
30/09/2026
02225296-0001